1 (overleaf)   *Muker: in the Kearton country, Upper Swaledale*

YORKSHIRE

G. BERNARD WOOD

The first of England
That spoke to me
　　　　　Laurence Binyon: 'Inheritance'

B. T. BATSFORD LTD　LONDON

To My Wife

First published 1967
Second impression 1968

© G. Bernard Wood 1967

MADE AND PRINTED IN GREAT BRITAIN
BY WILLIAM CLOWES AND SONS LTD, LONDON AND BECCLES
FOR THE PUBLISHERS B. T. BATSFORD LTD
4 FITZHARDINGE STREET, PORTMAN SQUARE, LONDON W1

CONTENTS

ACKNOWLEDGMENT

My thanks go out to many: to the owners of various country houses for so kindly allowing me to record interesting items of family history; to the staffs of several art galleries and museums; to not a few librarians, church authorities, and to innumerable persons mentioned by name in the ensuing pages.

For practical help and unfailing encouragement I am deeply grateful to my wife. Many visits and re-visits to different parts of the county have been facilitated by our motoring friend, Harold Child. But I must also salute the memory of several who, in the carefree days of box cameras and walking tours, first stimulated my love for the far-spreading county that gave me birth.

THE ILLUSTRATIONS

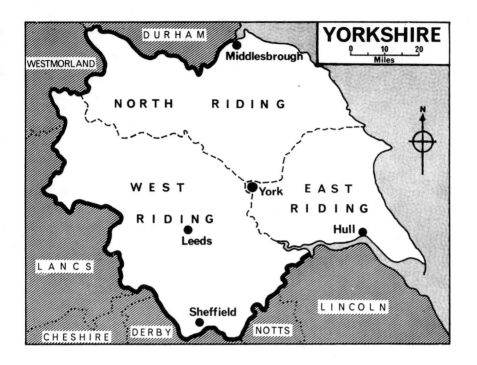

YORKSHIRE

0   10   20
Miles

DURHAM

WESTMORLAND

Middlesbrough

N O R T H   R I D I N G

N

W E S T

R I D I N G

York

E A S T

R I D I N G

Leeds

Hull

L A N C S

Sheffield

L I N C O L N

CHESHIRE   DERBY   NOTTS

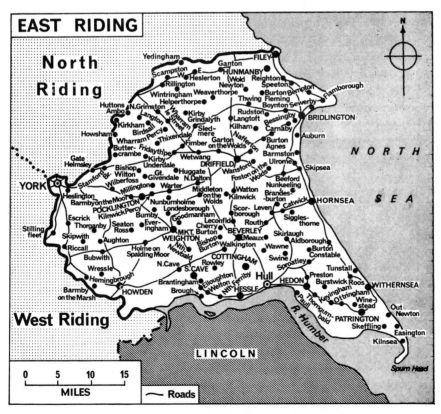

EAST RIDING

North
Riding

Yedingham   FILEY

Scampston   Ganton   HUNMANBY
E.   Wold   Reighton
Hesterton   Newton   Speeton
Rillington   Weaverthorpe   Burton Bempton
Wintringham   Helperthorpe   Thwing Fleming   Flamborough
Huttons   N.Grimston   Boynton Sewerby
Ambo   Langton   Kirby   Rudston   BRIDLINGTON
Kirkham   Wharram   Grindalyth   Langtoft   Bessingby
Howsham   Birdsall   Sledmere   Kilham   Carnaby   Auburn
Wharram Percy   Thixendale   Fimber   Garton   Burton
Butter-   Fridaythorpe   on the Wolds   Agnes
crambe   Wetwang   Nafferton   Barmston
Gate   Bishop   Kirby   DRIFFIELD   Ulrome
Helmsley   Wilton   Underdale   Wanston   Skipsea
Stamford   Bu.   Gt.   Huggate   Foston on the   Beeford
YORK   Wilberfoss   Givendale   N.Dalton   Wolds   Nunkeeling
Heslington   Warter   Middleton   Brandes-   Catwick
Barmby on the Moor   Millington   on the   Kilnwick   burton   HORNSEA
POCKLINGTON   Wolds   Watton   Leven   Sigglesthorne
Escrick   Kilnwick   Nunburnholme   Scor-   borough
Thorganby   Percy   Londesborough   Leconfield   Routh   Skirlaugh
Seaton   Everingham   Burnby   Cherry   BEVERLEY   Aldborough
Stilling-   Skipwith   Ross   Goodmanham   Burton   Meaux   Burton
fleet   Aughton   WEIGHTON   Bishop   Wawne   Constable
Riccall   MKT. Burton   Walkington   Swine   Tunstall
Bubwith   Holme on   Nth.   Cottingham   Sproatley   Preston   Roos
Wressle   Spalding Moor   Newbald   Rowley   Burstwick   WITHERNSEA
Hemingbrough   N.Cave   S.CAVE   Hull   Keyingham   Out
Barmby   Brantingham   Elloughton   Nth.Ferriby   HEDON   Ottringham   Newton
on the Marsh   Brough   Welton   HESSLE   Thorngumbald   Wine-   Easington
HOWDEN   Paull   PATRINGTON   stead
Skeffling   Kilnsea

West Riding

LINCOLN

R. Humber

N O R T H

S E A

Spurn Head

0   5   10   15
MILES

— Roads

N

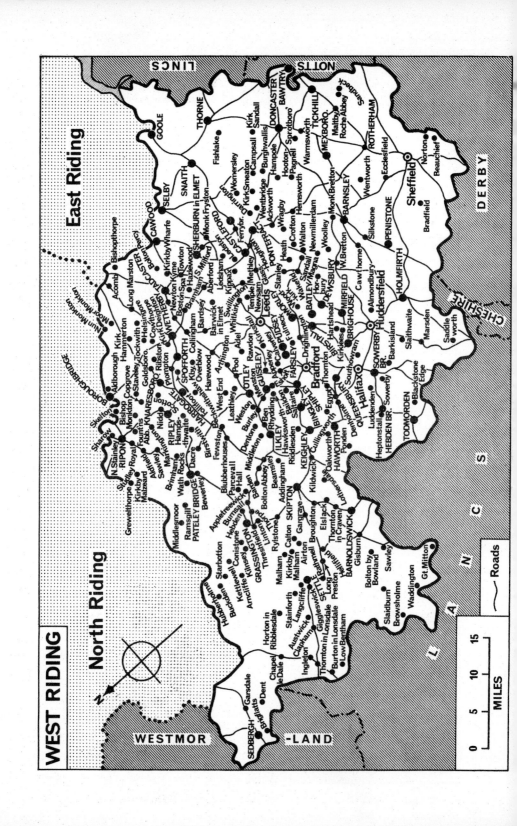

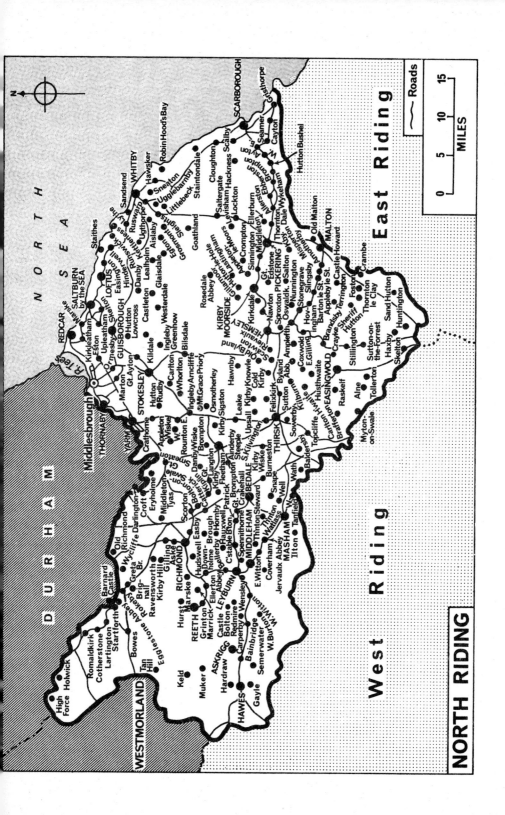

NORTH RIDING

The County

If any writer imagined he could encompass Yorkshire in one book he would be almost as foolish as those tourists who drive through an area and then claim to have 'done it'.

Not only is Yorkshire by far the biggest of the English counties, covering nearly four million acres; it is as varied as life itself, and as unpredictable.

It is bounded on the north and north-west by the Durham moors and the fells of Westmorland. Tack another ten miles to the Sedbergh countryside, and the county would have holiday resorts facing the Irish Sea as well as the North Sea. Around Richmond and Barnard Castle one begins to feel the magnetic pull of Hadrian's Wall, away there in Northumberland; around Sheffield, one is all but in the Midlands.

Within the intervening spaces—long divided by convenience into three Ridings—there is almost every type of scenery that England affords. A geological map of Yorkshire is a visual adventure, providing the key to our mountains and long, winding valleys or dales; our limestone caves and potholes; our smooth plains and extensive farmlands; our chalk cliffs and rolling Wolds; our coalfield—a murky slice of the West Riding, true, yet abounding with interest, as I hope to show.

It would be folly to dismiss this industrial belt with a mere shrug. Nobody expects it to be a picnic area, and yet there are places within a few miles of Sheffield and Leeds and Huddersfield that have miraculously escaped the blackening clutches of the Industrial Revolution. The steel-workers of Rotherham can 'get away from it all' by going along to Roche Abbey—a trifling distance of six or seven miles. Halifax is not half as

Stygian as it looks, at first sight; some of the county's finest moorland borders this lively textile town.

The industrial part of the West Riding contains many of these surprises, but scenic beauty is not the only criterion. Without its pit-shafts and looms and furnaces Yorkshire would not have produced such characters as Benjamin Huntsman, the steel pioneer; Rev. Samuel Marsden, the Farsley lad who left a blacksmith's shop to become a missionary to Australia and then sent back—to a weaving mill near my own home—the first Australian wool to reach England; Sir Titus Salt, who built a model village for his mill-hands at Saltaire; and, indeed, a number of writers and artists who have added their own colourful weft to the general picture. Even the Brontë family spread their roots around Bradford and Keighley.

The people of each Riding have their own distinctive dialects, which should be fostered. The plays written by such men as James R. Gregson (West Riding) and the late Austin Hyde (North Riding) have done much to capture the singular beauty of these ancient forms of speech.

Nowhere is the native dialect heard to better effect, however, than on the innumerable cricket grounds—whether these be of county status, the patch of green sward attached to so many mills and factories, or the field where some chapel team has to shoo away the cows before facing their rivals.

In Yorkshire, cricket is almost a religion. Its pantheon of gods include Wilfred Rhodes, Herbert Sutcliffe, Hedley Verity, and Len Hutton. Anywhere in the three Ridings it would be sacrilege to speak slightingly of them. It is hardly an exaggeration to say that whenever the Yorkshire team fares badly, a groan reverberates through the county. Hard-headed woolmen in Bradford will even forget their tops and noils for a moment to ask somebody, anxiously, for 't' latest scoor'.

But away there on his private cricket ground at Hovingham Hall, beyond York, Sir William Worsley remembers that cricket is primarily a game and invites some of the current 'stars' to remember also, and let themselves go, at his annual cricket festival. He even offers a prize to any batsman who can manage to hit the ball through one of the hall's topmost windows!

These country houses spell much of the county's history. I have been a privileged visitor to most of them, which explains why—in preparing the following pages—they have often been my principal textbook.

This love for architecture and the aesthetic values that go with it received a fillip during the last war, when the National Buildings Record entrusted me with the photographic survey of Yorkshire's rich architectural heritage. The experiences then gained provide something of this book's texture. Just one of its many strands. For I can never forget the people themselves—the fine, sturdy, often gruff Yorkshire men who built the manors and castles, the churches and chapels, and—yes—the funny little shops in some of the more remote market towns.

One of these shops comes to mind at this moment. It is set amongst the fells of Upper Wensleydale, where the local talk is bound up with sheep, and cattle, and cheese-making—but mostly sheep. The surrounding lanes are apt to be blocked with sheep, being driven to or from Hawes market. Yet right at the centre of this sheep kingdom there is a small bookshop—run, not for profit, but to bring a few gems of English literature to the dalesfolk at negligible cost.

The dalesman behind this delightful enterprise—Kit Calvert—is one of the characters who have helped to make the writing of this county book so pleasurable.

one

Sheffield and the Southern Fringe

When George Bickham sketched the bird's-eye-view map of Yorkshire for his atlas, *The British Monarchy* (1749–54), he looked north from Sheffield's picturesque turrets and gables and beheld vast, rolling acres of moor and farmland that merged, ultimately, into the distant horizon around Richmond and 'Yarum'. A delightful prospect. Michael Drayton's map of Yorkshire, in *Polyolbion* (1622), omits Sheffield altogether, substituting a shameless nymph wading knee-deep in the River Don. Drayton further personifies the neighbourhood by introducing several elegant ladies, well-clad this time!, each of whom balances on her head one or other of the surrounding churches, while over to the west stands another goddess—brandishing an axe to represent the once notorious Halifax gibbet.

Since those days, when map-makers could decorate fact with fancy, much has happened to Drayton's 'most renowned of shires', especially along its southern border. Coal has been mined extensively and steel produced. Industrial fortunes have been made—and beauty has departed from the affected countryside. Yet not entirely. Few English citizens are within such easy reach of fine scenery as are the people of Sheffield. Much of the scenery lies in the adjoining county of Derbyshire, true, but there are many rewarding places on the Yorkshire side.

It would now be impossible—except in imagination—to follow young Francis Chantrey as he whittled at a stick or modelled a lump of clay while leading milk supplies from Norton to Sheffield on a donkey, though some of the lanes he knew were still pleasantly rural when I was a boy, and the old village of Norton retains its attraction. The famous sculptor was born at Jordanthorpe Hall in 1781 and, by his own choice, rested at length—not in

Westminster Abbey, as was his due—but in the churchyard at Norton.

Behind him were a host of fine sculptures, some of the lesser-known ones being in Yorkshire churches: Sheffield Cathedral, Owston near Doncaster, Wragby near Wakefield, and Snaith near Goole. A commemorative tablet in Norton Church shows him, in effect, looking nostalgically upon the fascinating interior with its octagonal piers, Early English chancel arch, and the thirteenth-century font where he would have been christened. The font bowl is carved with a grotesque creature, recalling one of the dragons of Yorkshire folklore. What a contrast its crude lines provide with Chantrey's sensitive sculptures, of which one of the best examples is his Sleeping Children group in Lichfield Cathedral.

To the west, there are miles of unspoilt moorland, riven here and there with gritstone outcrops of almost Epsteinesque proportions. Stanadge, Ringinglow, Whirlow Brook and its delightful park—each has its own appeal. Several reservoirs bring a touch of civilisation to the wilder countryside, though a man could live the hermit's life thereabouts with nobody the wiser.

Monasticism early left its impress on the neighbourhood with the Norman abbey at Beauchief, though little of this now remains but the truncated tower. Far more satisfying is Roche Abbey, near Maltby, for here—in one of those oases of natural beauty spared by industry—sufficient of the original building has survived to evoke the past. Roche is reached from Maltby via A634.

It was in 1147 that a band of twelve Cistercian monks from Newminster, Northumberland, came to this cliff of magnesian limestone and decided to found under its friendly shade a daughter house. Today one looks in vain for the sign of the Cross—a natural phenomenon—on the beetling crags, which seemed to the monks a sure indication of Heaven's favour. They were subsequently known as the Monks of the Rock, and pilgrims came in great numbers to gaze upon the Cross—to them, a kind of stigmata.

What one can see, quite plainly, are the clefts and shafts made in the same obliging rock when the monks hewed from it the material they required for erecting the usual range of Cistercian buildings. The abbey church—now mainly represented by the transepts—rises in chaste splendour within a few feet of the parent rock, while some of the other buildings span the inevitable stream by means of small bridges. In these, as in other details, Roche Abbey resembles Fountains Abbey, near Ripon. It is natural to suppose that the Roche monks knew Fountains (a much larger house), of which Newminster was an offshoot, but practically nothing is recorded of their daily affairs. The only chronicle they left is their lovely abbey—not forgetting the vaulted gatehouse, still fairly intact, which admitted pedestrians through a narrow arch and wagons, or wains, through a broad archway. South of the church stretches the cloister walk, now marked by the footings of walls that once sheltered the monks as they studied their sacred books or meditated. In the small parlour, nearby, the vow of silence was lifted and conversation could flow—for a few precious moments.

It is odd that whilst records of the abbey's internal history are so scanty, a highly detailed account of the suppression of Roche, under Henry VIII, exists in the form of a letter written by a certain Miss Graham only thirty-one years after the closure in 1538.

Writing as an eyewitness, perhaps, she relates with horror that the common folk who only a few days before the handing over of the keys had come here to 'do great worship and reverence at their Matins, Masses and other Service', now went in and 'took what they found (and) filched it away'. Some intruders 'took the Service Books . . . and laid them upon their wain coppes to pice (mend?) the same; some took windows of the Hayleith and hid them in their hay'. The sense of tragedy mounts on reading further: '. . . the Church was the first thing that was put to the spoil; and then the Abbot's Lodging, Dorter and Frater, with the Cloister and all buildings thereabout within the Abbey walls; for nothing was spared but the oxhouses and swinecoates, and such other house of office that stood without the walls; which had more favour shown them (by the King's men) than the very Church itself . . .'

Some of the holy vessels (of pewter, not silver) had been hidden by the monks in the small, cup-like cavities, or vughs, that are such a characteristic feature of magnesian limestone, but there was no saving the choir woodwork: 'The person that cast the lead (from the roofs) into the fodders plucked up all the seats in the choir . . . which were like to seats in minsters, and burned them and melted the lead therewith; although there was wood plenty within a flight shot. . . .'

For Roche the Great Pillage had begun in earnest. The Norman doorway at Fishlake Church, near Doncaster, came from Roche, and much of Scrooby village, just over the border into Nottinghamshire, once echoed to the tread of the same brotherhood. If the pillaged stone was indeed taken down to Scrooby via the little stream in this vale, as tradition states, the stream must have been more navigable than now.

Silver-gilt cup (1896) bearing replica of the ...lers' Hall: Cutlers' Company, Sheffield

3 Georgian plasterwork in the Minstrel Gallery, Doncaster Mansion House

5 Woterton's sundial recording different times throughout the world; Walton Hall

The 'facetious door-knockers' at Walton Hall, ...e of Charles Waterton, nineteenth-century ...uralist

In the eighteenth century Horace Walpole declared that Roche Abbey was 'hid in such a venerable chasm that you might lie concealed there, even from a squire-parson of the parish. Lord Scarborough, to whom it belongs, and who lives next door, neglects it as much as if he were afraid of ghosts. . . .' Walpole could not know that within a few years (1774) the place was to be 'modernised'. The 4th Lord Scarbrough employed Lancelot ('Capability') Brown to 'improve' the 'Valley of Roach Abbey'. This entailed further sacrilege, as surviving parts of the ruin were demolished to make sham waterfalls. Another so-called amenity was a bowling-green. 'Capability' then proceeded to landscape the grounds of Sandbeck Park (occupying part of the old monastic purlieu) 'with Poet's feeling and with Painter's Eye', to quote his patron's instructions. Fortunately, his schemes at Roche were later considerably modified; the abbey is now in the more capable care of the Ministry of Public Building and Works and looks charming when the daffodils are in bloom.

Standing in the extensive grounds of Sandbeck Park—on the opposite side of A634—one might think there was not a single coal-mine, or a steel furnace either, within a hundred miles. The hall was designed by James Paine about 1763; its stately portico of Corinthian columns frames a view that embraces two ornamental lakes—Capability Brown's work—and the space beyond where the 6th Lord diligently, and sometimes successfully, trained his horses with the Doncaster Cup and the St. Leger in mind. An equal passion for music is attested by the organ he set up on the landing of the main staircase so that everybody in the house, presumably, could share his enthusiasm for Bach and Beethoven . . . .

This country house and others in the district are dwarfed by the palatial Wentworth Woodhouse, now a college, near Rotherham. It has a frontage of 600 feet—the longest of any English country house, and mainly embodies the Palladian work of Henry Flitcroft. When some friend or acquaintance enlarged their family mansion, so the story goes, Thomas Wentworth got Flitcroft or some other available architect to add another wing or projection to Wentworth Woodhouse so that he could retain the architectural supremacy. Neighbouring Wentworth Castle was a continual challenge. The result is such that one needs a map, indoors, to prevent getting lost. Of course it would be no hardship to flounder in such a maze of beautifully decorated rooms, bearing such enchanting names as Marble Saloon, Clifford's Lodgings, Van Dyck Room, and Whistlejacket Room— commemorating Lord Rockingham's favourite horse. But at night there may be a ghost to reckon with—the ghost of a former owner, the great

6   *Roche Abbey: one of the twelfth-century transepts*

Lord Strafford. He is said to strut about the mansion, holding beneath one arm the head that Charles I was the means of removing from his blameless shoulders in 1641.

The sheer size and grandeur of Wentworth Woodhouse, however, should not overshadow such neighbouring places as Tickhill Friary, two miles east of Maltby. The Friary is an unexpected survival from Chaucer's England, though later adapted as a private dwelling for Nicholas Booth, servant to George, Earl of Shrewsbury, who figures prominently in local history. If permission to view the house is granted, one can follow the beckoning of an external Early English arch and see how this is matched, indoors, by another lofty arch that encloses a crude doorway, beyond which a curved stone stairway leads down eerily to the original crypt. The only celebrity Tickhill Friary produced was Robert Worsop, who wrote a book of sermons entitled *Scholastic Questions*. He was buried here in 1350.

Tickhill Castle, of medieval tournament fame, is nearby, also the market town's splendid parish church, which belies its age by periodically ringing such cheerful tunes on its bells as 'The Minstrel Boy' and 'Home Sweet Home'.

Rotherham requires no signpost. Its chief aesthetic antidote to impinging industry is what Dr. Pevsner rightly describes as 'the largest and stateliest of parish churches in Yorkshire'. Its Perpendicular tower and spire dominate the town—but the Bridge Chapel, another gem, could so easily be overlooked. Provided by the master of the local grammar school about 1483, the tiny chapel stands partly in the River Don. Another medieval bridge chapel will be noticed at Wakefield.

Back, now, to the Sheffield area—nucleus of an uncharted kingdom known for centuries as Hallamshire. It has nourished the growth of many trades, some already well established in Shakespeare's day. In the chapter house at Sheffield Cathedral a modern window commemorates characters and scenes from the *Canterbury Tales*, all because Chaucer's Miller of Trumpington wore in his belt a 'Sheffield thwitel' or knife.

The focal point of Hallamshire is the Cutlers' Hall, opposite the Cathedral. It is the third building owned by the Cutlers' Company on this site. Presided over by the Master Cutler, members of the Company hold functions here that recall Merrie England at its most convivial. At one of their annual gatherings, however, they partake of brewis, traditionally a thin broth sprinkled with oat-cake; this, in bygone times, was the staple diet of a Sheffield apprentice.

What has aptly been called the 'true heraldry of Hallamshire' are the various trade marks, some still in common use—a bearded hermit, an acrobat, a swimmer, men playing bowls, a witch riding her broomstick, Guy Fawkes; an elephant, a walrus, a kingfisher; an angel sounding a trumpet, a stave of music.

In 1604 the Earl of Shrewsbury, Lord of the Manor of Sheffield, was drawing revenue in respect of twenty-eight 'cutlers' wheeles', including some on Sharrow Moor—now known as Hunter's Bar—and others in the valleys of the Rivelin, the Don and the Sheaf. The Shepherd Wheel beside the River Porter, in Whiteley Woods, is still in working order—a fascinating reminder of the 'little mesters' who depended on water power to drive their grinding apparatus. A round walk of ten miles takes enthusiasts through some lovely scenery which embraces Whiteley Woods and skirts Abbeydale Forge, near Beauchief. The Forge is an eighteenth-century scythe works complete with furnace, tilt hammers, warehouse and offices, all grouped around an open courtyard, and waiting for somebody to bring them to life once more. To this commendable enterprise Sheffield Corporation has recently set its hands. I hope the restoration scheme will not only liberate the water-wheel from its long rest, but also bring into use the swing seat I noticed here many years ago. The seat is suspended from the roof. It was occupied by a forgeman, who worked himself to and fro with his dangling legs before placing a scythe blade beneath the huge tilt hammer.

Norton, Chantrey's birthplace, was one of a small cluster of villages inseparably linked with this ancient rural craft. Ford, Ridgeway, Eckington and Hackenthorpe were amongst those villages. At Hackenthorpe—where I once watched scythes and sickles being made, largely by hand, for the overseas market—Staniforth's manager spoke of the old days when village craftsmen would use grinding wheels common to them all or to some small group. Thus the Broomheads and Haslams of Ridgeway resorted to the Never Fear Wheel; the Websters and Foxes used the Ford Wheel; others—including the Staniforths, one of whom kept a pack of harriers—ground their sickles at Field's Wheel in Eckington Wood. It is only a century or so since Staniforth's work was taken to and from this same wheel on the back of a white donkey!

The Weston Park Museum in Sheffield contains many mementoes of those leisurely days. Of the smaller exhibits one of the most attractive is a pair of scissors filed last century by Peter Atherton, a local craftsman, in his seventieth year. They are ornamented with the arms, supporters, crest and motto of the Cavendish family, over at Chatsworth.

Even the increasing use of coal for local industry left some chinks for romance. At Strafford Colliery, near Penistone, about fifty years ago, a certain youth was given the task of selecting the brightest lumps of coal and packing them carefully in straw. They were then despatched by the wagon load to Buckingham Palace.

Doncaster, Pontefract and Wakefield. Historic associations lend to these three towns a glamour which time has only partially dimmed. A traveller might not wish to linger much in modern Doncaster, though Sir Gilbert Scott's cathedral-like parish church is worth seeing for its pseudo-Gothic extravaganzas.

A few rather faded Georgian houses and inns which line the old Great North Road recall the coaching days, but the best period piece is the Mansion House, designed by James Paine. Construction was delayed because of the general upset created by the 1745 Rebellion, but by 1748 all recollections of Bonnie Prince Charlie's invasion, and the butchery that followed, could be charmed away by attendance at one of the Mayor's parties. In the ballroom a fine music gallery—high above the entrance—awakens the bygone atmosphere; this is epitomised by some of Joseph Rose's lovely decorative plaster work, with a floral swag enclosing a lyre, a flute and a page of music. Another music gallery was erected in the banqueting hall of 1806; it is slung dramatically between some lofty Corinthian columns.

South-west of Doncaster is *Ivanhoe* country—the land of Wamba the jester and the holy clerk of Copmanhurst. It is sadly changed, however, since the time envisaged by Walter Scott when he wrote: 'In that pleasant district which is watered by the River Don, there extended in ancient times a large forest, covering the greater part of the beautiful hills and valleys which lie between Sheffield and the pleasant town of Doncaster'.

Luckily, Conisborough Castle—in the heart of this countryside—has managed to survive, and does so with a touch of Norman arrogance. Its splendid circular keep and the curtain walls ride above the small town as a constant reminder of the De Warennes. Earlier favoured by William the Conqueror, this family built the castle about 1180. In *Ivanhoe* Scott makes 'Coningsburgh' the home of Athelstane. Just before I recorded the place for the National Buildings Record, in 1948, this paragon of castles could have been bought for £25! It was a relief to everybody when the Ministry of Works assumed custody and, after careful restoration, gave back to

Yorkshire and England such a vivid touchstone of north-country history. It is on A630, half-way between Rotherham and Doncaster.

Conisborough Castle invites exploration, from the deep tree-lined moat to the ninety-feet-high keep with all its ingenious living and defensive arrangements. There are beautifully contrived fireplaces and—in the thickness of one buttress—a tiny chapel graced with water-leaf capitals. It was from this chapel that the revived Athelstane emerged, still in his grave clothes, to the consternation of those assembled for his burial. One can reconstruct every incident that follows, to the moment when Athelstane vents his spleen against the rascally abbot responsible for his ghastly condition, by declaring: 'He shall hang on the top of this castle . . . in his cope and stole; and if the stairs be too strait to admit his fat carcass, I will have him craned up from without.'

Like a bedesman, the parish church at Conisborough keeps faithful attendance beside the old fortress, and has lineaments of its own from the twelfth century onwards.

One of the most curious churches in the neighbourhood, however, is at Sprotborough, three miles west of Doncaster. The presence, here, of a fourteenth century stone chair carved with a man's bearded face would alone satisfy anybody of an antiquarian turn of mind—but the bench-ends also pose their riddle. A local man once deciphered this for me.

First one sees a carving of a man and a woman about to exchange a kiss; then, on the adjoining pew, they stand aggrievedly back to back. These carvings represent Marriage, Before and After, with serpent-like scrolls symbolising the evil gossip that has come between them. The man's mother-in-law is shown next, then father-in-law wearing a strange, tapering hat like a candle-snuffer. Another carving, opposite, portrays a woman who fell in love with the parson; he turned out to be worthless and was later unfrocked. The woman's eyes are closed to signify that she feared to face the truth. As for the parson himself, his shortcomings are sufficiently indicated on the pulpit door by a tankard, a flask and a playing card. The bench-ends are said to have been provided, in Tudor times, by the village carpenter in lieu of his tithes. They are also supposed to relate something of his own life story and that of his foolish, purblind sister.

Several villages hereabouts retain their ancient integrity. The Countess of Rosse has written in almost idyllic terms of her own village of Womersley, five miles south of Pontefract. It is mentioned in Domesday Book, has an old moated farm, a fine Early English church, and a hall that reaches back to Elizabethan times. It has had its characters too, including the

Lord Hawke who once galloped horseback up the hall staircase for a wager.

Darrington, three miles to the west, centres upon a church fashioned from magnesian limestone, and therefore of a rich, creamy white appearance. J. S. Fletcher, who beguiled an earlier generation with his stirring historic romances, came from this village, though he was born in Halifax. Fortunately, the Great North Road just misses Darrington, so that one can comfortably enjoy such curiosities as the eighteenth-century dovecot in the churchyard, and a small arcaded gallery, like a bridge, high above the north aisle. Its purpose has never been satisfactorily explained.

Brought up on his grandmother's farm nearby, Fletcher absorbed the spirit of the neighbourhood and never tired of re-telling its tales. One of these concerns some local gypsies. When one of their number was charged with horse stealing the rest of the tribe offered the magistrate £5000 for his release! The same gypsies used to 'ride to hounds with the Badsworth Hunt, the men clad in scarlet waistcoats, and the women in gay riding-habits'.

One of the great surprises of this area is to find a village which is still very largely the agricultural community of medieval times. Coal seams burrow beneath the surface, but all around Hooton Pagnell—this lovely village on B6422, seven miles north-west of Doncaster—wide spaces are devoted to arable farming. The stone-built cottages cluster about a fine church having several Norman features, and the old hall.

Some years ago scholarly tribute was given to this place by Ruston and Witney, in their monograph, *Hooton Pagnell—The Agricultural Evolution of a Yorkshire Village*. The late Col. Warde-Aldam put a copy of the book in my hands when I visited the hall. At first it was rather puzzling to find its references to local crops and farming methods illustrated by drawings from the Luttrell Psalter. The explanation was most unexpected.

Hooton Pagnell embodies the name of the first owners, the Paganels, one of whom was so generous toward mother church that the family were at length compelled to seek financial aid from Josceus, a Jewish money-lender of York. When William Paganel's daughter and co-heiress, Frethesenthe, married Geoffrey of Lutterell, Hooton Pagnell passed into the hands of a wealthy family who revitalised the estate—and sponsored the now world-famous Psalter, kept in the British Museum.

It was the third Sir Geoffrey (1276–1345) who had this psalter made, presumably by a school of painters in East Anglia. Although he spent most of his time at Irnham, his Lincolnshire home, he must often have ridden over to Hooton Pagnell and it seems quite likely that some of the marginal scenes in the psalter were suggested by agricultural pursuits and village pastimes Geoffrey saw here in his youth. Among these scenes are a woman milking a ewe in a wattled sheep pen, the miller handling sacks of corn, a farmer using his sling against two troublesome crows, villeins ploughing with oxen, womenfolk reaping with sickles, and a comic wrestling match.

A striking reminder of the Lutterell period of ownership is the hall's fourteenth-century gatehouse. Their coat-of-arms—a bend between six martlets or martins—appears over the archway, and from the north-west angle a charming oriel window looks down the entrance drive. What lies behind the much smaller window below I saw later—on the owner's prompting—by descending through a trap door. A narrow passage soon debouched me into a medieval dungeon. The side-walls are curiously corbelled in to support the stone-flagged roof; this is pierced by a circular hole through which food would be dropped for some luckless prisoner.

One other token of the past is the tithe barn. This contains a 'bin' where corn for tithe settlements was weighed out. The barn is best seen from the front lawn—when the gardens are open to the public. On the opposite side of the house, last century, Mrs. Julia Warde-Aldam built a gazebo overlooking her beloved rock garden. These rocks are heterogeneous masses of the native magnesian limestone and have, for company, the rutted remnants of a road which is ancient enough to have brought the Paganels and the Lutterells home from the wars long ago.

Pontefract has several places worth exploring, notably the Plantagenet castle rendered doubly famous by Shakespeare in *Richard II*; also a little fourteenth-century hermitage hewn from the rock in Southgate.

In the diary of his travels John Evelyn (1620–1706) omits any mention of one local peculiarity—the liquorice growers of Pontefract and their plantations. One would expect his botanical interests to have prompted some entertaining comment on this activity, which was probably intro-duced by the Black Friars in the thirteenth century. Most people are familiar with Pomfret or Pontefract Cakes, the juicy lozenges made from liquorice and stamped with an impression of the old castle. When I was a boy they vied with dolly mixtures and tiger nuts for our few pennies, but the trade is now on the decline.

A subject which Evelyn does introduce is Robin Hood's Well. He wrote: 'We all alighted in ye highway to drink at a cristal spring which they call Robin Hood's Well, neere it is a stone chaire, and an iron ladle to drinke

out of, chain'd to the seate'. A few years later, about 1711, the owner of
Castle Howard commissioned his own architect, the great John Vanbrugh,
to erect a canopy over the well and it became the recognised thing for
travellers to stop here and regale themselves—not only with the 'cristal'
water, but with tales of Robin Hood. Near this part of the old Barnsdale
Forest the outlaw once relieved the fat abbot of St. Mary's York, of his
purse, gave this to the impoverished Sir Richard of the Lea, and then—
adding insult to injury—made the abbot dance a jig on the turf.

The heavily rusticated well canopy has lately been set back from the
verge of A1, near Barnsdale Bar, to prevent damage by passing lorries. But
it still looks remarkably like a detached fragment of Vanbrugh's colossal
masterpiece, Castle Howard.

The whole district rings with tales of Robin Hood. He is said to have
been born at Wakefield, and his last bow-shot gave him a final resting place
at Kirklees, near Brighouse. But more of that later.

Something must now be said about the country houses that still spread
beauty and interest over a district that attracted Augustinian canons in the
twelfth century, and Quaker educationalists in the eighteenth. Tradition
paints a nice picture of Dr. John Fothergill forsaking his smart London
coach and his beloved flowers, for a time, while he came north to found
Ackworth School for the Society of Friends in 1779. To this day the
older school buildings are somewhat austere, befitting a régime dedicated
to noble ends.

Nostell Priory nearby presents a sharp contrast with its extensive deer
park and a Georgian mansion, which echoes the name of the original
priory, Nostla, founded here by Richard Adlave about 1110. While
recovering from an illness at Pontefract, Adlave—then chaplain to Henry I
—had noticed some hermits during a hunting expedition. Greatly impressed with their simple way of life, he asked the king's permission to leave
his service and establish a monastic house, with himself as prior. Henry not
only agreed but bestowed a shilling per day on the new venture. The
gesture was far more liberal than it sounds today.

The priory, of which practically nothing now remains—thanks to Dr.
Legh, 'the fattest and most pompous' of Henry VIII's commissioners—was
dedicated to St. Oswald. This dedication has given latter-day owners of
Nostell their resounding title—Lord St. Oswald. It should keep visitors
mindful of the older history of Nostell while walking through the sumptuous rooms of a mansion designed by James Paine—when he was only
nineteen years of age. Other artists whose work Nostell displays to rich

advantage include Robert Adam for architectural design, Joseph Rose for 'plaisterer's work', Antonio Zucchi for painted ceilings, and Thomas Chippendale.

Chippendale may have been apprenticed here before going off to achieve fame in London. A large doll's house modelled on this mansion by the Nostell estate carpenter in 1740 contains tiny pieces of furniture by the promising lad from Otley, in Wharfedale. Twenty-five years later he was furnishing the real Nostell; every room bears the stamp of his genius. One of Chippendale's invoices still preserved here shows that the beautiful library table cost Sir Rowland Winn the sum of £72 10s. in 1767. When the table went out on exhibition a few years ago it was insured for £12,000.

In 1817 John Winn of Nostell rescued some fine pieces of painted glass from Switzerland, where it was suffering through neglect. Members of the family later set it up in Wragby Church, which stands at the gates of Nostell Priory. The window subjects range from St. Cecilia playing an organ, to William Tell and the apple episode.

The appeal of Walton Hall, nearer Wakefield, resides not so much in the building—now a maternity hospital—as in the eccentric Squire Waterton who lived here early last century and turned the extensive park into a bird sanctuary, the first in England. A drawing by his friend Hawksworth Fawkes of Farnley Hall, near Otley, portrays tall, slender Waterton in customary attire—stove-pipe hat, blue swallow-tail coat with gold buttons, and black slippers. In this rig-out he would sometimes observe his birds, from a lakeside hide or perhaps the fork of a tree.

How he cherished those birds! Some old fish-netting from Scarborough would be thrown over his fruit bushes, but a few bushes were always left exposed so that the birds should not feel robbed. The estate is still enclosed by the stout wall—three miles long and varying in height from eight to sixteen feet—which Waterton completed in 1826 to afford protection against foxes, badgers—and poachers. Further to deter poachers he glee-fully set up 200 dummy pheasants round the edge of the park. 'In a dim light they looked most realistic and caused much fruitless expenditure of powder and shot.'

Waterton scornfully called his Georgian house a 'stone box'. It occupies an island in the lake and perhaps the mouldering boat I once saw beside the small landing stage was *Percy*, the Squire's bird-watching vessel. Descendants of his Canada geese were paddling around. An iron bridge leads across to the house, but a picturesque watergate survives from the earlier, fortified residence.

Charles Waterton ingeniously turned the watergate into a nesting site for starlings, jackdaws, blackbirds and owls. He provided twenty-four cavities with splayed edges as nesting boxes; some can still be seen. When he encouraged 'Mrs. Bennet' to roost here too, the ruin must have been an aviary in itself. 'Mrs. Bennet' was a rumpless fowl that won his affection.

This man who was full of jests and pranks left a comic reminder of himself at the hall's front entrance. It is a pair of 'facetious door-knockers'. One knocker is a dummy, resting permanently on a face that grins in consequence. The other, effectual knocker falls heavily upon a face that scowls as if in pain. This scowling face is supposed to reflect the Squire's look when he saw Captain Jones, one of his cronies, sketching him for this jesting purpose. But he was a kindly soul. W. B. Spurr, a local man whose father was an acolyte at the Squire's lake funeral, told me that Waterton dispensed charity to all in need and lived a life of extreme simplicity. Food of the best was always available at the hall for any stray beggar. 'Did Waterton really use a wooden block as his pillow?', I asked. 'Yes,' said Mr. Spurr, 'my father actually saw that block'.

John Carr (1723–1807), the architect, was a very different character. He is usually referred to as John Carr of York, but once, while giving a lecture in Wakefield, I got my knuckles rapped for using this title. John Carr, I was sharply reminded, came from the industrial West Riding— from Horbury, near Wakefield, and nothing of the architect's eventual success in and around York, where they made him Lord Mayor, would rob my Wakefield audience of their prior claims upon the local boy who made good.

Carr's fine classical work is seen at Harewood House, at Denton Park near Ilkley, at Farnley Hall near Otley, and at the charming though little-known Easthorpe Hall, near Malton, which Charles Dickens so enjoyed. The graceful Greta Bridge in Teesdale which sent John Sell Cotman into raptures is Carr's design. He also made grandiose contributions to the Wentworth Woodhouse menage, including stables to match the mansion and a mausoleum to ensure posthumous fame for his friend, Lord Rockingham.

Yet Carr, the doyen of eighteenth-century York and its social luminaries, often talked in his gruff manner about his early days as a stone-mason at Horbury. Doubtless Rockingham himself would relish Carr's tale of how he would leave home for a week's hard work during his youth, fortified with a large circular meat pie which he proceeded to divide with his compasses into six equal parts, so that on no day should he over-eat. When he died he left £150,000.

Horbury still remembers him with pride and gratitude. As a present he designed and built the fine village church, with a staged tower not unlike one of Wren's; the interior seems to echo one of his own country house designs. When Horbury County Secondary School was built in 1961–2, curtains were provided that portray John Carr and this same beautiful church.

Wakefield Cathedral is full of interest, but the city's other reminder of medieval times should also be seen. It is the fourteenth-century chantry on Calder Bridge. The original frontage was moved to the grounds of neighbouring Kettlethorpe Hall last century and adapted as a boat-house. The last private owners of Kettlethorpe allowed Girl Guides to use this most romantic façade for dramatic performances; its Gothic arches opening on to the lake-side rock garden made delightful entries and exits. Modern housing developments have changed all that, but purpose and meaning have returned to the original bridge chapel, for divine service is again held occasionally in this ancient, wayfarers' shrine.

Fortunately a modern road-bridge takes the roar of traffic mostly beyond earshot, and Wakefield here becomes, once again, the home of miracle plays, as half suggested by the carved stone panels above the chapel entrance. Some years ago, at Christmas, one of the Wakefield Miracle cycle—the Second Shepherd's Play—was broadcast from St. Mary's on the Bridge, to use its full name. While the shepherds are watching their flocks, in this fourteenth-century play, a thief steals one of their sheep, takes it home, and later gets tossed in a blanket for trying to pass it off to the shepherds, when they search his cottage, as a new-born babe in its cradle.

Perhaps the strangest episode in the chapel's long history was that prompted by restoration of the fabric in 1938–9. An auction was held and people from many parts of England sent gifts for sale. The gifts included musical instruments, a grandfather clock, a modern bedroom suite, a warming pan, and—from the late Princess Royal—a pair of eighteenth-century soapstone cockerels. How the chantry priest who once served here would have raised his eyebrows!

two

Around Leeds and Bradford

Coal-mining gives to the South Yorkshire landscape a peculiar profile—often stark and ugly, yet occasionally dramatic as when the pithead-gear, rampant against the sky, comes alive with the huge whirring wheels that operate the cages. When my wife first came north from pastoral East Anglia, she was thrilled with the sight and took the first opportunity of going down a mine. Those who live nearby sometimes find the mines a source of real inspiration.

One who has done so since his boyhood days around Castleford is Henry Moore, the sculptor. An exhibition of his work is almost sure to include several drawings made in Yorkshire pits—miners at the pithead waiting for the cage, miners at the coal face, or drilling in a drift, or eating their 'snap', etc. Henry Moore was born into a Castleford miner's home. Once—when asked what first made him think of sculpture as a profession—he replied, 'It was seeing the little corbel heads in Methley Church. An aunt of mine lived at Methley and we used to visit her when we were children. . . . Those carvings at Methley, though small, were big in feeling. I suppose they gave me my first appreciation of three-dimensional form.'

Visitors to this fine church, two miles west of Castleford, will be impressed by the reclining figures of former times—effigies in alabaster or marble commemorating the Watertons, the Saviles and other local families. In this funerary parade Sir Robert Waterton and his wife strike an original note. Though clad in armour, Sir Robert wears a bejewelled turban and has his beard curled in the French style. Not to be outshone, his lady has settled herself comfortably against her pet dogs and flaunts a gay, floral head-dress. Other interesting features include a fine, early eighteenth-century pulpit and a sixteenth-century lectern of rich foreign design. The tiny corbel heads that peer down, rather quizzically, from the walls were to be accompanied later, in the receptive mind of young Henry Moore, with some Romanesque heads in the splendid Norman church at Adel, on the northern margin of Leeds.

There is a lingering romance about coal-mining. Around Leeds coal-digging began on a small scale with the monks of Kirkstall Abbey. They employed a peculiar 'divining' method, having discovered that clover with unusually big leaves grew on the clay above the coal they sought. This they used in their forges to produce tools, hinges and even book-clasps.

In the mid-eighteenth century Charles Brandling could live alongside his pit at Middleton, near Leeds, and invite his friends to enjoy his beautiful estate—now a municipal park—and the excitement of cock-fights. The cock-pit is still preserved in his former home, Middleton Lodge. In 1758 he opened Middleton Colliery Railway. This is still kept going, for sentimental reasons, by a group of railway enthusiasts, and the surviving portion of the old track is preserved by the National Trust.

In Leeds City Museum there is a length of the original rack-rail introduced on this railway in 1811, also a fine model of the *Salamanca*, one of Matthew Murray's locomotives, showing the large toothed wheel that engaged on the curious rack-rails designed by Brandling's agent, John Blenkinsop. In his contemporary volume, *Costume of Yorkshire*, George Walker illustrates this pioneer railway, placing in the foreground a then typical miner equipped, like some agricultural hind, with wideawake hat, breeches, and lunch basket. Brandling might well have said, with another north-country squire, that his 'coal pit was the best farm on the estate'.

Some so-called 'coaleries' around Mirfield, in the Calder valley, were so shallow that 'cottagers could knock on their floors and be answered by the colliers beneath'. This information comes to me from Judge Nevin, of Rawdon Hall, some of whose forebears operated two Mirfield pits. In 1875 some of the older workings, near Balderstone Hall, yielded some curious relics—five stoneware jars which had evidently been used for food storage by people hiding there, probably during the 1745 Rebellion scare. The Rev. J. Ismay, then Vicar of Mirfield, was presumably referring to this episode when making an entry in his diary on 1 December 1745. He remarks that because the inhabitants grew alarmed by a rumour that Jacobite rebels were approaching, 'the coal pits at Mirfield Moore . . . were stocked with clothes and provisions, and this day few attended Divine Worship for want of apparel . . .'.

In 1960 the York Minster authorities paid a fine tribute to 'those who labour in our mines to bring power to our industries and transport, and comfort to our homes' by installing in the north choir aisle a fascinating model made and presented by George Hector of Sheffield, a disabled mining instructor. The model is deeply recessed in a fourteenth-century niche, so that all is comparatively dark; then, with the touch of an electric switch, the interior lights up to reveal a miner working at the coal face amid the pit-props of the Barnsley Main Seam. When the late Dean of York dedicated the model to the Glory of God 'for a perpetual Remembrancer of the Miners of Yorkshire', perhaps there were a few in the assembled company who thought back to the times I have mentioned, when abbeys like Jervaulx in Wensleydale could keep good fires burning from All Saints' Day until Easter because of the precious mineral that now causes man to probe ever deeper into the bountiful earth.

Everybody deplores the unsightliness this usually entails but Nature has a way of covering the scars of industry. The best example in Yorkshire is at Fairburn Ings, between Kippax and Ledsham, where a large lake has formed in some great hollows caused in part by mining subsidence. Many beautiful waterfowl and other birds have made it their home; its 690 acres are on a regular migration route. Against the distant smoky background of chimneys and slag heaps, the drumming of a snipe can sometimes be heard; swans, mallard and teal ruffle the water, and the sedgy margins come alive with foraging warblers and the colourful reed bunting.

Fairburn Ings has become a recognised Nature Reserve, with its own Game Warden and a hide capable of holding fifteen bird-watchers.

On reaching Leeds, however, coal-mines are left behind, and the only local industrial feature I need mention is the little-known edifice resembling an Egyptian temple. It stands in Marshall Street, off Water Lane, just outside the town centre.

Its erection was regarded as one of the architectural wonders of the mid-nineteenth century; sightseers came in their hundreds to behold Temple Mill, which achieved further affinities with the temples of the Nile through its proximity to both canal and river. What contemporaries were pleased to call the Grand Canal—part of the Leeds and Liverpool Canal—was opened into the River Aire in 1777. By the time John Marshall started building his Egyptian-style flax mill in 1840, the surroundings were still delightfully rural and any cultured person sauntering along Water Lane would feel the full impact of Marshall's aesthetic scheme. He

7   *The oak staircase, Temple Newsam, Leeds*

was a man of some learning, and the fact that flax was extensively produced for their linen articles by the ancient Egyptians evidently influenced him in his choice of design for his own flax centre. Ignatius Bonomi is named as the most probable architect.

The building's resemblance to an Egyptian temple is confined to the two main façades, which face east. Tall brick warehouses immediately opposite now shut off most of the early morning sunshine—a circumstance that makes the stonework, already begrimed, rather gloomy. As if in mockery, the winged sun emblem is several times repeated around the entrance portico, recalling—even for those who have browsed only a little in Egyptology—King Akhenaton's wonderful 'Hymn to the Sun'. Curious rows of serpents, each bearing the sun disc, rear up like so many sentinels between some huge columns with papyrus flower capitals; the 200-feet-long mill-block resumes the masquerade with an impressive array of palm-leaf capitals. Both structures display the pronounced batter, or inward slope, that characterises so much ancient Egyptian architecture.

Some of the people who work in the area and pass the mill daily must occasionally feel mystified. They would have been even more mystified to see some sheep grazing on the flat roof, yet that actually occurred when the place was new. Rural amenities were of great concern to John Marshall; hence his decision to have a roof meadow. Perhaps the use of a few sheep to crop the grass satisfied his country-loving nature, but the practice suddenly ceased when one of the sheep fell through a glass dome into one of the flax-making machines.

John Marshall knew the Wordsworths intimately and sought the poet's advice on a suitable house beside Derwentwater for his son. In his book, *Marshalls of Leeds, Flax Spinners*, W. G. Rimmer has also rescued from the Marshall family papers an interesting reference to William Wordsworth accompanying Marshall on a five weeks' Irish tour 'prospecting for business', and another to sister Dorothy's overture on behalf of a young friend; she hoped to secure employment for him in this outpost of ancient Egypt!

Other bygone worthies are remembered in several of the town's fine churches. St. John's, New Briggate, was founded by John Harrison in 1632-4. In a memorial window illustrating his many benefactions he is seen consulting the building plans for this church, and also presenting to Charles I—when imprisoned in Leeds—a tankard purporting to be full of right good ale. It was crammed, instead, with golden guineas so that the King could bribe his way to freedom. Charles was grateful but the ruse

8   *Caroline pulpit, St. John's Church, Briggate, Leeds*

failed. Despite restorations, John Harrison's church retains much of its excellent woodwork, in chancel screen, pulpit, and pews.

Of several local celebrities commemorated at Leeds Parish Church perhaps the one who most captures the imagination is Ralph Thoresby, seventeenth-century antiquary and traveller. Yorkshire topography would have been much the poorer if he had not braved the shocking roads of his day and kept a detailed diary. He and his horse often floundered in potholes and quagmires. Yet little daunted him. Rescuing from the mud any precious document entrusted to him, he would ejaculate a prayer, re-mount—and proceed to the next objective. He was *persona grata* with all the local gentry, and gloated with them over their heirlooms. At Kirkstall he was shown 'the Abbot of Kirkstal's stirrups, which are prodigiously great and of a very antique form'. The rare privilege of seeing the 'pedigree of King James from Adam' takes him one day to the Bowland district, but on returning homewards he finds 'the nymph Verbeia was so surly, we durst not pass her without the help of the bridge. . . .' This is Thoresby's colourful way of referring to the tutelary deity of the River Wharfe in a tantrum.

When John Warburton, map-maker, used St. John's Church tower to survey the district, Thoresby, his host, climbed with the surveyor 'as high as the bells' but durst not venture farther. Quagmires, swollen streams and other wayfaring hazards, yes, but not the one dizzy height that would have spread all mercantile Leeds and its ring of meadows before him. His name lives on in the Thoresby Society, an antiquarian body of international repute with headquarters in Queen Square, a surviving fragment of Georgian Leeds.

One envies Thoresby's privileged way of visiting country houses—and Warburton caught the idea, while seeking patrons for his maps. Warburton's record of his visit to Ripley Castle, near Harrogate, is typical. After being 'kindly received by Sr John Ingleby Bart.' he 'stayd all night, and beside a most sumptuous entertainment . . . and a generous encouragement of my affaire, was favoured with a sight of . . . rare MSS. on vellum.'

When paying half a crown for the pleasure of viewing Ripley Castle or some other stately house in Yorkshire, today, it is at any rate amusing to think of Warburton preceding one, early in the eighteenth century. In he would go with many courtly bows—and private expectations—while his assistant got on with the actual road-measuring by pushing in front of him a strange contrivance which Thoresby called 'the wheel'. Way-wiser, its proper name, expresses its purpose more imaginatively.

Leeds was then circled by several splendid houses of the gentry. Thoresby himself went often to Ledston Hall, a many-gabled dwelling above Ledsham village, near the junction of A1 and A63. He went there chiefly to enjoy the company of Lady Betty Hastings, of whom Steele once remarked that to know her was a liberal education.

Of one visit, in January 1723, Thoresby recorded: 'several poor neighbours and tenants were admitted, for whose instruction an excellent book was read, and afterwards we sung the 100th Psalm with great affection; some in the other rooms, for we had three at least, sang the bass very well. . . .' On a later occasion Lady Betty sent Thoresby home in her private coach, which caused him to confide a little mishap to his Diary: '. . . the harness broke, but the horse and charioteer performed well.' On her tomb in Ledsham Church, Lady Betty overshadows all by sitting up as large as life between two sisters who seem to be enthralled by the 'excellent book' she is apparently reading to them.

Another mansion that awed the neighbourhood was Temple Newsam. On 14 January 1710 Thoresby 'rode with the Mayor, Cousin Milner, and others to see my Lord Irwin about the erection of a hall for the white cloths in Kirkgate (Leeds). His Lordship gave all the encouragement imaginable.' On another visit Thoresby 'found the ways very bad so that I rode as usually in fear but received no harm, blessed be God'. The distance from Leeds is barely four miles!

Ever since my schooldays Temple Newsam has held a peculiar fascination for me. My first acquaintance with this glorious mansion on the eastern side of Leeds was the second-hand one of admiring it from a distance, through the trees. It was not then open to the public. A master would take a few of us on a school outing, and before walking around the extensive park we would step inside Whitkirk Church to see the tombs of bygone owners of this fabulous place. Recumbent marble figures with lace cuffs for the men and quaint headdresses for the sad-looking ladies conveyed little to a boy, however, and even if our mentor spoke of more illustrious folk who had lived at Temple Newsam—Thomas Darcy, for example, who was beheaded for taking part in the Pilgrimage of Grace, the Countess of Lennox whom Elizabeth I sent to the Tower for conspiring against the throne, or Darnley himself—what were they, just then, but paste-board, impalpable figures that trailed their dreary ghosts through our homework hours? Nevertheless, Temple Newsam left its mark. And when Leeds Corporation bought the property from Mr.

Edward Wood, the late Lord Halifax, a friend and I were among the very first to take advantage of public ownership.

Temple Newsam is an historical pageant in itself. One can stand within the Clock Court and visualise the continuing drama which the place has staged since Dunstan and Glunier, two Anglo-Saxon thanes, came on to the scene about A.D. 1066. Henry de Lacy, founder of Kirkstall Abbey, transferred the property to the Knights Templars about 1155. Then, in stately procession, come later owners, headed by Marie, Countess of Pembroke, who founded Pembroke College, Cambridge. The Darcys make a brave show, even though the estate was to pass to Henry VIII because of Thomas Darcy's defection. Henry's scheming niece, Margaret, later Countess of Lennox, now sweeps into view, attended by her son, Henry Darnley. Then follow the Ingrams and the Irwins—a long line of them, beginning with Sir Arthur Ingram whose robust person conceals a bewildering mixture of piety and fraud, and culminating in modern times with Mrs. Meynell Ingram's nephew, Lord Halifax.

When Temple Newsam was handed over to Leeds Corporation in 1922 the occasion was commemorated in the mansion chapel by the singing of the 90th Psalm—'For a thousand years in Thy sight are but as yesterday. . . .' A very appropriate choice.

Today, Temple Newsam is a happy fusion of two stories; one, the expanding story of a stately home; the other, a no less remarkable story embodying the rise of a provincial art gallery to international distinction. This fusion is apparent wherever one treads. A glance within two or three rooms will suffice to illustrate the point.

The Drawing Room Lobby is hung with a fine eighteenth-century Chinese paper. Gay with exotic birds and foliage, it was reputedly given to the last Viscountess Irwin by the Prince Regent in 1806. Today the Georgian and Regency flair for Chinese art is given abundant expression. Indeed, examples of Chinese craftsmanship keep one bounding from room to room until, at last, one stands before the crowning piece—a massive screen in coromandel lacquer depicting the quaint atmosphere of a mandarin's birthday reception. This screen was bought, largely by public subscription, in 1940.

Then the Darnley Room. Mary Queen of Scots fills such a tragi-romantic rôle in history that every visitor makes a bee-line for this room where Henry Darnley, her husband, was born in 1545. Although the room was completely re-fashioned about eighty years after Darnley 'muled and puked' here, the nimbus of his infancy remains. As his eventual marriage to Mary Stuart was plotted here, the room catches other overtones too.

In the Tudor Room, Temple Newsam's share in the turbulent affairs of King and State at the time of the Reformation gains colourful emphasis by recent developments. In 1947 the Henry VIII Room from Viscount Allendale's former home, Bretton Hall near Wakefield, was reconstructed here. Equipped with splendid furniture and richly carved panelling, it seems to bring Bluff King Hal very near. It is supposed to have been the royal apartment at Bretton during one of the King's Northern progresses.

What a place in which to feel the living pulse of England! Historic personages forever haunt the corridors of Temple Newsam, and their opulence and taste are fulfilled in works of art of almost every genre. Even Sir Arthur Ingram—who once owned forty houses in Yorkshire, besides Temple Newsam—would have been impressed.

I once asked the late Lady Bingley, who lived at Temple Newsam in her youth, if her family did not find so palatial a house difficult to manage. 'To us', she thoughtfully replied, 'it did not seem too big.' And that, I suppose, is the gist of the matter. Considering its rôle in the story of England, Temple Newsam could never be 'too big'.

And yet there are features that convey the simple humanities. I think in particular of a gravestone lovingly erected to a pet squirrel oddly called Bunnie by Isabella Ingram when she was nine years of age. The epitaph breathes with a child's pathos:

> The sun that sets
> The next morning gets,
> But Bunnie gone for ever.
> The flowers that dye
> Next spring we espye,
> But bunnie we shall never.
> Here lyeth a favourite
> Squirrell of Isabella
> Ingram—who (the squirrel) dyed
> 11th of January, 1729.

When Henry Ingram, 7th Viscount Irwin, was creating the Long Gallery at Temple Newsam its ceiling was strengthened with timbers brought over from Kirkstall Abbey. Lovely plasterwork, portraying George II and members of his family, soon hid those timbers from view, but the abbey continued to be used as a 'free-for-all' quarry until the estate was acquired for Leeds in 1890. Basically, Kirkstall Abbey is as picturesque a ruin as any eighteenth-century virtuoso could have wished. J. M. W. Turner painted it before industry crept up the River Aire to tarnish its old walls, yet within the last twenty years the Cistercian monastery of A.D. 1152 has found new and sympathetic friends in the staff of Leeds City Museums. Several exhibitions on the spot have re-created the daily life of the Kirkstall monks and lay brethren, in church and cloister, at their forge and pottery, or working their extensive sheep farms.

The story of Kirkstall took a fresh turn when the monastery's inner gatehouse—a fine Norman building—was adapted for use as the Abbey House Museum, branch of Leeds City Museum. After surrendering the abbey in 1539 John Ripley, the last abbot, had come to live here, and although much has been altered since his time, the spiral stairway still exists by which he would sorrowfully mount to his bed-chamber, musing upon days gone by and listening for the sanctus that never rang. . . .

Yet the monastic heritage did not entirely vanish. Dispossessed monks and conversi found new outlets for their craftsmanship in the neighbourhood. In 1954 the museum was enlarged to accommodate Abbey Fold—a 'street' of old workshops representing some of those same trades, ranging from tanning and weaving to smithing. A few years later a corner of old Leeds, the town that had grown up almost alongside the abbey, was reproduced. Here is a goodly selection of quaint shops, with Edward Baines, stationer, offering almost everything from quill pens to etchings of Kirkstall Abbey; an apothecary blandishing strange nostrums such as Congreve's Balsonnic Elixir which 'annihilates Hooping Cough'; John Dyson, watchmaker, and his whirring collection of curious timepieces; and Mark Dearlove, musical-instrument maker.

All these were Leeds tradesfolk long ago and all have left interesting anecdotes. To celebrate the Leeds Centenary Musical Festival in 1958, many of Mark Dearlove's musical descendants held a family gathering around this museum shop. I was lucky enough to be invited and Jack Dearlove of BBC fame spent a lot of time showing me Mark Dearlove's violins and playing tunes of his own upon them. Even the miniature violin—five inches long, and the double-bass—fourteen inches long, which Mark made for the Great Exhibition of 1851, give out their sweet music. The bow for the tiny Cremona violin is fitted with black hair snipped from her own curls by Mark Dearlove's wife.

The latest addition at the Abbey House is a 'street' named Stephen Harding Gate after the Englishman who was closely associated with

Bernard of Clairvaux in the pioneering stages of the Cistercian Order. His paternal rôle is here stretched to cover many strange sights, from a Victorian ironmongery shop to the Leeds Pottery, as founded in 1760 by the Green brothers. A fine collection of Leeds ware can also be seen at Temple Newsam House, but here are some of the wheels and moulds and other apparatus used in producing those tureens, dishes and tea-pots often bearing curious mottoes. Facing down the street is the 'Hark to Rover' Inn. On the signboard Kirkstall Abbey forms the background to a lurid scene which inspired Southey's poem, 'Mary, the Maid of the Inn'. Despite such little incongruities, Stephen Harding—and John Ripley too—may rest content in the knowledge that Leeds, the vast modern city, has here turned aside to honour their memory.

Some delightful country that fans out to the north of Leeds will be mentioned later. Meanwhile the Bradford area offers much of interest, centring upon the Cathedral, elevated from parish church status in 1919. Within its fifteenth-century walls a few local men of bygone fame happily relate their achievements in carved stone or marble. Joseph Priestley, 1817, presents a relief carving of the Leeds and Liverpool Canal he helped to construct, and one may suppose the top-hatted figure watching the approach of the first two barges to be his own proud self. Abraham Sharp, 1742, who assisted John Flamsteed, the Astronomer Royal, displays some of the instruments he would use in his own curious observatory above the porch of Horton Hall; intimate friends were admitted to this observatory on giving the secret sign—the rubbing of a stone against the outside wall. Soon there may be nothing to rub. The hall is in danger of being eclipsed by town development.

Bolling Hall, not far away, echoes much of Bradford's fascinating story in a series of lovely old rooms, which I have briefly described in *Historic Homes of Yorkshire*. Tong village, four miles south-east of Bradford, ushers one into the squirearchy of eighteenth-century Yorkshire with an estate that long flaunted its peacocks, an adjoining church in which Squire Tempest's family toasted their toes—during sermon time—before a fire blazing in their private, boxed-in pew, and, abutting on the churchyard, a charming stone cottage whose lantern finials have prompted an entertaining variety of tales. People who talk about the lights once burned up there, as guide or warning, never account for the blowing of the wind. To be effective as lanterns the finials would have to be glazed.

From Tong it is but a short walk to Fulneck, where the Moravian

School throws an interesting range of eighteenth-century buildings across the ridge of a half-hidden valley. It is pleasant to think of Richard Oastler—the man who agitated against child slavery in the local mills, and James Montgomery—poet and reformer, pondering here over their algebra and Latin and singing with the others in the little turreted chapel over the entrance. One 'old boy', Christian Ignatius La Trobe—who commenced his schooling here soon after reaching his second birthday!—slept near this chapel, but often kept awake at night so that he could hear the organ pealing forth and the choir singing their liturgies. He became a great Church musician. But school had other repercussions for him. He related how once, when standing in the corner for some misdemeanour, the title of a fresh book met his idle gaze—*A new Account of Guinea and the Slave Trade*. Reaching it down, furtively, he scanned a page or two, and what he gleaned in those few punitive moments gave him a lasting concern for the slaves. When Parliament first investigated the matter of slavery, it was this ex-Fulneck boy who drew up a report on West Indian slaves, furnishing William Wilberforce—his personal friend—with one of his most convincing arguments for emancipation.

There is something to be said, after all, for sending a naughty boy into the corner.

On their countryside jaunts the Fulneck boys of those days sometimes visited Kirkstall Abbey, or the Five Rise Lock on the 'Grand Canal' at Bingley, near Keighley, which gives a fifty-nine-feet lift for the Leeds and Liverpool Canal. There are other attractive portions of the canal a few miles north of Bradford, around Apperley Bridge. The boys of Woodhouse Grove School nearby once went by barge to Leeds along this same waterway. Their objective, that day, was the Wesleyan Conference! The school is a Wesleyan foundation and the canal was then the readiest mode of transport. When the railway came along, in 1846, the school surrendered some land for the purpose. But the boys were not forgotten. The Railway Company undertook to leave a gap in the dividing wall so that they could enjoy watching the passing trains. The gap is still popular with the school's train-spotters.

Woodhouse Grove School developed from the 'elegant Mansion House' built for himself in 1799 by Robert Elam, a Quaker. Elam's Tower is still a prominent feature of the grounds and provides an unusual school-cap badge. It was while Rev. Patrick Brontë, then Vicar of Hartshead, was visiting the school as its first examiner that he met his future wife—Maria Branwell, the headmaster's niece. Picnic parties in-

9   *Ribbed vaulting in the nave aisle, Kirkstall Abbey*

cluding 'Uncle, Aunt and Cousin Jane'—schoolmaster Fennell and his family—sauntered down the banks of the Aire to Kirkstall Abbey, about which Patrick later wrote a poem. Maria was soon talking about her 'dear saucy Pat', and they were married a few months later—29 December 1812—in Guiseley Church, two miles farther up the valley. This beautiful old church is 'clipped', annually, by parish children forming a ring around its sturdy walls and singing hymns. One church window shows this ancient ceremony being observed, also, at the adjoining Elizabethan rectory, where Patrick and his Cornish bride would make their wedding plans with Rector Willoughby.

In subsequent years, when Charlotte Brontë came to Apperley Bridge as governess to the White family of Upperwood House—now supplanted by a preparatory school for Woodhouse Grove—she referred to the Aire as a 'pleasant trout stream'. In these reaches it is hardly that today! She seems to have found some relief from the troublesome White youngsters by keeping silkworms. A lovely woodland walk would take her uphill to Rawdon Hall where, I am told, the tenant's daughter, Mary Bingley, kept her supplied with mulberry leaves. A great-nephew of Mary Bingley has inherited a silk tassel—Charlotte's gift to Mary—spun out of that charming, little-known episode.

10   *Georgian chapel, Fulneck Moravian School, near Bradford*

three

The Brontë Countryside

Charlotte Brontë at Rawdon Hall is a theme to conjure with. This early seventeenth-century house of millstone grit has many of the ingredients that the future author of *Jane Eyre* and *Shirley* was to enjoy so much. In the inner hall she would see a finely carved stone frieze from Kirkstall Abbey. She would also see an imposing bread cupboard which Francis Rawdon had made for the same room, declaring his piety to all future generations by the legend painted round the top edge: 'Give God al praise, For to Him it is Dewe, Love God above all thing, and thi neighbour as Thiself'.

If she ever stepped with Mary Bingley into the Dining Room Charlotte might hear of the secret religious gatherings once held within its wainscoted walls, under the guidance of Rev. Oliver Heywood, one of the pioneer nonconformists, and of the white cloths spread on the garden bushes to summon the faithful from both sides of the valley. And so one might ruminate, Brontë-wise, here at Rawdon Hall, prompted still further by the sight of a long-handled wooden ladle which was actually used to take up the collection in Patrick Brontë's church at Hartshead, near Brighouse.

The moorland area familiarly known as the Brontë countryside radiates from Haworth and Keighley, a few miles to the west, but the Brontë enthusiast will find much of interest *en route*.

At Thornton, on the outskirts of Bradford, there is the simple terrace house in the main street which was the home of Patrick and Maria, and the birthplace of their four younger children. A strong friendship developed between the parson's family and the Kayes and Firths of Allerton Hall, in the same parish. This small Georgian hall is noteworthy on account of a rear courtyard, partly enclosed by former weaving sheds. To confirm a tradition that Charlotte Brontë stayed here several times, the present owner once produced for my inspection a letter written by a cousin of the Kaye family. It refers quite simply to the timid young girl who was being nursed back to health here after her tragic experiences at Cowan Bridge School: 'Charlotte was sitting in a large four-poster bed with a nightcap on.'

Of several other Brontë memories recalled here for my benefit I can best visualise the scene when Joshua Firth dispatched a few of his horse-drawn carts to help convey the parson, his ailing wife, their lively young family, and all their household chattels from Thornton to Haworth—Patrick's next appointment. It is interesting to follow in the wake of that strange cavalcade, for the seven carts trundled along via Denholme, a region of stone quarries which has produced two curiosities—a tiny hamlet of quarrymen's cottages called Egypt, served by a road that almost tunnels between lofty containing walls wittily embedded into local speech as the Walls of Jericho.

Over much of the area local stone is greatly in evidence. The millstone grit stolidifies the cottages; it provides field walls, barns, stepping stones and many a delightful pack-horse bridge. Some country houses are built of millstone grit, and where there was any surplus a few sizeable blocks might be used to improve the grounds. At Bierley Hall, two miles south of Bradford, the second Dr. Richard Richardson paid his man a shilling a day to arrange some boulders into a Druids' Circle and a couple of 'subterraneous caves' that would amuse his guests, especially by moonlight. Gritstone was fashioned into banks in Bradford and Leeds, to say nothing of castles, churches, and monasteries in earlier days. Thornton's Old Bell Chapel, where Patrick Brontë had impressed Elizabeth Firth of Allerton Hall with his initial sermon on the Parable of the Sower, was also a gritstone edifice. And here Patrick was—on an April day in 1820—facing yet another of these toughly sinewed villages, Haworth.

Not a pretty village, then or now, yet so full of gruff character that one asks for nothing more. The steep main street is still the cobbled way up which those borrowed horses toiled so long ago with the new parson's family and effects. Once round the corner by the 'Black Bull', and the worst was over. A short rumble past the gaunt old church, and there was the Parsonage, with the churchyard gravestones crowding near on two sides as if anticipating, already, the next few fateful years.

A plain Georgian house of two storeys, the Parsonage has become the Brontë Society's Museum, and how well it is administered. A wrought-iron sign near the entrance shows one of the literary trio—it could be

Charlotte, Emily or Anne—writing at a pedestal table. The door that admits visitors once admitted the Brontë family and all their friends— parsons, curates, school-chums, and the gay Mrs. Gaskell herself. Imaginatively, therefore, a strange hubbub greets one on the threshold, and if one adds the growl of Emily's dog, Keeper, and the fussy attentions of Tabitha, the servant, the past soon takes command. This process is aided considerably by the chief downstairs rooms having been arranged as Mrs. Gaskell described them in her *Life of Charlotte Brontë* (1857).

On the right is the Parlour where Patrick Brontë studied, wrote his sermons, and ate his meals in complete solitude. Some of his belongings are disposed about the room in a manner that suggests he is just about to enter. The Dining Room, immediately opposite, vividly recalls the now motherless children as they marched around the table in the evenings, reciting some of their little tales and poems, though some of the pictures and furnishings here are of a later day, when Charlotte was famous—and Emily, the dissolute Branwell, and Anne were all dead. The stone stair-case has not materially altered since Patrick Brontë used to stop at the half-landing, on retiring each night, to wind the grandfather clock and tell his children not to stay up too late.

Of the various rooms reached from the stairhead perhaps the most nos-talgic is the sparsely furnished Nursery, later Emily's bedroom. Charlotte describing it wrote:

> There have I sat on the low bedstead, my eye fixed on the window; through which appeared no other landscape than a monotonous stretch of moorland, a grey church tower rising from the centre of the church-yard so filled with graves that the rank weeds and coarse grass scarce had room to shoot between the monuments. . . .

Beneath the wallpaper of this room, some years ago, many tiny drawings were found on the plaster which clearly testify to the fanciful world created for themselves by the Brontë children in their tender years. Equally evocative are some toys found below the floor-boards in 1950—a tin trumpet, an engine wheel, building bricks, a silver medallion.

Another room contains the Apostles' Cupboard, described in *Jane Eyre* as 'A great Cabinet—whose front, divided into twelve panels, bore in grim design the heads of the twelve Apostles'. Branwell's Room is hung with several of his paintings, including a good study of John Brown, then sexton at Haworth. While I was gazing at this portrait on a recent visit, a local joiner doing house repairs edged near and remarked, 'He was my grandfather.' It did not seem strange, but only natural in this village of close-knit families and long memories. The village blacksmith who fashioned the entrance sign once told me that his grandfather made several items for the Brontë family, including the curious toasting iron in the Parlour. One of my informants even remembered short-sighted Patrick Brontë peering into his father's clock shop, in the main street, to get the correct time. A terrifying sight for a little boy—that stern face pressed against the window-pane, but a treasured memory later on, when fame descended upon the Brontës. I myself once met a very old lady, out Oxenhope way, who recalled being in Charlotte Brontë's Sunday School class. The possibility of hearing such first-hand, intimate memories of the Brontë family is, of course, rapidly diminishing.

Except for the tower, the present church at Haworth is unfortunately not the one Patrick Brontë knew. It was built in 1881, years before the Brontë cult developed. A Brontë corner has lately been arranged as a family tribute, but some of the original pews have found their way into the Parsonage, like faithful parishioners seeking their old minister's protection. One pew bears musical inscriptions based on Tennyson's 'Ring out the false, Ring in the new'. Part of Patrick Brontë's three-decker pulpit is now to be seen in the village church at neighbouring Stanbury, which can be reached by road, or by the 'lone green lane' beyond the Parsonage which was Emily's approach to—

> A distant, dreamy, dim blue chain
> Of mountains circling every side.

These 'mountains' are the Pennine moors of *Wuthering Heights*. They harbour charming little ravines like the Sladen Valley, near Stanbury; sprigs of the heather that grows here, among the boulders, used to be sent every year to American admirers of the Brontë sisters, who loved this particular spot. They had friends, nearby, in the Heaton family of Ponden Hall, generally regarded as the house Emily had in mind when creating the Thrushcross Grange of her great novel. The owner here today, Sam Dyson, breeds sheep-dogs that would have delighted Emily; he also farms her favourite bit of country between Ponden and Brontë Bridge in the Sladen Valley.

According to an inscription over the entrance, Ponden Hall was built by Robert Heaton in 1634 and rebuilt in 1807. The result is a curious medley of architectural styles. Many stories are told about the five Heaton bachelors—locally known as 'the five brethren'—who grew up here during the Brontë period. Two of these shy bachelors eventually became trustees of Haworth Church. Extreme shyness seems to have been a family weakness. It is recorded that John Heaton, who lived at one of the Stanbury farms, once went courting, but his heart failed him when he approached his lady-love's cottage. He simply stood there, watching the smoke curling from her chimney, then fled, fully satisfied. Perhaps it was as well that the Heaton boys were younger than the parson's girls, though they were all good friends.

As the Heaton family library—a magnificent collection, including a Shakespeare first folio and many travel books—was made accessible to their Haworth neighbours, it is hardly surprising to find the first-floor room that housed the library figuring as Edgar Linton's Room in *Wuthering Heights*. The books—a great rarity for these parts—have long been dispersed, but the beautifully panelled bookcases remain as a built-in feature.

Another interesting survival is an outhouse once used by the Heatons for band practices. They were keen exponents of church music. A contemporary thus described the scene here on the day of the Scar Top Anniversary: 'There's Will Feather with his trombone as clean as a pin and as breet as silver, with his black coat, white waistcoat and checked trousers . . . and Jim Feather with his clarionette, and Will o' Ponden the ophecleide, and there was Jim Brigg o' Deanfield with his big bass fiddle. . . .' Not on that day could the neighbourhood be regarded as the 'Lonely Valley' served by a 'Silent Inn' which figures in Halliwell Sutcliffe's novels; though one can go along there at most times and hear nothing but the bleating of sheep or the plop of a fish in the reservoir that now stretches between Ponden Hall and Scar Top Chapel.

From Ponden a stiff foot climb over the peaty uplands takes one to Top Withens, a now derelict farm that most literary enthusiasts identify as the original 'Wuthering Heights' of Emily's searing novel. Five or six miles beyond, to the south, the lovely wooded valley known as Hardcastle Crags winds away towards Hebden Bridge, a small manufacturing town where houses, chapels and other buildings are terraced above one another —giving a curious pick-a-back effect—on the steep hillsides. This district is served by the A6033 from Haworth.

The Brontë story emerges again around Brighouse, via A646 and A643, where Kirklees Hall stands aloof from surrounding industry, looking south-east over the Calder Valley.

Various episodes in *Shirley* take place in and around this fine Jacobean Hall, which is the 'Nunnely' of the novel. History had already clothed the

place with romance, for the hall is linked by Nun Brook—as by an um-
bilical cord—with the Cistercian nunnery that provided the stone. It was
from the Priory Gatehouse that Robin Hood, after being bled too freely
by the Prioress, his vengeful kinswoman, shot his last arrow, asking to be
buried at the spot where it fell to earth. His supposed grave is at the top
of a neighbouring hill, within the grounds of Kirklees. Michael Drayton,
personifying the Calder, wrote in his droll manner:

> She in her course on Kirkley cast her eye,
> Where merry Robin Hood, that honest thief, doth lie.

Charlotte Brontë was fully aware of these traditions, which also embrace the 'Three Nuns' Inn nearby. This hostelry was originally the guest
house provided for visitors to Kirklees Priory and the Three Nuns' sign
commemorates the last three nuns at the Priory when this was dissolved
in 1539. Although entirely rebuilt in 1939, the inn jealously preserves
former associations.

In the colourful medium of stained glass, various figures appear at the
windows—Little John, Friar Tuck, Robin Hood and the wicked Prioress.
There is a Luddite also—one of the desperate men who, at the beginning
of the nineteenth century, went about in gangs, storming the local woollen
mills and breaking up the new, hated machinery. Automation is not confined to modern times. For their destructive purpose the Luddites were
drilled at this inn, and then forgathered at midnight round a roadside
monument known as the Dumb Steeple. Charlotte Brontë had heard her
father reminisce from his Hartshead days about the Luddites, who conse-
quently provide some exciting scenes in Shirley. Oddly enough the Dumb
Steeple originated for the very peaceful purpose of ushering wayfarers
into the sanctuary area that once enfolded Kirklees Priory. This Steeple—
'dumb' because it has no bells—occupies the traffic roundabout on the
road from Bradley to the 'Three Nuns'.

About five miles to the north-east, at Birstall, there is another hall that
dovetails into the Brontë narrative. It is Oakwell Hall. While Charlotte
and Emily attended Miss Wooler's school in the same little township
there would be ample opportunity for them to see and admire this Elizabethan manor house. Later, Charlotte stayed here as a guest. Her lively
portrait of Oakwell occurs in Shirley, and even now one could almost use
the book as a guide to the house.

Notable features are the balustraded gallery, reached by a charming
staircase fitted at the bottom with a pair of dog-gates. They evidently

suggested to Charlotte that famous episode in which some visiting curates found refuge there from the attentions of Shirley Keeldar's fierce hound. Fascinating also is the small, household dairy. To comply with the regulations for window-tax exemption, in George III's reign, its tiny wooden grille was suitably labelled outside, but the spelling is odd enough to have caught Charlotte Brontë's observant eye. It is in the simple vernacular—DIRY.

Today Oakwell Hall is owned by Batley Corporation and opened regularly to the public. It is always as well, however, to keep alert for any evening concert arrangements here. Sometimes a programme of madrigals might be given, with all the performers dressed in Elizabethan costume. Once, some friends and I formed part of an audience that watched, enthralled, as *Jane Eyre* came to life in the old panelled hall. It seemed as though Charlotte was looking on, too, from her 'curates' gallery'.

The supposed West Riding dourness is often belied. A touch of poetry may colour some otherwise drab scheme as when, early last century, Colonel Edward Akroyd provided terraces of sombre dwellings for his Halifax workpeople, but named all the streets after great English cathedrals. The church, All Souls', which he commissioned Sir George Gilbert Scott to build for Akroydon—his little 'kingdom' on the fringe of Halifax—caused the architect to say, later, 'It is, on the whole, my best church'. Certainly the magnesian limestone gave him a pliable medium for its wealth of pseudo-Gothic carving. Then, instead of decorating his mansion, Bankfield, in conventional manner, this enterprising mill-owner exploited the Renaissance for his grand staircase, his pillared rooms and his lovely ceilings.

By a twist of fortune Bankfield has become the town's principal museum, and Akroyd's former Dining Room now accommodates many architectural features from houses built in the local vernacular styles, mainly of the seventeenth century. There are some beautiful plaster decorations, gable windows that once lit the handloom chamber of an old moorland farm, a fifteenth-century half-timbered wall from a homestead near Brighouse, a curious painting from the now demolished High Sunderland—whose external sculptures Emily Brontë had faithfully described in *Wuthering Heights*, and a reconstructed room from Scout Hall with a portrait of John Mitchell, its first owner, over the fireplace.

High Sunderland and Scout Hall were close neighbours in the diminutive Shibden Valley, which retains its rural appeal, being shielded from

11 Haworth Parsonage—home of the Brontë family

the chimneys of central Halifax—only a mile away—by a fortunate ridge. John Mitchell of Scout Hall was a constant thorn in the flesh to Rev. Oliver Heywood, that pioneer nonconformist whose preaching tours were perforce of a clandestine nature. 'Few dare own me', he once confided to his diary, yet he was 'sweetly entertained' by several of the West Riding gentry and, as at Rawdon Hall, allowed to hold secret services below their roofs.

But John Mitchell was certainly not of this select few. Heywood's diary vividly presents the tale of his shortcomings: 'Mr. Jo. Mitchell of Scout . . . to season his new house, entertaining all comers, had fearful ranting work drinking healths freely, had forty three dishes at once. I have scarce heard the like in our parts; his wife was the musitian. Lord put a stop.' Also, there are fulminations against Mitchell's addiction to horse-racing and gambling. Eventually, the owner of Scout Hall shocked the neighbourhood further by acquiring a kind of glider. In seventeenth-century Shibden a flying contraption would certainly be regarded as devil's work. Proof of this soon came, for while testing the device near his home, Mitchell crashed and broke his neck. Heywood—doubtless with great restraint—simply records in his diary that Mitchell's way of life had 'shortened his time'.

Mitchell's semi-classical house of 1680—a complete novelty for the district—is now empty and desolate. An amusing fox-hunting scene over the front door alone reminds one of Mitchell and his sporting interests.

Architecturally the most important house in the neighbourhood is Shibden Hall. It is an early fifteenth-century timber-framed dwelling later encased with stone, and commands a good view of the lower valley. Emily Brontë—who was governess at Southowram nearby for a time—may have breathed something of its character into *Wuthering Heights*. The house-body, or central room, is still furnished in a manner that enables one to visualise a scene recorded by Heywood on 13 July 1664:

> Being at Shibden Hall . . . I was desired to tarry dinner. They had invited some friends, and amongst the rest, Dr Hooke, Vicar of Halifax, who would not stay to dine because, as he said, he was bound by the canons not to eat with an excommunicated person, and, though he would have gone away, yet I thought that I would rather quit the place than that he should lose his dinner or be defiled, or his own conscience perplexed.

So it was Heywood, after all, who went empty away.

12 *Countryside pattern near Sowerby Bridge, West Riding*

The pseudo-Norman tower added last century is certainly a peculiar sight, yet nothing can rob Shibden Hall of its intrinsic appeal. Could anybody resist the naïve charm of its little picture gallery, devised in stained glass and presenting all kinds of oddities from a bird playing a dulcimer to the devil gleefully carrying off a sole, or soul? The entire Shibden estate is now owned by Halifax Corporation, and the seventeenth-century outbuildings accommodate the West Riding Folk Museum. This contains many craftsmen's workshops such as an estate of this kind would once foster; in the saddlery there is a set of packhorse bells which represent the tuneful mode of transport in vogue when the Listers of Shibden Hall were prosperous cloth merchants.

Of the once dreaded Halifax Gibbet nothing now remains except its stone platform, enclosed within a small court off Gibbet Lane in the town centre. Up to about 1650 this vile instrument dealt irrevocably with cloth stealers and other offenders. In Bankfield Museum there is a working model of the gibbet, but Moll's map of the West Riding, dated 1724, has a marginal illustration showing the whole grim procedure, with every part of the instrument—including a victim waiting for the axe to fall—lettered for detailed comment below. Some Frenchmen had once come over to Halifax to see the real thing. Traditionally, a long-term result of that visit was another Sharp Maiden, more generally known as Madame Guillotine.

To the west of Halifax there is some glorious hill country, dotted with attractive villages like Norland—perched on a windswept plateau above Sowerby Bridge; Cotton Stones, near Sowerby, which some touring maps do not even show; and Luddenden—miraculously wedged in a deep clough or ravine. While engaged as a railway clerk at Luddenden Foot, nearby, Branwell Brontë frequented the 'Lord Nelson' Inn at Luddenden and joined its library. This contained over 1,000 volumes and demanded of its members sobriety and decorous conduct. Drunkenness or swearing cost the culprit twopence for each offence. The library, housed in an upper room, petered out completely by 1915, but some of the books are now kept in Sowerby Bridge Public Library. The books cover all manner of subjects—travel, moral precepts, the aristocracy. I wonder what Branwell Brontë would make of *Chrystal, or the Adventures of a Guinea*, by Charles Johnstone (1775)? It was a very early example of the English novel. Perhaps the *Newgate Calendar*—with its graphic account of crimes, trials and tortures—was more in his line?

Not far away the Ryburn Valley, which William Wordsworth knew and loved, takes the A58 towards the Pennines. Near the county boundary on Blackstone Edge the moors are crossed for a short distance by a Roman road. Antiquaries still argue about its authenticity. Several reservoirs emphasise the grandeur of these solitudes. Defoe found the neighbourhood weird and perilous when riding into Yorkshire by this switchback route on his celebrated Tour through Great Britain (1727). The account of his adventures, up here, makes rather comic reading for today. For example: 'We thought now we were come into a Christian Country again, and that our Difficulties were over; but we soon found our selves mistaken in the Matter; for we had not gone fifty yards . . . but we found the Way began to ascend again, and soon after to go up very steep, till in about half a Mile we found we had another Mountain to ascend, in our apprehension as bad as the first. . . .' I am glad he got down to Halifax safely, for it was here that he began to write *Robinson Crusoe*. The local wool trade which interested Defoe comes alive today in the novels of Phyllis Bentley.

It would be well worth joining Woodsome Hall Golf Club if only for the privilege of seeing, repeatedly, this lovely house and estate near Almondbury, on the southern fringe of Huddersfield. Although the hall has become the club headquarters, its past lives on, largely unspoilt, in some of the finest domestic architecture which the district ever produced.

Three families preceded the Kayes at Woodsome—the Nottons in the thirteenth century, the Tyases in the fourteenth century, and for a short time afterwards the Finchendens, whose emblem—the finch—still adorns rain-water-heads, etc., as though to perpetuate the memory of Dame Alice Finchenden. In 1378 she granted the manor of Woodsome to John Kaye for twenty years, but when John married Dame Alice's daughter the emblematic bird was snared for posterity, so to speak, and Woodsome became a Kaye possession. The Kayes retained ownership until 1726, when Sir Arthur Kaye's daughter married George Legge, Viscount Lewisham, eldest son of the Earl of Dartmouth. Even now that little finch persists— in the crest of the present Earl of Dartmouth, the club's president.

The half-timbered dwelling to which John Kaye brought his bride evolved into a grand, stone house. One 'meets' the couple responsible on entering the Great Hall, for their names—Arthur Kaye and Beatrix Kaye —are carved in fancy lettering a foot high over the large, open fireplace. The Tolson Memorial Museum at Huddersfield now has custody of some treasures that once graced this noble room, notably a couple of curiously painted wooden panels. John Kaye is portrayed on one, along with the alliterative family motto *Kynd, Kynne, Known, Kepe*. The other panel, dated 1567, shows Arthur Kaye reclining like a second Adam while from his breast issues a family tree supporting nineteen figures. I wish Charlotte Brontë could have seen them!

These panels formerly hung on brackets from the minstrel gallery, which spans one side of the panelled room. High above the fireplace a quaint old clock plumed in Cavalier style chimes away the hours, and on the opposite wall there are two lattice windows through which the ladies once looked down on the after-dinner merriment of their menfolk below. The open courtyard at the rear of the building is equally charming, but the warm, convivial atmosphere of this Great Hall best suits the Christmas Song of Woodsome which used to be sung here:

> *The Master of this house, where now ye are met,*
> *Doth think you all welcome, and much in your debt;*
> *That with him you are pleased to use honest mirth,*
> *And with him rejoice in Jesus Christ's birth.*
>
> *The Master of this house, simple tho' he be,*
> *Doth care for his neighbours in every degree;*
> *And earnestly biddeth you turn wrath to mirth*
> *By the Godly embracing of Jesus, His birth.*

The 2nd Earl of Dartmouth was a man of whom Oliver Heywood—interrogated here in 1672 by Sir John Kaye—would have approved. The poet Cowper appraisingly wrote of the Earl as 'one who wears a coronet and prays'.

four

The Pennine Dales: I
from Airedale to High Craven, Dent and Bowland

In my early youth the Yorkshire Dales usually meant a day trip to Ilkley Moor, with an exhilarating walk from Hawksworth and the 'Gaping Goose' amongst the heather and the bilberry 'cushions'. Or, leaving Otley behind, we might trudge through the Washburn Valley. On one ambitious school outing we even explored Bolton Woods—keeping out of the Strid's clutches as best we might, and reaching as our *ultima thule* the grey stone tower of Barden. It really seemed like the edge of the world.

But then, of course, there were very few cars on the roads. Our own neighbour still ran one of the pioneer steam cars which had to stop every few miles to be re-filled with water from well or village pump! The Dales remained largely undiscovered.

How different today! The whole of the dales country, with its wonderful rivers, fells, villages and lonely spaces, is accessible to all, and the roads are mostly excellent. If I had to name the best that England has shown to me, I should try to forget the Cotswolds, and a lovely bit of North Devon, and—putting the Lake District into a special category—plump unreservedly for those same, far-spreading Yorkshire Dales.

It is odd, but many people who have lived in Yorkshire for years have yet to see Bolton Priory shimmering in the River Wharfe, High Force in spate, or the limestone crags and caves around Malham and Settle with all their archaeological appeal. They cannot realise how impoverished they are! Needlessly impoverished.

Thanks to the National Park movement and other vigilant bodies the dales country is, on the whole, remarkably unspoilt. The chief dales are Airedale, Wharfedale, Nidderdale, Wensleydale and Swaledale. Teesdale is shared with Co. Durham, and there are many delightful offshoots—all scooped out and pummelled into shape by geological action millions of years ago.

Skipton is a good centre both for Airedale and Wharfedale, but the old town itself must first be given its due. All the dales' farmers from miles around assemble here on market day, bringing not only their produce, or the price of a good heifer, say, but a picturesque dialect that would have been familiar to Lady Anne Clifford, away back in the seventeenth century.

About a hundred years ago one local firm whose ironmongery shop still overlooks the market place in High Street patronised the Abbeydale works in Sheffield—already mentioned—for scythes and sickles. These often came to Skipton by canal. This same firm sold quantities of Wensleydale cheese, supplied tools to the local lead-miners, and at length produced one of the first motorcars. Horse nails were also made here; in one of the old account books shown to me there is this droll entry:

> End of old Tom Bishop's nailing account—he is now dead and buried and if he is lucky (has) got a good block and good work in Kingdom come with a new Pair of Puffers (bellows).

The same kind of humour is heard in the market today. It does not seem long since the shoppers were all agog about a certain fifty-year-old farmer who, after being engaged for fifteen years, had just married the lady. 'Well, there's one thing aboot it,' declared the man's neighbour, 'it's noan so long to go if it doan't turn oot too weel.'

Standing protectively at the head of this broad street are the old parish church and the castle. Both demand homage in the form of a quiet hour's exploration.

The church draws upon six or seven centuries of history with many fascinating items, including the chancel screen supposedly from Bolton Priory; but the Clifford family tombs are the great attraction. When referring to the tomb of the 3rd Earl of Cumberland, the 'Sailor Earl', Dr. Whitaker pulled out all the stops of his antiquarian zeal by exclaiming, 'I much doubt whether such an assemblage of noble bearings can be found on the tomb of any other Englishman.' It is certainly an heraldic feast and worthy of the man to whom all these ancestral alignments were but a spur to exuberant living. George, the 3rd Earl, was a man after Queen Elizabeth's heart, revelling as she did in daring exploits. This scion of the Clifford family fought with distinction against the Spanish Armada and was the first to acquaint the Queen of its defeat. But he also had ideas of turning Puerto Rico, which he had earlier captured from the Spaniards, into a pirate kingdom, with himself at the helm. The pearl-mounted glove Elizabeth gave him appears in his well-known portrait at the British Museum and can be construed as a token of her overt pleasure in his risqué escapades. A grotto in the castle gateway represents a more creditable performance. It comprises sea-shells and fossils which the Sailor Earl is said to have collected during his voyages.

The castle, also, has its heraldic displays, from the family motto, *Desormais* (meaning Henceforth), spelt out in huge letters above the gateway, to the armorial cognisances carved on the walls of the Conduit Court. On first entering the court visitors invariably express delighted surprise, for this is a lovely fragment of Tudor England. The Clifford ladies must often have sunned themselves here while their menfolk were away at the wars. Immediately opposite the entrance arch one coat-of-arms catches a shaft of sunlight. Dr. Whitaker seemed rather puzzled by some of its devices, but surely there is no mistaking the wyvern supporters, and the checky coat quartered with three chain shots on the shield. These are the arms of John, Lord Clifford—Shakespeare's 'boist'rous Clifford', who eventually fell at Towton Field.

Today the lofty yew-tree here—traditionally planted after the Civil Wars by the Sailor Earl's daughter, Lady Anne Clifford—has reached full maturity and spreads a tapestry of feathery green fingers against the creamy-white walls. Many other parts of the castle are open to public view—including a particularly horrid dungeon!—but a comparatively little-known spot is the old moat, picturesquely incorporated with a canal that stretches its leafy way behind the west side of High Street.

Airedale is losing most of its industrial trappings by the time one turns aside from A650, just outside Keighley, to see East Riddlesden Hall. Over each entrance porch there is a very fine specimen of wheel window, peculiar to the West Riding. This lovely place, now owned by the National Trust, is the most convenient for recalling a long, expensive law-suit which ruined the Murgatroyds who once lived here. The family were supposed to pay Lady Anne Clifford one boon hen, annually, in addition to their rent. For two generations the Murgatroyds refused, but Lady Anne hung on until the courts awarded her this particular boon. Then, having won her point, she invited the losers to a banquet at which the restituted hen was served up, piping hot.

Other stories about this redoubtable woman will emerge later. Meanwhile, upper Airedale is calling.

For some miles the A59 from Skipton is a continuous avenue of beeches. Enchancing the scenery are the grounds of Broughton Hall. This house was founded in Elizabethan times, the famous Sailor Earl of Skipton granting Henry Tempest the necessary timber. No outward sign of the Elizabethan dwelling remains; its outer walls were enclosed by the remodelled centre portion when, in 1810, William Atkinson added the Ionic wings. The Italian gardens, designed by William Nesfield, followed in 1855.

A strange sense of furtiveness lingers from earlier days, however, for the Tempests suffered repeatedly for their staunch adherence to the Catholic faith. The present owner once showed me some of the licences, or passes, without which the family could not budge more than five miles from home. This meant that Skipton was just within bounds, whereas Malham, Settle and Grassington were forbidden country unless some magistrate, convinced of genuine intentions—such as unavoidable business or even paying court to a lady—issued the required licence. One licence, issued from the Council Chamber at Windsor on 9 July 1705, permitted Stephen Tempest of Broughton to keep a certain number of horses, for necessary estate work. Normally, at that time, no Catholic was allowed to possess a horse worth more than five pounds.

Any kind of intolerance may seem completely foreign to the neighbourhood opening out ahead, yet local Quakers and other Protestants had their share of persecution too, as time and place will reveal. At Airton there is an attractive Quaker Meeting House built in 1700 by William and Alice Ellis four years after putting up their own cottage, immediately opposite. In the gable end of this cottage a large pigeon cote reflects the simple ways of bygone village husbandry. Along with Eshton and Kirkby Malham, Airton forms part of a little network of delight between Broughton and Malham.

The early tourists were 'horrified' by the limestone scars that envelop Malham. After visiting Gordale Scar in 1769 Thomas Gray wrote to his friend, Dr. Wharton: '. . . and came to Malham (pronounce Mawm) a village in the bossom of the mountains, seated in a wild and dreary valley . . . on the cliffs above hung a few goats; one of them danced and scratched an ear with its hind foot in a place where I would not have stood stock-still for all beneath the moon.' The 'principal horror' of this gorge was its magnificent waterfall. 'I stay'd there (not without shuddering) a quarter of an hour, and thought my trouble richly paid, for the impression will last for Life.' No poetic Elegy here!

A few months later Gray was to tell Dr. Wharton of a trip to Kirkstall Abbey, whose 'lofty towers . . . were the truest objects for my glass I have yet met with anywhere. . . .' With this same curious device—'a plano-convex mirror of about four inches in diameter, on a black foil'— he had evidently tried to get an adequate view of Malham's overhanging rocks, about 400 feet above ground. They 'gave much employment to the mirror', he wrote, but some drips of icy water and a few loose stones that threatened to crash upon him from the same dizzy height made him rather nervous. Lunch at the village inn restored him, especially on hearing that a few landscape painters had lodged there recently while producing pictures of the same 'savage' Gordale.

How different today, when gaily clad youths and girls scamper up the gorge with the agility of Gray's goats and photograph each other in the same precarious places!

Malham owes most of its glorious scenery to the mid-Craven Fault, 'a great dislocation of strata, running east and west from the neighbourhood of Pateley Bridge to Ingleton'. Several visits would be needed to explore all the limestone ramifications around Malham Cove and Gordale Scar, and the astonishing pavements and disappearing streams on Malham Moor. They form a natural playground and must have made many a person into a lifelong geologist.

The bird and plant life, too, are engrossing. Not for nothing has Malham Tarn House become a Field Studies Centre. Down in the village these interests are beautifully characterised in the design of the garden gates at Dale House, in Cove Road. The wrought-iron motifs represent the natural life of the area—flowering grasses, swallows and swifts, a young leveret feeding off the wayside sedges, a curlew from the moors. Dominating the gates as their kind dominate the limestone fells are a Swaledale ram and a ewe suckling her lamb. Not only do these creatures reflect the district but also the mind of William Wild, the versatile artist and craftsman of Malham who works in the old village smithy; an up-to-date Thoreau for ever trying to catch the beauty and significance of the fleeting moment.

I have not attempted to describe Malham's attractions in any great detail, yet this must be said—some of us would never be satisfied until we had trodden that boulder-strewn way to the Cove and drunk of the water that bubbles like a faery thing from the very base of this huge amphitheatre of rock. Whether one regards this stream as the infant River Aire, or the tributary it really is, its sparkling water is essential vintage amongst Yorkshire ramblers.

14 Limestone grandeur at Malham Cove, Upper Airedale

Another splendid springboard for this High Craven area is Settle. Despite its restful name this busy little market town on A65 is one of the most stimulating places I know. Situated in the Ribble Valley, it is flanked by a wide arc of limestone hills whose baroque contours and hanging precipices demand exploration. Fortunate are they who discover the district while physical agility still enables them to climb the fells on foot, or to enter the caves and potholes that abound. Indeed, the youthful rambler, the caver, and the hill shepherd are the true inheritors of High Craven. Even so, there are numerous lanes that weave amongst the hills, offering motorists some intimate share in the general enchantment.

While still at valley level, in Settle, it is a good plan to visit—though only by prior arrangement with the owner—the Pig Yard Club Museum at Town Head. This converted fifteenth-century house is aptly situated at the Settle end of an old pack-horse track heading for 'Malham Mere' or Tarn. I enjoyed many a talk with the late owner, Mr. Tot Lord, who began caving as a sport and then graduated by sheer force of interest to its scientific and archaeological aspects.

The museum collection includes early-British dragonesque brooches and other bronze trinkets from Victoria, Attermire and Kelco Caves; part of a Roman chariot probably seized as loot by hill tribesmen; a short sword or *gladius* as used by a Roman foot soldier, and a pair of bronze eyebrow tweezers from a camp site in front of Attermire Cave. Victoria Cave has also yielded Roman coins of two distinct periods, suggesting that in the second and fourth centuries A.D. the local caves were occupied by Romano-British refugees. Of the earlier occupation of the caves there is ample evidence. Thus, from varying levels among the talus and laminated clays of Victoria Cave, remains of the woolly rhinoceros, hyena, great cave bear, straight-tusked elephant and red deer have rewarded the searchers.

Up on the fells around Attermire an imaginative person could mistake the solitary figure one often sees there for the traditional Brown Man of the Moors. He is probably the shepherd from Stockdale Farm, rounding up a few sheep with the aid of his collie. They have to keep a vigilant eye on their animals in High Craven. On dogs especially, for their questing instincts often lead them into some limestone cavity that may burrow far underground. It was such an escapade that led to the discovery of Victoria Cave, on Queen Victoria's coronation day, in 1838. Privately explored at first—after somebody's dog had nosed its way in—the cave was systematically excavated with British Association support in 1870–8; it proved to be one of the most important in the North of England.

A motorist can get fairly near the cave by following the Kirkby Malham road out of Settle for a mile, then branching left along the narrow Stockdale Lane for another mile. Magnificent country opens out ahead but without the help of a one-inch Ordnance Survey map one could soon be lost amongst its crags and miss Victoria Cave altogether. Other caves occur in Attermire and Langcliffe Scars nearby, but to the ordinary fell walker Victoria Cave is the safest and perhaps the most satisfying.

No special tackle is needed, though an electric torch is advisable for the innermost recesses. When I was last up there the cave was occupied by a number of wild goats. They seemed as thoroughly at home as those remarked upon by Thomas Gray, and lent an air of fantasy to the rock chambers, whose walls glisten with water seeping through from above. On the drier ledges, a few years ago, a young recluse clad in monastic habit passed several days in quiet contemplation. Unknown to him, he was repeating a sojourn spent here in the eleventh or twelfth century A.D. by one Ramric, probably a hermit. A Silurian slate slab bearing his name in runic characters was found in the cave during the 1870 excavations. It is now in the Pig Yard Club Museum.

When in High Craven I do not wonder that Michael Drayton invested the area with 'Topick Gods', as earlier writers did with their 'Pennine host of demons'. The famous triumvirate—Ingleborough, 2,373 feet, Penyghent, 2,273 feet, and Whernside, 2,419 feet—presides over the whole domain, each in its primeval splendour, just as though nothing had happened since the dawn of Creation. From Horton-in Ribblesdale, Penyghent looks like a huge sphinx. And Ingleborough—when it deigns to doff its cloud-cap—lifts an even nobler profile to the northern sky. After viewing the mountain once from this aspect, in a gale-force wind, John Ruskin recalled 'the vague sense of wonder with which I watched Ingleborough stand without rocking'.

Once, when I stopped to admire Penyghent afresh, a local bus drew up and the driver joined me by the roadside. Without any kind of preamble—it wasn't the occasion for any formalities!—he launched into a very creditable geological account of the mountain and its peculiar, awesome structure. Was not this limestone colossus, capped with millstone grit and marked with dark transverse bands, part of the background against which he lived his mortal span? I expect his regular passengers knew the phenomenal story off by heart!

Ingleton, the village at the western foot of Ingleborough, is justly famous for its glens and waterfalls. Let nobody think he has exhausted Yorkshire's touring possibilities until—preferably after rain—he has walked through the whole labyrinth and then swung round via the moraines to Thornton Force.

Much less popular today is Weathercote Cave, just wide of Chapel-le-Dale in the little Greta Valley that runs north-east from Ingleton. Nothing is required here but sure feet. It is a cave and pothole combined, with a stream bursting into the vertical shaft and then as quickly disappearing underground, like so many other streams in this fascinating countryside. A beck may flow merrily along, with cows wading leisurely through its transparent coolness; then, without warning, the fissured stream bed becomes deserted. Even the cows look round in surprise! Ears to the ground, I have spent hours trying to follow the course of these subterranean waters. Great fun when one is young. And the wagtails are always good company.

South of Ingleton and Settle lies Bowland Forest, which Yorkshire shares with Lancashire. It is forest no longer, nor was it ever forest in the accepted sense of the word, though there is much beautiful woodland—and several other features—to take one back in spirit to the days when the king came north to hunt deer.

Clapham, half-way between Settle and Ingleton on A65, is a beautiful spot in its own right, with some grey old cottages and a couple of quaint bridges spanning the beck that tosses down from Ingleborough. The village also provides a south-bound road to Bowland. Mountains are abruptly left behind as one crosses the exhilarating Burn Moor, where the River Hodder and innumerable lesser streams have their lonely birth. Describing the different effects of limestone in Craven on the one hand, and Bowland on the other, the geologist Tiddeman amusingly compared them to the Jews and the Samaritans—having origins in common but determined to live separately. In Bowland the limestone rarely comes to the surface. Even a novice must notice the dramatic change of scenery, especially around Buckhaw Brow—the steep hill leading down towards Settle. On the north side—the glorious limestone bastions of Giggleswick Scar, stretching for a mile or so and hiding a tiny hamlet, Feizor, which has its own 'private' view of Penyghent; immediately to the south—a far-spreading countryside reduced to low ridges and grassy hummocks. A lane from Giggleswick village curls round via Rathmell to enter Bowland from the north-east.

The first Bowland village to appear, about ten miles from either point on the A65, is Slaidburn. It has a fine church, with three-decker pulpit and squire's pew; and the 'Hark to Bounty' Inn. The inn's exterior staircase leads directly into a panelled Court Room where offenders against the old forest laws received whatever justice the times could manage.

Browsholme Hall, near Whitewell on the Clitheroe road, is the key to this countryside, for its present owner, Col. Robert Parker, is descended from the hereditary Bowbearers of Bowland. In fact the name, Parker—first adopted in the fourteenth century—signifies the highly important office of Park-keeper, a kind of local suzerain. Today one looks in vain for the herds of deer that once made Bowland famous as a royal hunting ground. The wild cattle of former times have also vanished. But Browsholme—pronounced Brewsome—has its own eloquence.

Presiding from one end of the Tudor entrance hall there is an interesting portrait of Thomas Parker, Bowbearer in 1592, wearing a magistrate's dress of that period. Nearby, Edward Parker, Bowbearer about 1690, holds a staff tipped with a buck's head, and a bugle horn hangs from his girdle. Their watchful gaze seems to rest on many relics of the chase hung around—hunting horns, spurs, antlers, etc., but the chief item is an iron dog-gauge, or stirrup, first used by the Bowbearers at the end of the fifteenth century. Any dog which could not pass through this stirrup was regarded as a menace to the king's deer, and its owner had to pay a fine or even destroy the poor creature. The gauge measures only nine inches across the widest part!

'My forebears were responsible for enforcing this law, and it was never revoked,' Col. Parker tells his half-crown visitors. 'The gauge was last used in 1780 when John Parker was elected M.P. for Clitheroe in opposition to the nominee of the Duke of Buccleuch. The Duke's ladies, out of spite, insisted that a pack of beagles kept at Browsholme should be tested in the stirrup. Failing to pass the test the hounds were destroyed!' The hound called Bounty after whom Slaidburn's old inn was named, in earlier times, presumably had better luck.

The present house dates from 1507, though its red sandstone frontage was added by the Elizabethan architect, Thomas Holt of York. J. M. W. Turner once stayed here during a painting expedition, which turned out to be 'very wet'. He and the Fawkes party from Farnley probably spent much time indoors, looking at Squire Parker's treasures. Early in the nineteenth century Thomas Lister Parker had spent a fortune on the house and grounds. Now that the hall is open to public view, one shares Turner's privilege—without having to bother about the weather.

There are some fine portraits, including a Romney and a Lely. John Carr, connected to the Parkers through marriage, is seen in a painting by Sir William Beechey; the architect cuts a very elegant figure and rests one hand on his plan for the Crescent at Buxton. A pair of sofas from his York home seems to bring Carr right into the Drawing Room, though he would probably have been discomfited to find himself surrounded here by so many Jacobite relics. These include garters and a tartan handkerchief—once belonging to Bonnie Prince Charlie—sent to Elizabeth Parker by her Jacobite sweetheart. Even more embarrassing, for a patriot, would be Charles Edward's portrait. Worked in silk, it is one of those smuggled into England in the heel of somebody's jack-boot.

Browsholme is also notable for its variety of beautiful furniture. There are court cupboards, livery cupboards, and bobbin chairs of Henry VIII's time. A finely carved reredos from Whalley Abbey, beyond Clitheroe, occurs in the Great Hall, also a monk's chair fitted with a heavy head-piece which knobbled the sitter if he should nod. This is a copy made by Richard Alston; the original thirteenth-century head-piece seen nearby shows that its function was not his own invention! Chippendale is represented by some lovely and rare pieces, Grinling Gibbons by the fine panelling in the Oak Parlour, while the Velvet Room contains the wonderfully designed Guest Chair in red walnut, c. 1720, known by repute to most connoisseurs. The Richard Alston mentioned above was a gifted wood-carver employed by the Parker family for over fifty years. He helped to refurnish the house after a series of disastrous fires. It is a delight to see so much evidence of his skill, mingling with that of acknowledged masters. He died in 1909.

Browsholme Hall stands on the very threshold of Lancashire. Nearby the beautiful River Hodder plays hide-and-seek with the boundary and the famous Trough of Bowland starts its long, winding ascent through the Pennines. Several little lanes on the Yorkshire side twist around some of Bowland's reef knolls—low, conical hills built up in remote times in the manner of coral reefs, for the whole area was then under water. One soon begins to recognise these knolls. Whitewell and Slaidburn both have good examples, almost on the doorstep, though the best Yorkshire ones known to me are several miles across country, near Linton in Upper Wharfedale.

From Browsholme itself a very interesting road zigzags via Bashall

Eaves to the pretty village of Waddington. The restored Perpendicular church contains two modern windows whose full significance only becomes apparent on crossing the little beck to Waddington Old Hall. One of those windows portrays the Saxon giant Wada, and the other Henry VI preparing to yield up his crown.

The Waddington family derived their name from Wada, as indicated on the hall's entrance gate set up as part of his general restoration scheme by John Waddington in 1900. Evidently, while sheep farming in Australia, the thought of the old place falling into ruin irked his soul. After all, Wada, founder of the family, had built Mulgrave Castle, near Whitby, somewhere about the year A.D. 798 so it was up to this wealthy sheep-farmer to set about the ancestral Waddington Hall—which he did, chivying himself with the ancient tag:

I will raise up his ruins,
I will build it as in the days of old.

Though he may have overplayed his hand a little, this son of a noble family saved the hall for posterity. Original features still remain, memorably the Tudor windows and a fourteenth-century doorway in the Monk's Room. The hall's most evocative feature is a restored spiral stairway leading from the Dining Room to a chamber immediately overhead. . . .

After the Battle of Hexham, Henry VI found refuge here for twelve months, 1463–4, but at length a 'black monke of Abyngtone' betrayed his secret to Sir James Harrington. When Harrington and two of the Talbot family came over to seize him, Henry was dining with the Dean of Windsor. Rising hastily he rushed up this stone stairway, and if the staircase was as well concealed then as it is today, one can well understand how the king gained temporary advantage over his enemies. As they were searching below, Henry and a faithful retainer climbed out of a window above stairs, by ladder, and made off. They were overtaken, however, while crossing the River Ribble—a mile away—by the Brungerley Hipping, or stepping, Stones. The unhappy king, who loved learning and architecture rather than the butchery of war, was put on a horse with his 'legges bound to the stiroppes' and led in ignominy and shame to the Tower of London.

Succeeding owners of Waddington Old Hall tried to give Henry a better deal, if posthumously. The King's Bedroom was hung with tapestries and its walls painted with various martial frescoes. But these, and the knights in armour that used to terrify servants as they crossed the dark entrance hall, have now disappeared, along with Henry's ghost. What does survive from that adulatory period is a carved oak cupboard in the Dining Room. Appropriately, it stands next to the concealed door of the spiral stair and illustrates a couple of episodes from that old story—the flight by ladder, and the capture on the stepping stones.

Before going into hiding at Waddington Hall the hunted Lancastrian king had found brief sanctuary at Bolton Hall, adjoining the beautiful village of Bolton-by-Bowland. This hall was unfortunately demolished some years ago, but the man who there befriended Henry can be seen in the village church with all the panoply of family pride those days could muster. He was Sir Ralph Pudsay. His tomb is understandably famous, for on this exceptionally large slab of grey Craven limestone his figure is engraved in full armour, along with his three wives and their twenty-five children. The costume details are incised, somewhat after the manner of monumental brass-work.

Among much else of historic interest, here, the font merits more than a passing glance. It is shaped like a five-pointed star—the Pudsay emblem—and dates from the early sixteenth century. Later that century the same device distinguished the 'Pudsay shillings'—coins made illegally in a family mint from silver obtained locally. When the Government got wind of the affair and sent a number of soldiers to arrest William Pudsay, the offender, a magic bit supplied by the Bowland fairies enabled him to escape on horseback. Rainsber Scar marks the place where he made his renowned leap across the Ribble.

Pudsay galloped straight on for London and, hoping for the Queen's pardon—was she not his godmother?—located her eventually on a boat in the Thames. At this point the story is best taken up in an old ballad:

Queen Bess she laughed, Queen Bess she smiled,
She thought on many a bygone day;
And then she pardoned her own godchild
Who on the deck before her lay.

She gave him then her hand to kiss;
So, while the tears stood in his ee,
His heart was brought from bale to bliss—
'But no more Pudsay shillings,' said she.

The Sailor Earl, and now William Pudsay—Elizabeth seems to have had a soft spot for our erring Yorkshiremen!

I doubt whether archaeologists have ever found a 'fairy bit', in the glacial drift of Bowland, but a few Pudsay shillings are said to be in existence, even now. Let collectors look for that five-lobed star!

Two Pennine dales that escape the rough symmetrical pattern of the rest are Kingsdale and Dentdale.

Before the motoring age Dentdale was almost inaccessible except from the Westmorland side. Only thirty or forty years ago local guide books referred to other approaches as being little better than the cart-tracks once used for leading peat down from the enclosing fells. Several good motoring roads now lead to Dent. One strikes across Newby Head Moss— six miles south-west of Hawes—and, after passing beneath Dent Head Viaduct, plunges through beautiful miniature gorges to join the valley at Lea Yeat and Cowgill.

From the mountainous country around Ingleborough another route offers itself. Half a mile beyond Ingleton one turns right, at Thornton-in-Lonsdale, for Kingsdale. This wild valley makes its way through limestone escarpments and moraines that hide several caves and potholes—Rowting Pot, Marble Steps Pot, Bull Pot, Gingling Hole, etc. The easiest and safest to explore for those not linked with any recognised pothole club is Yorda's Cave—noted for its waterfall chamber and weird limestone formations.

Scenically, Kingsdale is an embryonic valley, belonging rightly to the early days of Creation—an impression emphasised by the huge massif of Ingleborough, to the south-east, crouched on its primeval pedestal like an all-knowing deity. Throughout its length of some seven miles, Kingsdale supports no village, not even a hamlet, only two isolated farms, one with a name—Braida Garth—of Viking origin. The being after whom all those fantastic stalactites are named, in Yorda's Cave, was himself a mythical Scandinavian god. It is said, locally, that with the first appearance of full moon, psychic folk can hear the sound of voices and the marching feet of Vikings going over the pass from Kingsdale to Deepdale, a little way ahead.

Gradually, as the altitude increases, Ingleborough drops behind, leaving Whernside and Gragareth to cradle the pass that winds over White Shaw Moss for Deepdale and Dentdale. From the pass summit, 1,583 feet, a striking forward view reveals several Westmorland fells, but the foreground is dominated by Rise Hill, a whaleback ridge running transversely between Garsdale and Dentdale. The road finally cavorts among the rocky ravines of Deepdale—where Lockingarth Fall and its dark pool seem just right for mountain trolls—before joining verdant Dentdale between Cowgill and Dent Town.

I can never pass the River Dee, in these upper reaches, without marvelling afresh at its freakish behaviour. Every trick of Nature, where a limestone stream is concerned, here finds dazzling expression. Among queerly-eroded rock-ledges and boulders, the sparkling water cascades, glides and swirls in a dozen different ways, then flows underground for a change, reappearing lower down to perform fresh capers.

Dent Town—in size a small village—was the birthplace of Adam Sedgwick (1785–1873), pioneer geologist. His love of open-air pursuits won him the nickname, Robin Goodfellow. It stuck to him even in later life when he was studying the Whin Sill of Teesdale, the flints of the Yorkshire coast, and the Palaeozoic rocks of Lakeland. But many knew him best as Adam o' the Parson's. His father was vicar and schoolmaster of Dent, and Adam always recalled with pleasure his time at the little Free Grammar School, built in 1603, which still stands in the churchyard. Immediately in front are some of the gravestones over which Adam and his schoolmates used to leap as a relaxation from Latin and arithmetic.

During Dent's great knitting era in the seventeenth and eighteenth centuries the first thing a child had to learn at school was one of the local knitting songs. Some years ago an old Dent worthy recalled the following song, which took priority in his own schooldays, early last century:

> *Bell wether o' Barbon goes baa, baa, baa,*
> *How many sheep hes ta lost today?*
> *Nineteen hev ah lost, and one hev ah fun* (found),
> *Run Rocky, run Rocky, run, run, run,*

Barbondale is a Westmorland offshoot of Dentdale, and Rocky is the sheep-dog who 'chases' through all the verses, which are slightly reworded—eighteen lost, and two found, etc.—until every lost sheep is accounted for, by which time one round of a stocking was completed.

Hosiery, caps and other articles were continuously knitted by the men, women and children of the entire community. Never a moment was idle. Small wonder that Southey referred to them as 'the terrible knitters of Dent'. His account was amply borne out by Sedgwick, who described their nightly sittings beside peat fires, or—in summer—on the exterior galleries which then graced many of the cottages.

A painting dated 1820 shows some of Dent's unique cottage architecture. Only one gallery—and that a modern reproduction—now exists, but Dent still offers the highway hazards Hartley Coleridge once described:

> There is a town, of little note or praise;
> Narrow and winding are its rattling streets,
> Where cart with cart in cumbrous conflict meets;
> Hard straining up and backing down the ways
> Where, insecure, the crawling infant plays . . .

Today the 'straining and backing' are best demonstrated when the Sedbergh bus lurches along the cobbled Main Street, which has almost as many twists and turns as a typical stretch of the River Dee. Personally I hope that, despite an occasional conflict with some farm tractor or a few startled sheep, this undulating cobbled way, with its whitewashed cottages and two cosy inns, will survive any drastic change. A fountain memorial to Adam Sedgwick—hewn from a block of Shap granite—thrusts its bulk into the street, near the church gates, as if it were the grand old man himself resisting so-called progress.

In the church, founded in Norman times, perhaps the finest survival is the set of seventeenth-century box pews, arranged in the south aisle and near the organ. They were formerly used by the Statesmen of Dent, a relic of the old yeomanry. The Lake District also had its Statesmen, but here the title was applied particularly to 'the twenty-four' who had constituted a form of local government from as far back as 1429. They had beautiful carving on their pews and often adorned them with their monograms, all picked out with brass-headed nails. In a church restoration of 1889 the Jacobean three-decker pulpit, from which Adam o' the Parson's sometimes preached, was reduced to its present size, and many of the Statesmen's pews were unfortunately dismantled. Those pews that do remain serve as a two-fold reminder; first, of the earlier Statesmen—some of whom acted as agents for the Dent knitters in their dealings with the buyers in Kendal; and then of the Statesmen appointed in these days to fulfil certain parochial duties. A true appraisal of this 'land of Statesmen'—Sedgwick's phrase—makes it natural after a time for a visitor to fall in with local custom by calling the valley itself Dent, and its parental community, Dent Town—not village.

A hand-written document in the 'Sun' Inn, opposite the church, gives an interesting account of the riding of the local boundaries as organised by the Statesmen in May 1671. The account mentions several places with intriguing names, such as Cablerayke, Backstonegill and Henside Keld, which would take the party up Deepdale to the summit of Whernside; westwards to Dent Crag, within sight of Lakeland, then across upper Barbondale and 'so downe Alicegill' to Dent Town. To the particular kind of limestone that predominates for miles around, Sedgwick gave the name by which it is still known today—the Great Scar Limestone.

It is not surprising to find that the Quaker movement flourished in this narrow, secluded valley, which is barely ten miles long. Victims of religious persecution early sought refuge in Dent, occasionally sheltering within the thick belts of trees that formerly clothed Rise Hill. When George Fox visited the district in 1677 there were over 500 people to greet him—at Brigflatts, near Sedbergh. Brigflatts, then a hamlet of flax-weavers, still maintains its Meeting House of 1675. Externally, it is a charming stone building in the local vernacular; indoors there are quaint furnishings, particularly the dog-pen at the foot of the gallery stairs. So frequently were these Brigflatt Quakers taken off to prison, sometimes at York Castle, that one of them anticipated events by always carrying his nightcap to meeting with him.

A sharp contrast is provided by Whernside Manor—or rather the story of its origin. Known first as West House, it was built in the late eighteenth or early nineteenth century by a Liverpool merchant called Sill whose trade with the West Indies had been culled to provide him with a retinue of negro servants. Some of these were traditionally employed in making part of the road between Sedbergh and West House. Echoing their forebears, some Dent people say that one of the negroes, quarrelling with another man over a white sweetheart, was killed and had to be buried nearby in secret.

Certain tree circles on the hillsides increase the general air of mystery. They are supposed to mark other black men's graves—yet nobody knows for sure. The local council is most reluctant to remove any of these tree circles, even when they occur at an awkward corner of the road. What is their real significance? T. Wray Milnes of Lea Yeat, Dent—to whom I am indebted for much local information—believes that the circles may be vestiges of pre-Christian rites. His belief is coloured by the curious fact that 'in a similar ring of trees, just south of Kendal, a pascal lamb was found mysteriously sacrificed every Easter morning right up to the 1940s. Nobody could or would say who did it'.

Concerning Whernside Manor many other tales have gained local currency, not forgetting that of the negro-lover's ghost. But one is on sure ground in recalling that in later years this large, rectangular house became the home of Miles Mason, who achieved renown with his ironstone-ware pottery. Whernside Manor stands near the foot of Deepdale, half-way between Dent Town and Cowgill Bridge.

five

The Pennine Dales: 2
Wharfe, Ure and Nidd

Settle also provides a lovely approach to Upper Wharfedale. A little time should first be spared for the curious adjoining village of Giggleswick, where there is a fine church, then the Ribble is followed for two miles to Stainforth—which has its own wonderful variations on the waterfall theme. Here one strikes north over the slopes of Penyghent. The views are stupendous. An alternative road leads in equally fine mood from Langcliffe, near Settle, to Malham Tarn and Arncliffe, where the other road comes in.

Arncliffe belongs more to the past than to the present—which is not criticism, but full-hearted appraisal. I have a great fondness for Bridge End, the seventeenth-century house Charles Kingsley visited when gathering ideas and impressions for *The Water Babies*. He was the guest of Walter Morrison at Malham Tarn House and walked over to Arncliffe, one day, where he was given tea by Miss Elizabeth Hammond; she was to appear in the forthcoming children's classic as the 'woman in a red petticoat'. One can see her house and garden from the hump-backed bridge. The River Skirfare which gurgles beneath the bridge is the place where Tom, the chimney-boy hero, slipped in to join the other water babies.

Kingsley's tale was written primarily to amuse his own little boy, but his knowledge of local conditions is something to marvel at, even today. The 'great patches of flat limestone rock, just like ill-made pavements' which young Tom had to negotiate during his flight, are the spectacular limestone formations fringing the summit of Malham Cove; whilst Tom's aquatic abode within 'beautiful caves of tufa' derives from the travertine, or lime-saturated moss, which Kingsley would see in abundance around

Malham. A curtain of tufa behind Janet's Foss at Malham conceals a cave—
the traditional home of Janet, a water elf. Need one look further for the
origin of *The Water Babies*?

The Vendale of the story, however, centres upon this peaceful Arncliffe, where the riverside church reigns as patriarch—and artists' easels
often dot the village green. This must surely be the place where a certain
young lady caused a minor sensation some time ago. On showing her landscape effort to the tutor he became very enthusiastic, praising in particular
the 'marvellous brushwork'. His pleasure turned to wrath when the girl
roguishly explained that it was due to an inquisitive cow having licked off
most of the paint during her brief absence!

The River Skirfare joins the Wharfe three miles away, near Kilnsey
Crag, but it is now time to leave this little tributary valley, Littondale,
and follow the Wharfe up from its lower reaches.

Otley is a small market town in mid-Wharfedale. It is famous for printing
machinery, paper mills, and Thomas Chippendale. J. M. W. Turner also
left an abiding stamp on the place by staying repeatedly at Farnley Hall as
the guest of Squire Walter Ramsden Fawkes and painting there some fine
water-colours, including several architectural studies of the Hall.

But Chippendale was a native. He was baptised at Otley Parish Church
on 5 June 1718, but has had to wait a long time for full local recognition.
A commemorative plaque has at last appeared in the Council Chamber,
and outside the Boroughgate premises that occupy the site of Chippendale's
birthplace, a bronze tablet displays one of the ribbon-back chairs which
were to take his name, and the style he initiated, all over the world. The
tablet states that Thomas Chippendale was 'the son of an Otley carpenter'.

Known facts about Chippendale's local connections are few. However,
as his surname—according to a Harrogate descendant—means 'chip-in-
dale', or one who 'chips or cuts wood in the dales', the family background takes recognisable shape. Around Otley and Ilkley the term 'dale'
naturally signifies Wharfedale, the little offshoot—Washburndale, and the
southernmost stretches of the old Forest of Knaresborough.

In bygone days many a farmhouse chair or table was hewn by some
humble carpenter from local timber and, seeing some of them, young
Thomas must often have wished they were better designed. Chippendale
senior is said to have practised his 'joyner's' craft at Farnley Hall. Somebody may one day discover precisely when, and in what circumstances,

Thomas prospered by exchanging this attractive countryside for that work-shop in St. Martin's Lane, London, where the gentry began to clamour for his exquisite creations in mahogany.

Perhaps the Lascelles family of Harewood helped Chippendale to achieve his ambitions. The riverside route from Otley to Harewood is delightful, even today, and I like to think of the young craftsman saunter-ing in that direction when Edwin Lascelles, Esq., was about to muster his team of architects and artists to design and decorate his new home above the Wharfe. There would be John Carr and Robert Adam, of course, with Angelica Kauffmann and Antonio Zucchi for the painted ceilings, and Joseph Rose for the decorative plaster-work. Who would be commissioned to provide the furniture and other fittings ? One glance within Gawthorpe Hall, before this was demolished in favour of the present Harewood House, would have given the answer. By this time Gawthorpe Hall had simply become a repository for the latest, contemporary furniture—all of it fashioned by the erstwhile Otley youth. How fine it was can be seen to-day by visiting Harewood House, home of the late Princess Royal and of the present Earl and Countess of Harewood. One of Chippendale's great-est achievements—specially pointed out to me by the Princess Royal—occurs in the Long Gallery. It is the set of tastefully draped window pel-mets and hangings. They deceive everybody, being modelled entirely in *wood*.

The Washburn Valley branches away to the north of Otley. It was once bedevilled with witches, especially around Timble and Fewston. An old resident told me that his two great-uncles, who farmed nearby, would never pass Bland Hill in the Norwood area without first protecting them-selves from witchcraft by putting bits of rowan wood in their pockets. He also disclosed a family tradition about one of the Timble witches who once called at his house, Tatefield Hall, Beckwithshaw. The farm-lad who answered the door should have known better than to mock her. As punish-ment she caused him to be levitated to the kitchen roof, and he had to stay there, impaled on a meat hook, until somebody came to his aid.

But all the talk in Washburn Valley these days is of the new reservoir and how it will affect the landscape. Three reservoirs have already en-chanced the beauty of this valley, and although one regrets the passing of old, well-loved landmarks like West End, Thruscross Reservoir* should provide abundant scenic compensation. Just before West End Church was

* Opened September 1966.

15   *Bolton Castle—Mary Stuart's Wensleydale 'prison'*

finally engulfed a man swam through the rising waters and sat on the belfry. When in later years he yarns to his grandchildren this feat will make a nice change from the witches.

There are several interesting country houses in this area. Leathley Hall, in lower Washburndale, was the home of Anne Hitch who built the eighteenth-century almshouses on the green and now lies, 'much lamented', in the Norman church. The fine old water-mill at the head of the village seems to belong more to her day than ours. Hawksworth Hall occupies a gritstone ridge called Odda, above Menston, near Otley, and has a large room splendidly decorated by Walter Hawksworth in the fond hope, not realised, that James I would favour him with a visit. I hope the spastic children now living here find some happiness in following Walter Hawksworth's comic little figures stuccoed round the wall of this Royal Room. Perhaps they invent tales about them ? One arm of the central pendant, on the ceiling, is supposed to drop off when the reigning monarch dies. A pleasant thing to remember here is that although the Hall became a refuge in times of religious persecution, Protestants as well as Catholics benefited. Nothing ecumenical occurred, of course; the fugitives would be of different periods.

Menston itself—that is, the old Mensington which has the rolling contours of Burley and Ilkley Moors as backcloth—is crowded with memories. Many of them cling to Fairfax Hall.

Two impressions of this small, seventeenth-century hall stay in my mind—one of the place heralding spring with bursting leaf-buds and clumps of snowdrops; the other in high summer, with roses and delphiniums spilling a riot of colour against the grey stone walls. Three hundred years ago the same garden would gladden Charles and Mary Fairfax; it would please their fourteen children, too, especially the giant pear-tree which now overtops the house and still bears fruit.

The Fairfax children lived in turbulent times. They grew up during the Civil Wars and would often see their father retire to his private room with bundles of strange-looking documents. Among them were monastic papers and charters which he and Roger Dodsworth, a fellow antiquary, rescued from St. Mary's Tower at York when the city was besieged in 1644. Fire had damaged many of them, but the two zealous antiquaries pieced together the charred, scattered fragments, here in the tranquillity of Menston.

Despite an eventual commission under General Monk, Charles Fairfax was no soldier. He left fighting to the more illustrious members of the family—notably his brother Ferdinando, and 'nephew Tom' who became the great Parliamentarian Leader. As a youth Tom had often ridden over from Denton Hall, near Ilkley, to be tutored by his scholarly uncle. Yet Charles had a bravery of his own. He was one of the local gentry who in 1649 swam against the tide by establishing the tiny chapel for nonconformist outcasts in the grounds of Bramhope Hall. Oliver Heywood once preached here 'with abundant enlargement' for four and a half hours! Visitors can feel the impact of that wonderful oratory by gazing up at the three-decker pulpit from one of the crude oak benches. Bramhope is on A660, near Otley Chevin.

A fine piece of restoration at Ilkley has given back to this bracing moorland town its Tudor manor house, an oak-raftered building where succeeding generations of the Middleton family dispensed local justice. Being free tenants, many of the families already noticed in these pages could come here in their miniver and gold-trimmed gowns and look on with varying degrees of rectitude. There would be the Vavasours of Weston, near Otley, the Fitzwilliams of Wentworth, the Plumptons of Grassington and, on occasion, George, Earl of Cumberland—the Sailor Earl himself.

Some of the early Middletons repose in the Parish Church nearby, but Ilkley's origin as the Roman *Olicana* accounts for two items of far greater antiquity than their grizzled effigies. These are Roman altars formerly built into the north wall of the church tower. One shows what appears to be a flask for sacrificial libations; the other is carved with a figure often described as Hercules strangling the serpent though it is more probably a representation of Verbeia, that goddess of the River Wharfe which Ralph Thoresby found so hampering.

Verbeia was to influence the Middletons when they laid out the grounds at Middleton Lodge, high above the opposite shore of the Wharfe. On the north side of the Tudor house some Roman altars and other relics of *Olicana* form a sort of Appian Way. Beyond, in a separate enclosure, one enters a Via Dolorosa—an avenue comprising fourteen Stations of the Cross—leading to a Calvary. This shelters an oratory containing a stone altar, reputedly from Bolton Priory. Surrounded by tall beeches, the whole area takes on the character of a sacred grove.

The Passionist Fathers who acquired the Lodge in 1923 have made a Lourdes grotto in the East garden. Enclosed by oak, chestnut and beech-trees, the grotto commemorates the vision granted to Bernardette Soubirous, the French peasant girl, at Lourdes in 1858. Amongst the bushes at one side of the grotto I noticed a Roman altar dedicated to Verbeia. This is a replica made for William Middleton in 1608; the original, which was dragged from the Wharfe, stands in the North garden. The siting of the Lourdes grotto, near these pagan altars, was singularly apt, for the people of *Olicana* regarded Verbeia as primarily a goddess of *healing*.

Across the valley the Cow and Calf Rocks tempt people of almost every age to do a little climbing, while the surrounding Rombalds Moor provides walks through ling and bracken that never lose their appeal. This is the moor of the famous song that extols the virtue of being up here 'baht 'at'—without a hat. All very well for summer, but the winter aspect of these moors can be severe, especially when the snow freezes into a shimmering mantle of 'glass' and the gritstone outcrops become tiny, polished igloos.

The main road up Wharfedale, B6160, offers continual delight. It branches from the A65 at Addingham, three miles west of Ilkley, and within another three miles Bolton Priory breaks into view, beside the Wharfe. The history of this Augustinian priory—often mistakenly called an abbey—ranges back to 1151, when it was founded by Alicia de Romilly. Despite the Scottish raiders of future centuries, the inevitable ravages of time, and of course its despoliation after the closure in 1539, the building has come through with considerable grace, and part of it is still in regular use for divine worship. Offset by some beautiful interlaced arcading, the monastic choir now grants splendid views of the river and of Bolton Woods—through the empty window tracery. This surrounding scenery is amongst the finest in Yorkshire, or in England for that matter. Its loveliness inspired Wordsworth, Turner and many others. The neighbourhood has hardly changed since then, thanks to the Duke of Devonshire's protective care.

A little-known link with the Priory is Beamsley Hospital, about two miles away, on the Harrogate road, A59. The Hospital was founded in 1593 by Lady Anne Clifford's mother as some compensation to the poor, who in the previous generation had been badly hit by the closure of the monasteries. A touch of heraldry on a roadside arch marks the place for most wayfarers, but behind the surrounding cottages there is a remarkable chapel which should be seen.

A long flagged path leads up to the low, stone-built chapel, which is circular and has a startling array of chimney-stacks rising like minarets from its cupola. These chimneys and several small mullioned windows serve some cottages that surprisingly form a rotunda and enfold the chapel in a perpetual embrace. The diameter of the building is only thirty feet. When we last stepped up to the chapel the Reader, a clergyman, came along to take the Wednesday afternoon service for the widows who form this little community. He had come from Bolton Priory Church. Behind him I seemed to see many who once supervised this place, including the Sailor Earl (how he keeps returning from the high seas!), and Lady Anne who 'more perfectly finished' the building.

This indomitable woman also added a valuable estate at Harewood to the Hospital endowments. When this property was sold back to Harewood many years ago the deed of conveyance had to bear the Beamsley Hospital seal, but as this had disappeared a fresh one was specially made. Lady Anne Clifford, that stickler for correct procedure—as witness the Murgatroyd hen—would certainly have demanded no less.

Two miles up river from Bolton Priory the Wharfe accomplishes a rare feat by squeezing tempestuously through a narrow rock channel—the Strid. Foolish people try to jump across; drowning fatalities are not uncommon. Earlier this century a Strid Escapists' Club was formed, but membership was naturally very limited! Local sub-aqua clubs have introduced a new era; their members sometimes jump into the river, higher up, and float like corks through the seething cauldron. It seems an affront to all bygone traditions, though the place is as perilous as ever.

At Barden Tower—the old shooting lodge of the Cliffords—my wife and I were once shown an engraved silver jug presented to the housewife's grandfather, Sylvester Lister, by friends and neighbours in recognition of his courage in 'rescuing Eliza Williamson from the Waters of the Strid, May 23, 1868.' There have been Listers at Barden for centuries. One of them accompanied Henry Clifford, the Shepherd Lord, to Flodden; the halberd now slung over an inner door is supposed to be the very one John Lister used in that far-off battle. A surer link with him is the sheep brand still used hereabouts. It comprises Lister's initials—J. L.

Students of architecture will find more to interest them in the Tudor cottage than in the semi-ruined tower just opposite. This retainer's cottage adjoins the old chapel and two of its rooms are actually embodied in the squat, chapel tower. An exterior stone staircase serves one of these rooms, entry being made through a series of stone arches stepped up within the thickness of a six-foot wall. The chapel itself is entered through a tunnel-like porch. Divine worship is conducted here periodically from

Bolton Priory—a reminder that in the old days a few of the Augustinian canons would come over and mount the roof to study the starry heavens with the good Shepherd Lord. Because of his secret upbringing amongst shepherd folk, after the Wars of the Roses, this heir to the Skipton estates filled his manhood with rural and scholarly pursuits. Dorothy Una Ratcliffe wrote a charming one-act play, *Desormais*, about this fine character and the way his spirit lived on to help local shepherds.

This part of Wharfedale is perhaps the most enchanting of all. The upper reaches around Kilnsey Crag, Buckden and Hubberholme have still to contribute their own particular charm, but this stretch of woodland, river and inter-folding fells, between Bolton Priory and Burnsall is, for me, the nearest thing to Heaven. Others have felt the same, as may be judged by some of the dwellings, both old and new.

If this book were twice its size places like High Hall at Appletreewick —which has a fine minstrel gallery—could be given their full due. Here lived the Craven family whose fortunes began with that William Craven who helped to drive a pack-horse team laden with woollen pieces to London, in the sixteenth century, and stayed there to make his fortune and be acclaimed Lord Mayor. Monks' Hall, in the same village, stirs many more memories, from the canons of Bolton dispensing alms here, to a late owner's children riding in the little dirk gaits—a kind of trolley— that passed through her garden after carrying lead across the moors from the local lead-mines.

One house that crystallises much of the all-pervading charm, and adds its own peculiar romance, is Parcevall Hall.

It has lately become an Anglican retreat, but the wonderful rock gardens—frequently open to the public—sufficiently evoke its interesting story. The hall occupies a spur of cragland that thrusts its way dramatically between Appletreewick Pasture—a mile or so east of the village—and Simon's Seat. It has all the appeal of a mountain refuge, which the last, winding approach only serves to strengthen.

Originally the place was a rest-house for the monks of Fountains Abbey. It stands almost athwart an old route through Trollers Ghyll which many of them used when visiting the great sheep-farms and other property in Wharfedale and around Malham in Airedale. Those Cistercian monks, or their lay brothers, must often have been glad to reach this haven, for Trollers Ghyll was the abode of the Barguest hound and other supernatural creatures. Even today, the wind rushing through this limestone gorge can play tricks with the imagination.

As the manor, together with its profitable lead-mines, had once belonged to Bolton Priory—even nearer than Fountains Abbey—this old
house was doubly associated with monastic life. In 1928 the hall was
bought by Sir William Milner. As an architect delighting in old buildings,
Sir William adopted the Tudor style of the place for his own extensions,
of which the chief block faces west to form an entrance courtyard. The old
south porch overlooks the terraced gardens, with Simon's Seat raking up,
beyond, into the sky. This splendid view made its own impression on
Chiang Yee, who was Sir William's guest while he was preparing his
Yorkshire volume for the well-known 'Silent Traveller' series. Simon's
Seat reminded Chiang Yee of the Fu-Chou mountain in Nanking; a Chinese
sage sitting in contemplation on this rocky Wharfedale summit is one of
his word-pictures which seems not inappropriate to the hall's new régime.

How the Bradford diocesan authorities handle the hall's less reputable
episodes is their own affair. I am thinking of the strong tradition that in
the seventeenth century Nevison, the highwayman, found frequent refuge
here. Bygone owners loved to explain that while the sheriff clamoured at
the outer door, Nevison could slip from his first-floor room—the Council
Room—and mount his waiting horse unseen. It was one more tale to
charge Sir William's 'armoury' when, on winter evenings, he drew his
guests close to the solar fire—fuelled with huge logs from the Bolton
Priory estate—and worked up his siege on their willing credulity. With
the ghostly 'knockers' of the lead-mines, a spectral monk of Bolton
Priory, Pam the Fiddler from Threshfield nearby, and a cowled figure he
sometimes glimpsed in his own dining-room, the district yielded plenty
of scope for those nocturnal occasions.

Sir William Milner gloried also in the more tangible world of dales
architecture. Some of Wharfedale's most beautiful buildings are in this
same neighbourhood. At Burnsall there is a fine church which Sir William
Craven 'repaired and butified' in 1612; only a few yards away stands the
Grammar School, built and endowed by the same benefactor in 1602 and
still looking more like a stately manor house than a place where sons of
local farmers came to learn English and Latin. These subjects were taught
free, but arithmetic cost one shilling per week.

Apart from the telephone kiosk, I cannot recall one strident note in
Linton, two miles up river. Grey stone cottages border the village green,
a clapper bridge and one of pack-horse design span the little stream, and
Fountaine Hospital looks on from one side as though Vanbrugh himself
had planted it there in a moment of preoccupation. Actually, the architect

is unknown. The benefactor it commemorates was Richard Fountaine, a local lad who—like William Craven—amassed wealth in London and then made this gift to his birthplace. Behind the village are the reef knolls mentioned earlier.

Linton also has a lovely old church, with Norman and later features, but it stands away from the village, down by the Wharfe, and looks rather squat, as though still hiding itself from the attentions of Scottish raiders. Other dales' churches have the same air of secrecy. Some places, usually the hamlets, have no regular church at all. I remember looking for the place of worship in Thorpe, between Burnsall and Linton, and being told by a resident that there was no proper church, though services were sometimes held in an old building opposite her house by the Vicar of Hebden, just across the river. At that time the Wharfe—which has the typical dales habit of rising quickly after rain—had to be crossed hereabouts by stepping stones, hence the wording of the Vicar's announcement on the previous Sunday. 'Next week', he would tell his Hebden congregation, 't' sarvice will be at Thorpe if t' weather's fine and t' watter's low.'

Dalesfolk show a strong individuality of speech and action. I thought Grassington, the old lead-miners' country town, was beginning to look a little too smart, but we went along one summer evening, not long ago, and found the old market place absolutely jammed with all the impedimenta of a travelling funfair. Everything—hotels, shops, cafés, even the public lavatories—became temporarily engulfed by roundabouts, swings and dodgems so that Grassington youth should have its fling.

How the form of local amusement has changed since the days of Edmund Kean and Harriet Mellon! As barn-stormers hired by Tom Airey, the postmaster, they attracted eager audiences of farmers and lead-miners to the little 'Girston' theatre. There is some talk of reviving local drama, but never again will it be possible to see the Duke of Devonshire—owner of so much surrounding country—ceremoniously ushered into a ducal box improvised from bits of wood decorated with brown paper.

Years later Tom Airey would say, with a twinkle in his merry eye, 'The Girston folk thought it a great condescension for His Grace to look in, but I told 'em to bide till two of ours came into their own. There were a good few dukes about, but only one Edmund Kean and never another Harriet Mellon.' Then, when Harriet had become premier actress of the day and also wife of the Duke of St. Albans, that old wiseacre would drop this remark with the morning letters: 'She can hob-nob with our Duke at his own game now, but what sort of show would *he* make if he had to take the boards ? Ha, ha!' I can still catch Airey's amusing echo in Grassington's cobbled market place—on quiet days!

Behind the main street, Grassington Old Hall—an attractive survival from medieval and Tudor times—preserves memories of the monks who sojourned here—as at Parcevall Hall—on their way from Fountains Abbey, near Ripon, to the monastery's great sheep-farms. One wall of the house is pierced by a dole window, through which alms were distributed to the needy. Among those passing monks there would be the Fountains cellarer, bound for the annual sheep-shearing at Kilnsey Crag. It must have been a wonderful sight, with all the monastic sheep gathered from miles around. Today rock-climbers try their skill on the forbidding overhang of this huge limestone cliff. Its curious elephantine profile caused Chiang Yee to compare the crag with one of the giant stone animals adorning the Ming Emperor's tomb at Nanking.

The last few miles of Wharfedale bring their own reward. Beyond Kilnsey the left turn for Littondale is soon passed; then comes Kettlewell, neighboured by the modern Scargill Church imaginatively designed by George G. Pace of York in Norwegian style so as to merge with the steep, wooded slopes behind. A fine upland road from Kettlewell leads north through Coverdale into Wensleydale. An even finer pass, Kidstones, branches north from Buckden. There is yet another north-bound pass; the road first sports with the infant River Wharfe and then careers into Wensleydale via Fleet Moss. Before surrendering to its magnetic appeal, however, one should step into Hubberholme Church, a mile from Buckden along the Fleet Moss road.

With its rough-hewn pillars, rugged arcades and rood loft, the interior of this old forest chapel betrays the same, sturdy, forthright spirit that animates most Yorkshire dalesfolk. Just think, a painted rood loft dated 1558—almost twenty years *after* the Reformation!

The parish records tell of fish having once been seen swimming in and out of the pews, due to flooding by the Wharfe. Much more recently some young lambs enjoyed the same kind of freedom. They were sharing in a thanksgiving service for a successful lambing season, but soon escaped from their pen in the chancel and were then allowed to gambol at will up and down the nave.

Perhaps that scene might be regarded as a natural rebound from an old custom which distinguishes Hubberholme from all other Yorkshire hamlets or villages. Every New Year's Eve the Vicar meets local farmers in the 'George' Inn, just over the bridge, to receive their bids for the annual letting of a plot of land known for centuries as Poor's Pasture. Two rooms are used for the ceremony. That occupied by the Vicar is temporarily named the House of Lords; the other one, used by the farmers, becomes the House of Commons. The Vicar's Warden has the pleasant job of go-between, placing each bid before the 'throne'. When the letting has been knocked down to the highest bidder, and farmer so-and-so has secured these church-controlled grazing rights for his sheep and cows, the local Parliament is prorogued for another year.

Nobody seems to know who bequeathed Poor's Pasture for this pur-pose. The parish records are silent. But the custom is jealously guarded. The only difficulty today, I am told, is to find enough 'local poor' to enjoy the proceeds of this strange auction!

Some years ago I travelled the Fleet Moss road in the company of Kit Calvert—cheese-factor, farmer, historian, and indeed 'father' of Hawes. It was a unique experience. Practically all that exhilarating way he was telling me local tales in Wensleydale dialect, of which he is a master.

It seems fitting that the man who has delved so deeply into the story of Wensleydale cheese—first made by the Jervaulx monks from ewes' milk—should also undertake the translation of parts of the New Testament into his own native speech. The Cistercian monks at Jervaulx Abbey, twenty miles down the valley from Hawes, used the Vulgate version of the Bible. And then, close by Jervaulx, there is the tributary valley of the Cover, where Miles Coverdale spent his boyhood. Miles Coverdale was to trans-late the Bible into boisterous English, as still reflected in the Prayer Book. Latin, English—why not also Wensleydale?

Kit Calvert's translation is, of course, far less pretentious than Cover-dale's. His sole desire is to present certain well-loved New Testament passages into the speech that has barely changed hereabouts since the days of the monks and, indeed, perhaps even of those who peopled the dale be-fore them.

It was a visiting minister who first suggested that Kit Calvert should attempt this worthy task. They were sitting beside Aysgarth Falls, watch-ing a salmon trying to leap its obstacle. The tale of a country preacher had just been told in the rich, fruity tongue of the neighbourhood, when the challenge came. 'Kit,' said his companion, 'why not translate the New Testament into your beautiful Wensleydale dialect?'

The idea simmered for ten years and then Mr. Calvert set to work, using every suitable bit of local colour for the purpose.

Typical of his method is the rendering of Christ's conversation with Peter, in the twenty-first chapter of St. John:

> Jesus sez t' Simon Peter, 'Simon, son o' John, do ye love Me maar than t' others dew?' 'I, Lord,' sez Peter, 'Thou knaas ah love Th''; He sez tew him, 'Then sarra mi lile lambs.' He assis him again a second time, 'Simon, son o' John, dew ye love Me?' Sez Peter, 'I Lord, Thou knaas ah tresur Th'.' 'Than bi a shipperd t' mi yowes (ewes),' sez Jesus. Fer t' third time He assis him, 'Simon, son o' John, yer seur ye love Me?' Noo Peter was a bit naaked (narked) at bein' asst a third time . . . 'Lord,' sez he, 'Thou kens ivverything. Thou knaas well eneuf 'at ah love Th'.' Jesus sez tew him, 'Than father mi pooer yowes an' lambs.'

Here the emblematic sheep of Palestine have become the ewes and lambs that roam the Wensleydale fells, forever cropping the limestone herbage.

When my Hawes friend translated that part of St. Luke's Gospel relating to the Lost Sheep, he wrote:

> 'Whars t' man among ye if he had a hunderd sheep, an' lost yan on 'em, 'at wadn't leave oat t' others on t' fell an gang an laat straggler till he finnds it.'

Surely he was thinking of the silly sheep which sometimes have to be rescued from dangerous places like the Buttertubs.

Several times these and other warm, homely passages have been broadcast by the BBC. A favourite is the Nativity scene, in which the 'swaddling clothes' of the Bible story become the 'barrie cooat' which Wensleydale mothers formerly put on 'a new babby'.

From this market town of Hawes, Buttertubs Pass is the shortest way into Swaledale. A good road has tamed Buttertubs somewhat, yet it is still majestic and rather eerie—especially where the road snakes past the limestone potholes that give the pass its name.

But first there is much to see in Wensleydale, for which Hawes is an obvious centre. Hardraw Force at the foot of Buttertubs is one of Yorkshire's most spectacular single waterfalls. Bainbridge, five miles down the valley, spreads itself comfortably around a spacious village green, and a tiny river, the Bain, splashes down from Semerwater to join the River Ure, or Yore, nearby. Another attraction is the Bainbridge horn-blower, who steps on to the green every night from Holyrood (27 September) to Shrovetide with his curious insignia. . . .

Originally, the Bainbridge horn emitted its long wail to guide wayfarers down through the surrounding Wensleydale Forest, lest darkness—and the wolves—should trap them. Succeeding centuries have banished those dangers, but Bainbridge still keeps the ancient tryst. Bolton Castle farther down the valley has custody of the old horn, but as an example of local pride and tenacity it would be hard to beat the ceremony which initiated the present horn for the custom in 1864. This great buffalo horn headed a procession through the village, with twelve white horses prancing along as a token of the local sovereignty of the Metcalfes of Wensleydale.

Many of the horn-blowers have come from that family. The senior branch lived at Nappa Hall, near Askrigg, two miles away. Thomas Metcalfe, who bought this land from the Scropes soon after Agincourt, 'waxed rich and builded . . . two faire towers', which gave his new abode the appearance of a small castle. The Metcalfes were estate stewards for Jervaulx Abbey and Wardens of the Forest of Wensleydale. Their coat-of-arms—three black calves on a silver shield—was known and respected all over the county. Perhaps the family's finest flourish was on that memorable day in the mid-sixteenth century when Sir Christopher Metcalfe, High Sheriff of Yorkshire, mustered 300 men of his own name, mounted them all on white horses, and then rode at their head to greet the Judges of Assize, whom they escorted in this more than princely fashion to York.

Thomas, founder of the Nappa line, certainly chose the site of his house well, being assured that never would a cold northerly blast chill his spine; an outcrop of rock rises like a miniature Malham Cove only a few yards from the back of the hall. The battlements of the higher, sixty-feet tower only just reach the level of the road that runs along the crag summit.

Here, Mary Queen of Scots slept for two nights during parole from Bolton Castle. Her room is in the smaller tower. Here, Lady Anne Clifford visited 'cousin Metcalfe' during the oft-repeated tours of her north-country possessions. And here in the eighteenth century came James Wilson of Askrigg to install one of his renowned grandfather clocks. It is built on to one end of a delf rack in the old kitchen—but I feel sorry it is not a Mark Metcalfe clock. He also worked in Askrigg. Chimes from one of his timepieces would have echoed very appropriately in this fine old Metcalfe home. The full story of the Askrigg clock-makers, the curious designs they produced, and the odd tools they used—such as the mouse's claw for smoothing edges, is a fascinating study. Several clocks by these craftsmen may still be seen in Askrigg cottages.

Semerwater, across the valley, awakens further memories of the Metcalfes, though revealing them in a rather despicable light. In 1667 Sir Thomas Metcalfe, the Black Night of Nappa, besieged Raydale House owned by William Robinson because he coveted the place. Robinson was away from home, but his wife secured help from York and the four days' siege ended in the complete rout of the Metcalfes.

The lovely, quiet vale that cradles Semerwater has sometimes been called Quaker Valley. Both George Fox and the saintly John Woolman visited Richard Robinson at Countersett Hall, and Dr. John Fothergill, founder of Ackworth School, lived nearby at Carr End—when he was not in London, or hurrying about 'perpetually from one sick-chamber to another'. At Countersett, Fox—the man who was to address spiritual homilies to the King of Spain, the Pope, the Emperor of China, and even Prester John—was pleased to occupy the tiny room over the entrance porch.

Hidden away amongst the hills, the Semerwater area—on weekdays— suggests a kind of Shangri-La; while here, Woolman must have rejoiced that England had at least one place where stage-coaches could not travel 'a hundred miles in twenty-four hours' and people could feel 'quiet in mind'. Speed-boats on the lake have become a noisy, week-end horror which must surely give way to enlightened public opinion!

The Metcalfes were also disturbers of the peace, being only too successful in persuading dalesfolk to inform against the local Quakers. Richard Robinson wrote a book that gives a long account of these persecutions. He himself sleeps in the Quaker burial ground beside Bainbridge green.

The geological architecture of Wensleydale is striking. Great bold scarps, sculped like inverted cornices, flank both sides of the broad valley. The rock ingredients—shale, sandstone, and limestone in ascending order— are popularly known as the Yoredales. They give the valley its innumerable waterfalls, of which the most famous are those plunging over massive rock terraces at Aysgarth. Near here, Kidstones Pass comes over the tops from Wharfedale.

Many writers have attempted to describe the wonder and beauty of Aysgarth's three falls—and failed. Even Wordsworth had to fall back, lost for words, on 'the yellow light of evening'—which conveys next to nothing. I shall only say this. The falls are more than a sight for the eyes; they come nigh to being a spiritual experience. But how different all would have been if the Skipton–Kettlewell railway had come through to Aysgarth, as planned, with a viaduct right across the Upper Force! John Ruskin and William Morris were not the only ones to raise horrified protests.

There are men of the Ruskin and Morris stamp in Wensleydale today— men who have spent most of their lives enjoying every phase of the dale's charm and mediating it for whosoever will take heed. I think of Fred Lawson, first coming to Castle Bolton village, near Aysgarth, on a week-end painting trip and deciding there and then to stay. In the colours and shapes and variable moods of the surrounding landscape he had recognised his life's work, though then but a student. His first winter here meant living with the local rabbit-catcher and his snares. He once told me that he has never regretted burning his pile of art certificates that would have secured him a 'safe' job. He had secured something better—a foothold along the route taken by Girtin, Turner, Cotman and other water-colour-ists when they rode horseback with their painting tackle via Semerwater and Wensleydale to Richmond.

He and his wife—Muriel Metcalfe, another gifted artist—now live in a house overlooking the valley, with Pen Hill on the southern skyline. In the 1930s the Castle Bolton group of artists grew up around them—which evidently inspired the children of the village too, for Lawson used to find them painting, avidly, but with the strangest equipment. One child's brush was made from a sheep's thigh bone; another was a tuft from a domestic broom. He would remedy the situation by taking along some of his own rather worn brushes—brushes that had helped to paint lovely water-colours, perhaps Bolton Castle in the snows, or a gypsy encampment. Fred Lawson has won his place, not only in art circles, but in the homes and affections of Wensleydale. And his daughter, Sonia, whose toys once amused my own children during a war-time visit, now exhibits paintings in her own right.

I once lunched with Fred Lawson and George Jackson—one of the Castle Bolton group—in a tiny, one-up-and-one-down cottage on the edge of Castle Bolton village. As war-time rationing was in operation the chief fare was a tin of sardines, but there was a feast of talk about local art and drama, for the neighbourhood then ran its own annual festival—produced by George Jackson and staged in the adjoining village of Redmire.

Mr. Jackson is just as proficient with brush and pen as with those delightful homespun plays that made his name a byword in the Dales. In these plays he presents local history and folklore. An old oil-painting picked up in Ripon market place for sixpence suggested the theme for *The Swan Inn*. The painting showed a humble cottage interior, for which an old house in Redmire—once an inn—provided the dramatic counterpart. It was a place to be feared because of the witchcraft practised there by Hannah, the inn-keeper's wife. She conjured the Devil into milk-churns, and made wax models of her intended victims—models to be thrown on the fire, later, when her horrible plans matured!

Other local strands in the play are from George Jackson's family background. His ancestors have been associated with Castle Bolton for generations. One of them celebrated her own wedding feast in the great, rambling castle at the head of the village, with the church band supplying music on fiddle, 'cello and wood-wind. The 'serpent' which gave the deep, bass undertones still survives, in the castle. Built in the fourteenth century by Richard, Lord Scrope, this feudal stronghold has found its historian, very appropriately, in this same Wensleydale virtuoso. Once he acted the part of Queen's lover in Dorothy Una Ratcliffe's play, *Mary of Scotland in Wensleydale*, when this was staged in the room traditionally occupied by Mary Stuart during her six months' semi-imprisonment here in 1568–9.

One can have tea in the castle today, and explore rooms and courtyards which battle and siege failed to destroy. From the towers there are glorious views of the dale, and of Leyburn Shawl—the natural terrace along which Mary Stuart tried to escape, it is fondly believed, with the help of Kit Norton, a young guardsman who was too susceptible to her charms.

From Redmire a woodland path to Wensley is made available through the courtesy of Lord Bolton. The path passes close beside Bolton Hall, seat of the family since 1678, when they moved here from the castle. The first owner of the hall seems to have lived mostly by night. He rode to hounds by torchlight, slept through the day, and only spoke towards evening when the air was pure.

Whether one reaches Wensley by this sylvan route, or by road, time should certainly be given to this lovely village, which bestows its name on the dale.

In the sixteenth century the Great Plague visited Wensley, then the dale's chief market town. Hundreds died 'by reason of the sickness' and the rest fled. The church is the chief surviving feature and a noble church it is, though much of the nobility derives from the Scropes, and the Boltons who succeeded to the Scrope estates. The Bolton family pew is approached through some screenwork that adorned the Scrope chantry at Easby Abbey, near Richmond, before the Dissolution. Various colourful shields remind one of the part played by this family in north-country history. Perhaps the best-known episode is the ninth Lord Scrope's custody—shared by Sir Thomas Knollys—of Mary Stuart at the castle nearby. The pew proper is in two halves, one raised a few inches above the other, the higher portion being used by Bolton Hall residents and guests, and the lower one by Lord Bolton's heir. Dr. Whitaker described its red pine arches and columns as a 'wretched piece of clumsy work', but at his time of writing, 150 years ago, there was little appreciation for this type of craftsmanship.

Actually the Bolton pew is a grand piece of carpentry, probably local, though not as finely conceived as the choir bench-ends here; emblazoned with the Scrope arms, these were fashioned in 1527 by the Ripon School of Woodcarvers. A wooden reliquary from Easby Abbey hangs near the church entrance as an offertory box, exchanging a saint's relics for visitors' contributions!

It is sometimes beneficial to view a well-loved place through another's eyes. When the place is Jervaulx Abbey, and the person one who lived beside it for a lifetime and walked daily through the ruins, something unusually illuminating may be expected.

William Lorenzo Christie's daily walk, continued almost until his death in 1962 at the age of 103 years, was not a mere 'constitutional'. It was his way of linking past and present. It had sparked off a monastic quest that eventually resulted in his fine little handbook to the abbey. In its pages one becomes, in turn, a monk of the Cistercian Order; a lay-brother concerned with the community's cheese-making, horse-breeding or farming; or a witness of the Pilgrimage of Grace. He could eruditely describe the large affairs of the abbey and its architecture—and then interpose a homely word about the monks being forbidden to crack nuts with their teeth, or wipe their knives on the table linen.

The story begins in that period of English history when, 'as the dreaded millennium had passed without world destruction', abbeys grew up as an expression of renewed religious fervour. In 1145 Alan, Earl of Richmond, had in his household a monk called Peter Quiniaco. Peter was a skilled physician and had saved the Earl's life. When he sought a plot of land for building an abbey he naturally won his patron's co-operation. This first abbey, known as Fors, was situated near the head of Wensleydale, perhaps at Bainbridge, though some antiquaries favour the region above Hardraw Force. In 1156, owing to lack of crops and other austerities that even a Cistercian monk could not long endure, Abbot John and his brethren moved down the valley to the present site near East Witton, given to them by Earl Alan and his son, Conan.

At length the monks of Jervaulx achieved renown for more than piety. They reared sheep, bred horses, made wonderful cheese, and worked lead and coal-mines farther afield—all of which yielded considerable wealth. Their recipe for cheese-making was kept secret, even by those who inherited the craft after the Dissolution. Its special flavour was at last traced, in part, to the fact that *ewes'* milk had been used in the process. Today this product is widely famous as Wensleydale cheese, though ewes' milk is no longer used.

Squire Christie, who celebrated his centenary year by winning the Pateley Plate at Ripon with 'Bengal Lancer', always showed particular interest in the monks' famous breed of horses. One of Henry VIII's inspectors, in 1537, just prior to the closure of Jervaulx, became quite ecstatic about these fine animals, referring to them as 'the trydd (tried) breed in the north'. He even suggested that a royal stud might be established at Jervaulx, where the King's highness 'shold have . . . the most best race . . . in England'.

Mr. Christie had his own bloodstock trained at Middleham, nearby, which reminds me that in Middleham Church, within earshot of the stables, one of the Jervaulx abbots is commemorated by a remarkable tombstone. It is carved with a rebus—a *thorn* penetrating a *tun*, or barrel—on his name, Thornton.

From his Dutch-gabled house in the abbey precincts Mr. Christie could look out upon Witton Fell and try to visualise the last abbot, Adam Sedbergh, climbing up there to escape those who would force him to join the rebellion of 1536 known as the Pilgrimage of Grace. At length, under duress, Sedbergh agreed to go with the insurgents—and was eventually hanged at Tyburn for his complicity. Surely an undeserved fate. But, in Mr. Christie's succinct phrase, 'the witnesses against him were a bad lot'.

For Jervaulx, as for other monasteries, the final curtain was about to fall. After the Dissolution the abbey changed hands and underwent the usual depredations. A few doorways remain, several altars and sculptured stones, and a number of broken walls from the Infirmary, Refectory and Cloister. The best feature is the Chapter House—roofless, of course, but yet retaining its octagonal roof-shafts with their foliated capitals, and some round-arched windows that give harbourage to a few tenacious wild flowers.

Time has also been unkind to Middleham—where the Coverdale road from Kettlewell enters Wensleydale. Because of its castle and the Nevilles who reigned here in almost regal splendour, Middleham was sometimes called the Windsor of the North. But one would have to be clairvoyant to sense this atmosphere today. A modern window in the church seeks to re-habilitate Richard III, traditionally held responsible for the murder of the Princes in the Tower. He married Anne Neville and lived at the castle, with musicians in frequent attendance. On a recent visit to Middleham I was pleasantly surprised to see two men repairing the Swine Cross. Centuries of exposure to the weather had reduced the boar emblem on this old market cross to an amorphous lump; on somebody's instructions the ancient Neville standard was being in effect 'raised' again.

Nidderdale has always been a cul-de-sac valley in this vast Pennine net-work, but very interesting to follow from the river's source on Great Whernside—not to be confused with the Whernside beyond Ingleton—to the lower reaches around Knaresborough. Angram and Scar House Reservoirs close the head of the valley, which is sandwiched between Wharfedale and Wensleydale. A comparatively new connecting route for motorists leads over the hills from Lofthouse to the Masham countryside, below Jervaulx Abbey. Pateley Bridge, six miles down the Nidd from Lofthouse, provides the first available road turning for upper Wharfedale.

At the dale head the Nidd indulges in some of those delightful antics associated with limestone country. Beside the road, as this loops from Scar House to Lofthouse, two attractive caverns are seen—Manchester Hole and Goyden Pot. Here the Nidd vanishes, only coming to daylight again—with fine frenzy—two miles away at Nidd Heads. Since Goyden Pot was incorporated with the Bradford Waterworks undertaking it has become almost impossible to explore, though I once spent a curious half-hour in the rocky entrance, trying to photograph the amazing barrage of spider webs.

More rewarding, scenically, is How Stean Gorge, near Lofthouse. Here the How Stean Beck puts on a really magnificent show, writhing and booming through the encaging limestone cliffs and creating, in the process, many hanging galleries, thick with dripping creepers and weird-looking ferns. A grotto of legend and fantasy. A fit limbo for all the boggarts and kelpies that used to plague this countryside. What the early tourists and map-makers would have made of this Stygian gorge! I don't suppose they knew of its existence.

At Wath, five miles down the valley, beyond Gowthwaite Reservoir, an old weaving mill by the roadside is still operated by water-wheel—a huge affair seen at one end of the building. When some friends and I were once being shown around, after closing time, we were startled to see the machinery giving occasional spurts of movement. This uncanny sight was due to some vagary in the water-wheel; even when the supply stream was shut off, the buckets accumulated enough dripping water to rotate the wheel spasmodically. The mill appeared to have its ghostly shift!

Water certainly plays some queer tricks in upper Nidderdale. Ramsgill used to have a spring with petrifying qualities, though the honours for this sort of wizardry go to Knaresborough's famous Dropping Well, to be described later. At Wath, again—a name signifying a ford—the river is spanned by a charming hump-backed bridge believed to have been built, in its early form, by the monks of Fountains Abbey.

This abbey is also recalled by a small roadside dwelling at Bewerley, near Pateley Bridge. The house was first built as a chapel and priest's cell by Marmaduke Huby, Abbot of Fountains (1494–1526). An antiquarian friend of mine bought the place many years ago, carefully restored it, and inserted a window emblazoned with Huby's coat-of-arms. Forgetting the Cistercian ideal of humility and poverty, this same abbot also rode about in his own private coach. His beautiful monogram—seen here and at Fountains—is partly a rebus, for one stroke of the initial *H* takes the form of a hobby, or small falcon. It is clear that, despite the inscription *Soli Deo Honor et Gloria* which distinguishes Huby's work at both places, the Abbot fostered very firm notions of his own worth.

Above Bewerley, on the Grassington road, B6265, one comes to Greenhow, Yorkshire's highest village. It is bleak country, part of the watershed between Nidderdale and Wharfedale. There seems little to warrant a halt, save a small, lonely hut bearing the words, Stump Cross Cave. If one happens to be looking the opposite way the existence of the caves would escape notice altogether—as they did for centuries until some lead-miners discovered them by accident in 1860. The barrenness overhead is amply compensated for by a fantastic display of stalagmites and stalactites. The caves they adorn are now illuminated by electricity.

Between Pateley Bridge and Ripley the River Nidd makes a wide sweep, followed closely by the main road. On the heights several by-roads exercise more freedom. One of them climbs up from Pateley Bridge to Guy's Cliff, which is surmounted by Yorke's Folly—a mock ruin erected by one of the Yorke family to provide work during a time of serious depression. The views from the cliff-top are glorious; Yorke evidently wanted people to enjoy them.

Equally fine views reward those who ascend the valley slopes from Summer Bridge, not far away, to Brimham Rocks, though here it is the rocks themselves that steal the show. Centuries of wind and rain have sculptured these masses of Millstone Grit—1,000 feet above sea-level—into many grotesque shapes. Indeed, Nature has arranged her own circus up here, covering fifty acres with rocks resembling an elephant, a dancing bear, an oyster, a hippopotamus's head, a frog, a tortoise, a tiger, a rabbit and many other creatures, with an Idol Rock and a Druids' Circle for good measure. Though some of the names are rather too fanciful, nothing can detract from the drama of the place. Brimham once belonged to Fountains Abbey; in view of this natural 'zoo' it is odd to read that Roger de Mowbray—donor of the property in 1280—also gave to Fountains the entire population of 'wild beasts and birds' in the Forest of Brimham. I wonder what the Fountains monks made of these Brimham grotesques. Did they cross themselves and hurry along to their nearest grange?

Francis Chantrey once visited Brimham Rocks. His comments on Nature's amazing sculptures, on this lofty windswept ridge, might have been very amusing, but one is simply told that Chantrey—the eminent Academician—won a thrashing contest on the local farm!

As Ripley and Knaresborough characterise the Nidd after it leaves the true dale country, they will appear in a later chapter.

six

The Pennine Dales: 3
Swale and Tees

Wensleydale and Swaledale—though separated by only five or six miles of exhilarating moorland, which rises to 2,213 feet at Lovely Seat—show markedly different characteristics. For most of its twenty-two miles Wensleydale is broad and spacious; the fells seem almost to lean back in timeless repose. Swaledale's hills crowd upon the numerous villages and the scenery is more rugged.

Richmond is undoubtedly the best centre for Swaledale, having a picturesque antiquity well-nigh unbelievable for these days. The town is also linked by good roads to most of the North Riding. From Leyburn in Wensleydale the A6108 zigzags over the intervening country, passing—near Downholme—one of Yorkshire's few surviving fortified farms, Walburn Hall.

In bygone times, starting about the twelfth century and continuing sporadically until the Union under James I, raiders from Scotland frequently ravaged the north country, seizing all kinds of plunder—chiefly cattle, but women too if they got half a chance. Several of the old peel towers built as some protection remain in the northern counties, but here at Walburn the defensive plan was rather different. Built of rough-hewn masonry, the house is L-shaped with a crenellated wall enclosing a cobbled courtyard. From within the courtyard the embattled wall is seen to be equipped, a little below the parapet, with a three-foot-wide stone platform reached by a flight of steps.

On hearing of an impending raid the men of Walburn would round up their cattle, drive them into the courtyard or an adjoining area also enclosed by the protective wall, ram fast the outer gate and then, mounting

the platform, prepare to open a volley of arrows upon the approaching foe. The soldiers who garrisoned the hall for Charles I during the Civil Wars probably manned the same platform.

Mary Queen of Scots is said to have stayed here for a short time; it was possibly a visit arranged for her by Lord Scrope as a change from Bolton Castle. Walburn was then Scrope property. But although Mary was given the hall's best room, lighted by a fine oriel window, she liked the place no better than her other 'prisons'. She attempted to escape by squeezing through the centre casement and jumping down to the road—and a waiting horse ?—ten feet below. It was one of several bids for freedom. Here I am simply quoting one of Walburn's traditions, which goes on to claim that Mary is still in residence—as a rather demure ghost. Sober history is disappointingly silent on the whole matter.

Dominated by its magnificent castle, Richmond has often been likened to a typical Rhineland scene, or to some romantic spot in Italy. For Swinburne it evoked memories of Toledo. But it is best to regard Richmond on its own individual merits. Comparisons are unnecessary.

The Richmond neighbourhood is rooted in two ancient civilisations. Applegarth, two miles west of the town, retains its British camp, while the earthwork known as Scots Dyke on the north-east is thought to have marked a boundary between two Celtic kingdoms. Later, the Romans—despite scant evidence on the point—probably used the strategic advantages of Richmond's massive rock which rises almost perpendicularly on the north bank of the River Swale; the more probably as their camp at *Cataractonium*, the forerunner of Catterick, was only six miles to the east.

With the coming of the Normans, Richmond began to take historic shape. At the Conquest the wide domain of the Saxon earl, Edwin of Northumbria, was rudely confiscated and given to Alan Rufus, a kinsman of Norman William. And in 1071 Alan proceeded to build himself a castle in the newly-named Rich-mont, meaning strong hill. The great rectangular keep was raised in 1146 by Conan, the fourth Norman Earl, and the castle became so formidable—being protected on three sides by its precipitous elbow of rock, and on the fourth by Conan's keep—that it assumed no spectacular rôle in future history. There is no record of any siege, but it has gained some glamour by having imprisoned several notabilities, including William the Lion, King of Scotland, David Bruce, and Constance of Brittany.

18   Georgian Theatre, Richmond, showing original boxes and stage

Legend—that ever-ready stand-by—has cast its spell upon the place, for one hears of a hidden chamber beneath the castle where—despite similar claims made for Tintagel in Cornwall—Arthur and his knights lie asleep until England again requires their particular qualities. A passage leading from the Castle Walk to this chamber was once found, so they say, by one Potter Thompson, but he was almost frightened out of his wits when one of the knights turned over in his age-long slumber. People also said that Thompson could never find the way in again. But I think he must have been foxing. Another premature entry might have stirred the whole company with wrath. He wasn't risking it!

Leland's description of the town, 'Richemont is pavid', meaning cobbled, applies to some degree even today. One has to step gingerly in Bargate, Newbiggin, and part of Rosemary Lane, but in the spacious Market Place there are concessions to foot comfort in the form of narrow macadamised strips which connect various corners with the quaint central block of buildings. Richmond folk are very jealous of their cobbled ways. Some years ago a certain individual had his application for the post of borough engineer rejected immediately it was learned that his first town-improvement scheme would be the complete abolition of the cobbles! In Richmond, 'Swale Rovers' does not signify a local football team; it is the name applied with dogged loyalty to those hard, unrelenting, though picturesque cobbles yielded up by the foaming river.

That central block of buildings is an architectural contradiction. Holy Trinity Church, originally built about 1150, stands at the west end; Corporation offices abut on the south side, while various shops—including a hairdresser's—are actually incorporated with the old north aisle. The interior has been considerably restored but the fifteenth-century tower serves as the town belfry. The eastern portion of this arresting block comprises shop and house property whose eighteenth-century aspect adds a further touch of incongruity to what must surely be the most curious architectural jumble in England.

Among the delightful labyrinth of streets and alleys either radiating from, or careering behind, the Market Place and down to the river, are several of medieval origin. One cobbled track which precipitates visitors into Bargate is spanned by Cornforth Bar, part of the old town wall, but the narrowest way of all is Friars' Wynd. It passes through a postern gate belonging to that same mural system, and leads direct from the Market Place to Greyfriars' Tower. Nothing of the original friary survives. The present tower, graceful and richly designed, represents one of Yorkshire's finest achievements of fifteenth-century sacred architecture. It was to have been the glory of a new Franciscan church, but the times were out of joint—the Dissolution intervened.

The Dissolution had its expunging influence also, at Easby Abbey, a mile to the east of Richmond. It is some compensation, however, to have the choir stalls from this Premonstratensian abbey of 1152 serving present-day needs in the chancel of Richmond Parish Church. The church was largely restored last century, but at the west end of the nave Norman pillars and arches give a truer time-scale. Also, there are two monuments of unusual interest, from former times. In the choir Sir Timothy Hutton of Marske, Swaledale—son of a late sixteenth-century archbishop of York—is seen with his lady and their twelve children. The costumes are of the early seventeenth century and below each child there is a rhymed inscription of a biographical nature. Two of those who died in infancy are thus commemorated:

> I liv'd, I dy'd, yet one could hardly know,
> I dy'd so soon, whether I liv'd or no;
> O what a happy thing it is to lie
> I' th' nurse's arms a week or 2 & die.

> Into this world, as strangers to an inn,
> This infant came guest-wise, where when 't had been,
> And found no entertainment worth her stay,
> She only broke her fast and went away.

The other noteworthy monument is a table tomb in the churchyard. It recalls the remarkable story of Robert Willance who, while out horse-riding one day, found himself suddenly enveloped in mist on the edge of neighbouring Whitcliffe Scar. The horse plunged over the precipice to its death, but the rider survived—at the cost of a broken leg, which had to be amputated. With a careful eye to the future, Willance had his leg buried in its own special grave. He continued his prosperous career as a merchant of Richmond, presented a beautiful silver goblet to the Corporation, and had three stones set up on Whitcliffe Scar to represent the three leaps his horse had blindly taken before that fatal plunge. Two of the stones bear the words, '1606, Glory be to our Merciful God who miraculously preserved me from the danger so great'.

Ten years later Willance died, whereupon his severed leg was disinterred and ceremoniously re-buried alongside its owner beneath the new tombstone. Willance meant to meet his Maker *whole*.

Friars' Wynd leads also to the recently restored Georgian Theatre. My wife and I first saw this place in the forlorn condition to which years of neglect and misuse had reduced it. Galleries and boxes that had once seated enraptured audiences were piled high with sideboards and tables and bric-à-brac—the faded stock-in-trade of a second-hand furniture dealer.

Then something fortunate happened. Richmond appointed David Brooks as Town Clerk—and he at once fell in love with this jilted theatre. There was much of the dramatic in his make-up for he would usually append to his official signature a little outline sketch of Conan's keep, at the castle. He set his seal upon the theatre by agitating for its revival and browbeating everybody for funds—even amongst the daughter Richmonds overseas. Gradually Richmond folk bestirred themselves about this forgotten gem in their midst and began to feel some nostalgia for the old jolly days. . . .

It was in 1788 that Samuel Butler, an actor-manager from York, asked the Mayor and Corporation of Richmond to allow him to build a 'proper theatre' in their beautiful Swaledale town, then enjoying the status of a fashionable social centre. By September that same year the playhouse was ready for the public! Amongst those who patronised the 'first night' were Sir Robert Dundas of Aske Hall, nearby, and—very probably—Frances McNally of Hill House, Richmond, lately married to the Irish barrister who had courted her in song as the Sweet Lass of Richmond Hill. All kinds of farces and comedies were presented, besides the inevitable Shakespeare, and the audiences cheered themselves hoarse when Edmund Kean, Sarah Siddons and Macready trod the boards. . . .

As a result of the recent restorations—directed by Dr. Richard Southern, the great authority on Georgian stage-craft—one can now catch authentic echoes from the past. Little has been changed. The boxes are separated by handsome Doric pillars, the galleries retain much of the original knife-board seating, and even the sunken pit—lost to sight for many years—has again come into its own. The theatre can be viewed at almost any time, and suitable plays are frequently staged, with an éclat that would have deeply gratified old Sam Butler.

The only serious blot on Richmond's escutcheon is the Gas Works, which enjoys a delectable site below the castle in a crook of the Swale, near some terraced falls. Mercifully, trees hide its shame, but only in part.

Otherwise the river and its steep banks are magnificent, and the views from Castle Walk superb.

The immediate Richmond countryside has no more thrilling place than Aske Hall, two miles north on the Gilling road. Though lately adapted by the Earl of Zetland to present-day needs, its structure still embodies a Border tower erected about 1130. Aske is a name that emerges repeatedly in Yorkshire history, for this family were great benefactors of religious houses. About 1150 Roger de Aske founded Marrick Priory farther up Swaledale. One of his descendants, Robert, led the Pilgrimage of Grace in support of the outraged monasteries. In 1465 Conan de Aske obtained a special licence to have Mass celebrated in a 'low voice' by his private chaplain here.

Eventually the property was bought by Sir Lawrence Dundas. The late Marquess of Zetland—Lawrence John Lumley Dundas—once explained to me that his family 'came down from Scotland and played their part in effecting the peaceful conquest of England'. A piquant remark to hear in a house built around a Border tower designed to *repel* the Scots!

The arms of three local families—the Askes, the Scropes and the Conyers—appear on the ruined masonry of Easby Abbey, and again over the south porch of Easby Church. Although restored, this fine church matches the adjacent monastery in antiquity, having been founded about the same year, 1152. I like to imagine the White Canons stepping into this church when its now famous thirteenth-century murals were freshly painted. Perhaps they even had a say in their subject and treatment?

The paintings are in the chancel and take the beholder through familiar Biblical episodes, from the Creation to Christ's Resurrection, with many an incidental glance at country pursuits like sowing, tilling and hawking. There is much humour too, as when the hand of the Almighty reaches down like a celestial surgeon to help Eve out of Adam's recumbent body. In the Nativity scene, Joseph drops off to sleep during his vigil beside mother and child. Attended also by a sheep and a cow, the baby Jesus lies apparently embalmed on a colonnaded structure behind the wakeful Mary, who is pleasurably fingering a tiny flower. A later century would have denied us all this charming naïveté and produced something formal and lifeless.

Swaledale takes one into country that gets wilder and wilder as the river's source is approached, on the moors beyond Keld. All the way from

Richmond, however, the Swale lives up to its Norse derivation—'flowing tumultuously'—and the main road keeps it close company.

There is a particularly fine stretch around Marske, where the Hutton family seat stands back amongst the trees. How sad that the two Hutton infants already mentioned never lived to enjoy these delightful gardens and water-meadows. Two miles farther on, Marrick Priory adds a touch of austerity to the landscape, for this house of Benedictine nuns boasted little ornament save its rather gaunt tower. To this remote spot, one raw October day, came Isabella Beaufort, one of Queen Catherine's maids of honour. She was seeking refuge from the amorous attentions of Henry VIII. The sisterhood entered into the little conspiracy and kept her here in secret for four years. After the Dissolution the beautiful girl was restored to her true lover, Edward Herbert, a Somerset squire. It is good to know that the insatiable Henry could be effectively thwarted; every account of this incident declares with romantic insistence that Isabella and her Edward were duly married and lived 'happily ever after'.

Great issues have sprung from this loop of Swaledale. The fells around Hurst have for centuries yielded quantities of lead; some of it is said to have gone abroad to roof the public buildings of Rome and Jerusalem in Herod's day. On the opposite side of the valley Swale Hall, now a farm, casts a fatherly eye on Grinton. It was Solomon Swale of this homestead who once directed the fate of Britain by proposing the motion in Parliament for the restoration of Charles II. He came back to Swale Hall with a baronetcy, a gift of £2,000 and—further to redress his losses during the Commonwealth—an interest-free loan of another £2,000. As if this were not enough fame for one small place, there is a strong tradition that the first tea to come into Swaledale was that drunk at Swale Hall. Perhaps Solomon Swale was still celebrating his restored fortunes!

At Reeth, the next up-dale village, the subsidiary valley of Arkengarthdale branches north-west, plunging deeper into the moors and luring tourists with such curious place-names as Booze, Whaw and Punchard.

But the main valley has its own fascination, beyond Reeth, with villages and country made known amongst naturalists, early this century, by Richard and Cherry Kearton. It was through their splendid books and films, and later by Cherry's broadcasts, that some people heard for the first time of Thwaite and Muker, of Swinnergill Kirk and the Buttertubs Pass, of Keld and its waterfalls, and Nine Standards Rigg. This was the enchanted land of the Kearton brothers' boyhood. Here they sought the

nesting sites of the ring ouzel, timed the migration of swallows, peered
into a weazel's underground larder, and 'learnt to imitate the call-notes
of most of the wild creatures inhabiting the hills around our home'. Here
also they developed the science of photographing birds from hides—then
a novel idea.

They were born in a tiny cottage at Thwaite and went to school at
Muker. Cherry rode the two miles on a 'penny-farthing', but Richard,
being lame, had to struggle along on foot. This was told to me by David
Harker and his wife, who were contemporaries. While in London writing
their books, years later, Richard and Cherry would often pine for the pure
air of Swaledale, for a sight of the fells, for the tang of homely 'Swardill'
speech. When nostalgia took complete command, Swaledale would see
one or other of them again for a few days, and Mr. and Mrs. Harker would
play host and hostess. Cherry's autobiographical film, which must have
gone round the world, was partly conceived in their humble cottage
beside Muker Church.

A lovely story is told about one of the earlier Keartons, who was a local
gamekeeper. It was part of this dour fellow's duty to catch a dish of trout
for his master's table. A new master had arrived but Kearton, being somewhat dubious about his worth, muttered this prayer as he cast his line:
'Oh, Lord, if t' maister's a good un, hook 'em on; if he isn't, gi'e t' fish
a chance'.

Keld, a delightful medley of old lichened cottages, is situated on the
Pennine Way and makes a first-rate walking centre. The limestone fells
soar up loftily on all sides and there are waterfalls and bosky glens to satisfy
the most adventurous soul. Swinnergill Kirk—a cave once used for secret
worship—is suitably difficult to find, but the one-inch map will help. An
acquaintance of mine, after once staying in Keld for a few days, asked a
native when church service began on the Sunday. No definite time was
stated on the notice board. The answer was quite unexpected, but entirely
characteristic of this secluded sheep country: ''T sarvice is in th' evening,
as soon as t' shepherds come down from t' fells'.

Just before Yorkshire peers over into Westmorland, from Nine Standards Rigg, the infant River Swale dances along towards Keld in a fine
series of leaps and bounds. The best exhibition—out of a possible eight
cascades—is at Wainwath Falls, where the river has eroded the encom-
passing limestone into a long corridor of fanciful shapes. These falls are
seen to full advantage from Park Bridge. Here an exciting road branches
north for Tan Hill and Stainmore—the gateway to Teesdale.

No Yorkshireman would dare forget that the little whitewashed building on the scrubby summit of Tan Hill is England's highest inn. It long served the men who worked the surrounding lead-mines and collieries. Fortunately these places were rural in character and, far from adversely affecting the countryside, even added features of interest, like the smelt mills of Arkengarthdale—rather ghostly nowadays—and the strange, harnessed waterways below Tan Hill.

The seam known as Crow Coal runs for many miles along the edge of the Pennines; between Upper Swaledale and Stainmoor it invades the peat mosses 1,700 feet above sea-level. The chief colliery was Tan Hill Pit, near the inn. During the thirteenth century some of these shallow pits belonged to Richmond Castle. They were later acquired by Lady Anne Clifford, who fuelled her castle at Appleby in Westmorland with 'coales from my owne pitts in Stainmoore'. Pack ponies were then used for transport, but much later a character called Elkanah employed a team of donkeys for the purpose. He would blow a horn to announce his approach to the dale's farms that gave him their custom. It must be about a hundred years since this curious cavalcade threaded its way among the hills, but the same manner of coal transport—later adapted for local milk supplies—was used at Castle Bolton and Redmire in neighbouring Wensleydale within living memory.

Stainmore is a grim, barren region, traversed in the Ice Age by a glacier which carried huge boulders from Shap and deposited them farther east, in lower Teesdale, for example, beside Semerwater, and in the Vale of York. Stainmore gave the Romans a fine road route across the neck of England, connecting Brough in Westmorland with their camp at *Lavatrae* (Bowes) and other places beyond. Scottish raiders found the pass very convenient; motorists can but follow in their wake, content perhaps to share for a few miles 'Stanmore's shapeless swell' which Sir Walter Scott cites as background to his eulogy of Teesdale, in *Rokeby*.

Bowes is chiefly noted for two things, separated in time by about 1,800 years. One was the Roman camp, to the south of the village street; the other, a boys' academy, exposed as a villainous place by Charles Dickens. Both phases are recalled at the Parish Church, a fine building which the Normans built inside the former Roman camp. One Roman inscribed stone refers to Emperor Severus as 'great conqueror of Arabia'; significantly, the name of one of his sons, Geta, has been erased—showing that even in far-off *Lavatrae* Caracalla's jealousy of the brother with whom he had shared the Imperial Throne had its repercussions. Geta was murdered; his memory had to be effaced throughout the Roman Empire. I wonder what the garrison thought about Caracalla, the guilty party, in this lonely outpost? And the mason who was told to chisel the name away and ask no questions?

Charles Dickens spotlighted Bowes in *Nicholas Nickleby*. William Shaw's so-called academy which he held up to shame is now a roadside café. Not long ago a man whose relatives ran their farm from this long, low house— early this century—told me the following: 'When repairs were being made to the kitchen a door in the floor was discovered which led to a cellar, and on inspection it was found that schoolboys had written their names on the ceiling . . . with the soot from tallow candles'. It sounds as though some of the pupils had been despatched to the lower regions in punishment. Or did they have to sleep down there? William Shaw, Wackford Squeers' prototype, was quite capable of imposing such 'internal economy'. Certainly the pump which Dickens describes in connection with the boys' morning ablutions still remains, in mute testimony of bygone austerities, for winter brought no alleviation. The pump stands in the flagged yard at the rear of the premises, next to the bleak, open moor.

Dickens saw something else, on that wintry day in 1838. After Shaw had shut the door of Dotheboys Hall in his face, he went over to the church, and wrote later: 'The first gravestone I stumbled on . . . was over a boy who had died suddenly. I suppose his heart broke. He died in this wretched place, and I think his ghost put Smike (in *Nicholas Nickleby*) into my mind on the spot.' The grave is that of George Ashton Taylor. He was about nineteen years of age when death overtook him, in that vile boy-farm.

Critics sometimes contend that Dickens exaggerated his case against this and other Yorkshire schools in the neighbourhood. Perhaps he did. But it was the local people who put him on Shaw's trail. And there was widespread relief when, after the publication of *Nicholas Nickleby*, the population of the Bowes' schools alone dropped with dramatic suddenness from 800 to twenty.

The River Greta which flows through Bowes joins the Tees near Rokeby in very pretty fashion, but the parent valley must first be followed from its head-waters near Cross Fell. This is essentially walking country, for—on the Yorkshire side of the river—only a determined plod below the Whin Sill crags of Cronkley Fell will take one to Cauldron Snout. The Snout is a sight both weird and majestic. After assembling its waters in a deep, mysterious pool known as the Weel, the Tees vaults down a succession of Whin Sill terraces with all the wild abandon of youth. Something of that same quality is required of its would-be explorers. The best views are reserved for those who do not mind wading across a very turbulent Maize Beck and then scrambling up beside the falls to the seductive Weel.

Yorkshire's highest mountain, Mickle Fell (2,591 feet), presides over this far corner of the county. The reward for a long, tedious climb is the magnificent prospect it unfolds. One who evidently 'collects' summit views, despite the hard work involved, declared of Mickle Fell that 'at daybreak the sun may be seen rising from the North Sea, whilst in the evening its last rays may be descried shining on Morecambe Bay'. In other words, the east coast and the west coast—here about a hundred miles apart—are visible from the top of Mickle Fell. On the *Polyolbion* map already mentioned, Drayton shows a lone stranger resting up there, presumably to admire this phenomenal view.

On the same companionable map one of Drayton's water nymphs stands almost waist-deep in the Tees, nearby; a meek version, perhaps, of the Peg Powler who was supposed to lure folk to their doom in this undeniably dangerous river. Peg Powler's Suds are the masses of peaty-brown foam that swirl below the numerous falls and rapids. They are seen at their most ominous where the Tees flings its entire bulk over the seventy-eight-foot precipice of Whin Sill, to create High Force. A huge crag which divides the waters in their headlong descent used to be regarded as the abode of the river-god—that same Peg Powler, I suppose, for it was always she who got the blame for exacting tribute in the form of a human life.

There is a good riverside walk to High Force, on the Yorkshire side, but motorists must take the Alston road, B6277, as far as High Force Hotel. Opposite the hotel a well-laid footpath serpentines down the steep, wooded bank, ending within a few yards of the waterfall. It is at all times impressive, but when the river is in spate people as far down the valley as Darlington will put everything aside and drive up to see High Force at its grandest.

While in Upper Teesdale it is always tempting to step over the county boundary into Barnard Castle, or 'Barney', where Dickens stayed—at the 'King's Head'—with his artist friend, Hablot K. Browne, in that memorable winter of 1838. Several Dickens mementoes are shown in the town's splendid Bowes Museum—but its main windows frame lovely views of the

Yorkshire countryside, beckoning us once again into the Teesdale which Walter Scott described so fervently, around Egglestone Abbey, Brignall Banks and Rokeby.

Egglestone Abbey—another Premonstratensian house—which Scott saw truly as a 'reverend pile . . . profound, dishonour'd, and defaced', is now in the care of the Ministry of Public Buildings and Works. The ruins are scanty, but anything that brings visitors to this part of the dale is to be commended. The Abbey Bridge crosses the Tees at a point which Scott at his most ecstatic could only describe as a 'mighty trench of living stone'. Local people have resorted to the name, Paradise Walk, for a lovely path that leads from this bridge to Rokeby and the Meeting of the Waters. Both Turner and Cotman felt inspired by the confluence of Greta and Tees, here, but Scott—using even brighter word pictures—went into rhapsodies about a 'shy maid' going 'all blushing to her bridal bed'. I can hear modern youth laughing in derision. Scott is more digestible when he describes Mortham Tower.

Although occupying such a fine site above the Meeting of the Waters, Mortham Tower was built out of the stern realities of Border warfare. A village had grown up within its protective shadow, but when the Scots swarmed south in 1346, after Bannockburn, Mortham was ravaged and set ablaze. Their scorched earth policy was only too effective. The tower alone survived.

Early in the fifteenth century the Rokeby family decided to rebuild Mortham Tower and make it their regular home. Before they could move across the parkland from Rokeby, the Tower had to be restored and battlemented, and extra accommodation provided by erecting additional buildings to flank three sides of a courtyard. Blackened masonry still bore eloquent witness to that early raid, so the whole place was fortified afresh. Was it economy of building material, or outraged sentiment, that caused the courtyard gateway to be strengthened with buttresses that incorporate clearly inscribed gravestones from the obliterated Mortham chapel? The courtyard is enclosed by a crenellated wall equipped with archers' plat-form—almost identical with that at Walburn Hall. In this miniature fort-ress the Rokebys lived for about 300 years.

When the Robinsons bought the estate more elegant architectural ideas prevailed, and Mortham Tower was forsaken in favour of the Palladian mansion which the family proceeded to build in Rokeby Park. Once again, Mortham Tower fell into ruin, becoming a forlorn pile, fit only for the spinning of eerie tales.

Under Rokeby's next ownership the Tower found its staunch champion—in the ever romantic Walter Scott. John Bacon Sawrey Morritt had furnished the novelist with many scraps of local history and legend. 'You have often given me materials for romance,' declared Scott; 'now I want a good robber's cave. . . .' Morritt obliged, with this and more. At length, in December 1812, the narrative poem 'Rokeby' appeared and a delighted public began to exult in 'Mortham's cavern dark', in 'fairy Thorsgill' nearby, and in the Felon Sow—a fierce beast which Ralph of Rokeby presents to the Grey Friars of Richmond. The 'Robber's Cave' is in the grounds of Mortham Tower. It overlooks the Greta and contains the table Scott used, here, when writing about the Tower and its hegemony of tales.

Mortham Tower was yet again restored, in 1939, but in general appearance it is still the fortified home of long ago. Within the courtyard the house is entered from the old 'barnekyn'—a lofty chamber with an open timber roof. A stone staircase leads directly into the Tower proper; first comes a short, straight flight, then—with a quaint sculptured head peeping from beneath one step—the long spiral stair begins. It serves the Great Chamber, still attractively Tudor, and two modernised bedrooms, before reaching the Tower roof. From the parapet, Greta and Tees are glimpsed far below through magnificent trees; some of the oaks supplied acorns for Walter Scott to plant around Abbotsford.

Whenever I shudder at what modern industry has done to the Tees estuary, thirty miles east, I let my thoughts run back to High Force, or to the boulder-strewn river at Egglestone, or to this fine panoramic view from Mortham Tower.

seven

Around the Great North Road: 1
from Croft Spa to Fountains Abbey and Ripon

Walter Scott seems to have found the Great North Road 'dull'. It might have been even less to his liking today when so many of the old coaching towns and attractive villages are being by-passed. Yet nobody can deny that the historic A1—be it stripped as clean as a willow-rod—serves a most interesting countryside as it shoots through Yorkshire.

In this chapter the highway will be joined at Darlington and followed southwards—but with plenty of deviations.

A glance at a geological map shows how the Great North Road clings to a central 'corridor' compounded of Permian and Triassic sandstones and marls. The Pennine dales are over to the west. On the east side, the Clevelands and the Hambletons model the distant skyline with their oolitic ridges. But this flat intermediate corridor is bordered widely with rich agricultural land, belts of timber, sleepy villages, and many landed estates.

After Darlington the first worth-while detour is via the A167 to Croft Spa, three miles south. Here the River Tees is spanned by a handsome bridge linking Co. Durham with Yorkshire. St. Peter's Church, just over the bridge, is burnished with the same kind of red sandstone, which the medieval builders took from the river bed, offsetting it in places with some white stone from a local quarry. The result is a picture that lingers in the mind—a picture enhanced in summer by the roses clustering around the south porch.

Two families—the Nevilles and the Places—have their coats-of-arms on the fifteenth-century tower, but their day was still in the future when another stone was tooled. This stone—now built into the inside wall, near the south door—portrays a curious figure supposed to represent Romanico, a Roman river-god. It was exhumed many years ago from the graveyard, which reaches down to the Tees. A pagan church may once have occupied this site. It is considered possible that Benedict Biscop of Jarrow and Monkwearmouth, and Wilfrid of York—two great church builders—may occasionally have met here, roughly half-way between their respective domains, and persuaded the local people to renounce their old gods in favour of Christianity. Hence, may be, the first Saxon church established in this neighbourhood.

I fancy that Romanico was set up in the church after the incumbency of one Victorian rector—Lewis Carroll's father, but the boy would still find plenty here *sub rosa* to fire his imagination. There is much quaint carving, notably on the medieval sedilia, but also on a long narrow stone in the Chaytor Chapel. This stone, bearing the family coat-of-arms, came from Croft Hall. The story goes that when the railway thrust itself across the neighbouring countryside, the Chaytors were so disgusted at the sight that they had their house re-orientated so as to face away from the abomination. In the process, this coping stone and two other heraldic sculptures were removed and taken to the church, doubtless as symbols of injured pride.

To Lewis Carroll, however, railways meant adventure. In the rectory garden he and his younger brothers and sisters ran a miniature railway, complete with signals, stations, refreshment rooms—and tickets. Years before *Alice* appeared, this and other juvenile delights helped to animate the little magazines he wrote here to entertain the family.

But the 'Great North of England' railway made another impact at Croft. If the owner of Croft Hall could have known that in later years George Hudson, the 'railway king', was to settle down with his wealth at neighbouring Hanlaby Hall, and attend the same village church, he would surely have thrown an apoplectic fit!

Hudson seems to have enjoyed his squirearchical rôle. It gave him and his the right to occupy the most fantastic family pew in Yorkshire. Originally built for the Milbanke family, the pew and its staircase fill two bays of the north arcade. The staircase alone is a fine sight; it could easily have been the *pièce de résistance* in some splendid Jacobean house. There are dog gates at the bottom and its three short flights are enclosed by a balustrade with spiral rails. The pew stands on oak pillars, which are echoed in the slender, fluted columns supporting the pew canopy, and within its panelled enclave—hung with red curtains to exclude draughts and the prying gaze of 'lesser' worshippers—the squire and his guests could sit in domestic comfort and actually look down upon the parson in his pulpit. This species of high churchmanship appealed to not a few gentry in the seventeenth and eighteenth centuries.

To Hudson, the elegant pew may possibly have stood for the sumptuous first-class carriages to which his railways would eventually aspire. Meanwhile, the ordinary folk below sometimes saw strange things up there, for Hudson usually sang with his back to the parson, while his wife—not to be outdone—settled herself daintily beneath her parasol for the sermon. It must always have been something of a peep show. When Lord Byron accompanied his bride, one of the Milbanke girls, to morning service— some years earlier, it was as if Don Juan himself was aloft and cogitating, perhaps, about the desirability of drawing the curtains across if the parson should turn over the hour-glass for another spell of oratory. Incidentally, the hour-glass is contained within a seventeenth-century engraved metal frame not unlike a basket.

Croft Church was indeed a stimulating place for Parson Dodgson's growing, dreamy boy. How the coming nonsense writer must have fed on these odd happenings—if only through hearsay, before his other half— the Oxford don and mathematician, emerged.

Eight miles farther south, via Dalton and North Cowton, the village of Scorton looks 'promising', especially when one first notices the 'monks'. These black-robed brethren belong to the Hospital of St. John of God, a Roman Catholic community dedicated to the welfare of cripples. The country lanes radiating from Scorton know them all well.

One of England's oldest archery societies—the Scorton Archers— originated from this same pleasant village, barely two miles from the tumultuous Great North Road. Samuel Henderson of Leeds, a prominent member, describes this society as 'an archery peculiar', for there are no headquarters and only the annual summer-time 'shoot' holds the society together, with those who compete forming the membership. 'The Society's existence hangs by a thread', says Mr. Henderson, 'but it has been doing so since it was founded in 1673.'

Of the present-day village Henry Calverley, first Captain of the Scorton Archers, would recognise little but the large, central green which is raised some three feet above the roadway and has to be reached by steps placed at intervals round the edges. The enclosing ring of stone-built cottages is broken at one point by the Grammar School of 1720. It is good to learn that at this attractive school—capped with a clock-turret—archery is a recognised sport for the senior boys; a graduation course, no less, for the annual contest that has taken the name of this small village throughout the toxophilite world.

Scorton's Silver Arrow—believed to be England's oldest sporting trophy—has been dubiously attributed to Elizabeth I, though it may have some connection with Roger Ascham, her tutor in archery and author of that famous treatise on the subject, *Toxophilus*. His amusing account of the 'winde' as a hazard that 'tryeth an archer' is related as part of an experience near his birthplace. For Ascham was born in 1515 at Kirkby Wiske, only twelve miles south of Scorton, and it is known that he took part in various archery competitions in Yorkshire.

The Scorton Arrow is awarded, with the Captaincy, to the archer who scores the first gold or bull's eye of the day's contest, the range being one hundred yards. He also receives a handsome badge, comprising a silver-arrow pin carrying a medallion and a miniature bugle. There are several other awards, one of the most coveted being a horn spoon, awarded for the 'worst white' at the extreme outer edge of the target—a very difficult shot, if intended! This booby prize is probably as old as the Silver Arrow.

Nowadays the Scorton 'shoot' may be held anywhere in Yorkshire, and it is usually advertised in the local Press. If or when visitors tire of watching the actual contest, there is an alternative interest—that of inspecting the trophies displayed on the scorers' table along with the society's record books.

The oldest of these books contains the society's quaintly phrased rules, drawn up at a time when Flodden and other memories of military archery were fading into armchair tales. One rule reads:

Forasmuch as the exercise of archery is lawful, laudable, healthy and innocent; and to the end that God's holy name may not be dishonoured by any of that Society, it is hereby declared that if any one of them shall that day curse or swear in the hearing of any of the company, he shall forthwith pay down one shilling, and so proportionately for every oath, to be distributed by the Captain to the use of the poor of that place or township where they shoot.

The poor would listen very intently that day.

For old times' sake, the rule is still substantially observed—though, in this affluent age, there would be few if any indigent persons to benefit! Even more interesting, to an onlooker, are the Society's later records, which become increasingly decorative, though Roger Ascham's phraseology breaks through with such delightful terms as 'loosing of shafts', 'piercing of golds', and 'nocking'. A particularly fine page, in the records, refers to a meeting of the Society at Settle in the Pennine country. It is bordered with a lavish display of the county's White Rose emblem.

The decorative pages for the current 'shoot' are the responsibility of the newly-assigned Captain, who will probably employ an artist for the purpose. If only this particular custom had been in vogue earlier one such page would most probably have been illuminated by the hand of Julius Caesar Ibbetson, the famous water-colourist, who was born at Masham nearby. I discovered that it was he who won the Silver Arrow in 1815, two years before his untimely death.

The neighbouring countryside provides yet another example of how some great event has sprung from obscure beginnings. In this instance the colony of Maryland, U.S.A., was the outcome. Scorton and the adjoining village of Bolton-on-Swale had a share in founding this state, for both places pro- vided colonists when Lord Baltimore of Kiplin sailed west on his great mission in 1630.

Kiplin Hall stands back from B6271, half-way between Scorton and Northallerton. The older part shows the influence of Inigo Jones. An his- torical novelist would revel in its stories and traditions, and above all in its characters, who have the place largely to themselves today as the present owner spends much of her time in the south. Yet this lady, Miss Bridget Talbot, wrote a masque not long ago which re-vivified the whole surroundings. Entitled *Farewell Kiplin*, it was enacted around the lake here and Mrs. Calvert-Pierce of Maryland took a leading rôle. She is a direct descendant of George Calvert, the first Lord Baltimore. A great moment in the masque occurred when models of the *Ark* and the *Dove*—the two ships that took the colonists overseas—sailed across the Kiplin lake in simulation of that momentous Atlantic voyage. I hope the masque will be repeated here many times.

Thornton Watlass is the kind of place one might dream about after reading one of Lord Dunsany's tremulous stories. Remote from modern life, as full of memories as an octogenarian, it has more than a hint of mystery in its quiet charm. It stands between Bedale and Masham, with Jervaulx Abbey only four miles away, across the River Ure. A house on the same site was mentioned in Domesday Book, but three or four cen- turies are sufficient for the present hall to set its stage. Built in the late sixteenth or early seventeenth century, and remodelled in 1727 after the

Vanbrugh manner, this large house of many rooms is surrounded by a park of a hundred acres.

Generations of Dodsworths have lived here. It was Lady Smith-Dodsworth who once showed me round, conjuring the past from her rich store of family anecdotes while Lorenzo, the peacock, preened himself in the old pump yard as if trying to lure us away from our absurd preoccupation with history. But I was hearing tales about priests in hiding, and martyrs, and ghosts—so Lorenzo took the huff, closed up his gorgeous feathers in disgust, and vanished.

The Scropes have already coloured these pages. When religious persecution was rife, John Dodsworth stabled Lord Scrope's horses at this place. Remaining true to the Old Faith, the Scropes were forbidden to keep their own horses—a Government attempt to exercise some control over the movements of the Catholic gentry. 'We have several recusant fine papers here', said Lady Smith-Dodsworth, 'all testifying to staunch religious observance in face of civil authority. The famous Edmund Catterick stayed at Thornton Watlass for a time,' I was told further; 'on hearing that the pursuivants were after him, he left, but was apprehended on the way to York—where he was martyred'. As a warning to others his head was spiked on Micklegate Bar. The 'good old days' seem to have been largely chimerical.

Roger Dodsworth was the antiquary of the family, and had as patron the Lord General Fairfax of Civil War fame. Fairfax himself was no mean antiquary. It was he who rescued the famous Horn of Ulf after it had been stolen from York Minster. Before the Siege of York, in 1644, Fairfax hired Dodsworth to make duplicates of the precious monastic papers kept in Marygate Tower, not far from the Minster. Acting against orders, a Scottish colonel blew up this old tower—but not before Dodsworth recovered some of the outstanding treasures, including the famous Rhyming Charter given by King Athelstan to John of Beverley. As already noticed at Menston-in-Wharfedale, Charles Fairfax played his own part in this salvaging of precious documents. At Thornton Watlass, 'nephew Tom' is remembered by a keepsake given to the zealous Dodsworth; it is a silver hip-flask embossed with the Fairfax lion.

Dorothy Dodsworth—whose portrait in the Drawing Room introduces one to a charming young lady of the William and Mary period—seems to have inherited Roger's collecting zeal, though her partiality was for old lace. Venetian, Flemish, Spanish, English—these and many other varieties swelled her collection, which she proceeded to mount on red silk in the form of curtains, tablecloths, bedspreads, etc. She then presented this unique display to Princess Charlotte of Wales who, however, died before being able to use any of it. Eventually the entire collection was bought back for the Dodsworth family.

Yet another with the true collector's flair was Lady Julia Smith-Dodsworth. Her speciality was old oak, some of which she incorporated with the main staircase about a hundred years ago. The balusters were adapted from some Wren-like altar rails at West Tanfield Church, but the panelling and the newels were purposely carved for her by the estate gamekeeper. This clever fellow first tooled a bit of family heraldry, then let himself go with a delightful set of ferns, grape-vines, oak leaves and acorns.

An arresting sight on the staircase-landing is a shillelagh hewn from bog oak—reminiscent of the one with which the Irish curate armed himself when facing the Luddites, in Charlotte Brontë's *Shirley*, except that here a grotesque face crowns the cudgel. The face is that of a man who has apparently come off badly in some shillelagh encounter. How many broken skulls it had accounted for, in its own right, before some Irish ancestors sent it over to Thornton Watlass, I could not discover. But the rôle of this ugly-faced club, here, has been peaceful, if a little waggish. 'When our children were young', said Lady Smith-Dodsworth, 'they would dress it up and then put it in the guest bedroom.' Awaiting a visitor's reaction was good fun!

Over to the south-west, on Ilton Moor, anybody might be deceived by a very different kind of joke. It is a Druids' Temple—erected early last century by William Danby of Swinton Hall, near Masham. The druids had been eclipsed centuries before Christ, yet here—as on other gentlemen's estates—the cult was revived so that guests could shudder to the full extent of their stimulated imagination at the sight of strange monolithic stones and sacrificial altars. The Temple is in excellent condition.

But in a countryside so rich in genuine monuments of the past there was little need of another Stonehenge—if that was the governing idea. In Masham churchyard there is a round pillar about seven feet high which still bears figures of Christ and his Apostles, carved some thousand years ago. Older again is the portion of tessellated pavement preserved in Well Church—a venerable place which entombs in its walls a lot of masonry from the same Roman villa.

Well village is a pleasant surprise. The Great North Road might be a hundred miles away, instead of a mere four as the crow flies—but there is no direct approach. People evidently had plenty of time on their hands when surrounding lanes were first trodden out, by villein or beast, and only a fool would mind having to twist about via Leeming, Bedale and Snape to reach this little hollow in the low hills, named after a holy well.

The outstanding residence—near the church—is Well Hall, though its original function was not to house some influential family, but a few 'needy poor persons'. Out of his generosity Ralph Neville, Lord of Middleham, built the place as the Hospital of St. Michael the Archangel. That was 700 years ago. By 1342, twenty-four men and women were in residence, under the care of a chaplain and two priests.

In due course, Warwick the King-maker would become patron of the Hospital, and—later—Richard III himself. Richard had married the Lady Anne Neville, Warwick's younger daughter, and one may try to visualise Richard riding over from Middleham—perhaps with some of his beloved musicians tuning the way—to see how the Hospital fared in this little outpost of his northern estates. Despite his supposed infamies, he was always popular in Yorkshire.

Eventually, Robert de Tateshall acquired the Hospital for his own private use, and a mean little almshouse was built nearby for the dispossessed. The reason for this nasty bit of work becomes apparent if one is privileged to view Well Hall, especially the Dining Room which is virtually the lower chamber of the thirteenth-century building. It is a long, low chamber with stone ribbed vault resting on three stout pillars spaced down the centre of the room. On the wall side the arches spring from corbels of varied design. It has the character of a church crypt, and at the east end a tunnel-shaped recess probably marks the site of a stair that would lead to the upper chamber.

Here lived the cremetts, as the inmates were called in Tudor times. Earlier they were known simply as bedesmen and bedeswomen. Few lords of those days could boast so fine a home. Little wonder that it later aroused Tateshall's envy. When, finally, he pounced, St. Michael's patronal care was dispensed with and he called his new mansion The Hond.

The village church is integral to the story of Well Hall; one can readily imagine all the cremetts following in procession as Sir John Neville, third Lord Latimer of Snape, was laid to rest here in 1543. And how the tongues would wag afresh over Sir John's family affairs—especially the marriage of his kinswoman, Katharine Parr, to Henry VIII. This wedding was as much local as national history, for Katharine Parr—a Neville by descent—had lived at Snape Castle, only two miles away. Lord and peasant alike, throughout the district, must have feared for Katharine as she left this fair countryside for London, there to walk the precarious path taken by Henry's previous wives. . . . Various sculptured stones in the front garden at Well Hall came from Snape Castle.

Two miles south the River Ure—now a river of the plain—swings through West Tanfield to create a scene which few painters or photographers can resist. Viewed beneath the arch of the old bridge, the red roofs of the village cluster above the Ure, dominated by the Marmion Tower and the tower of the church where the Marmions sleep. Walter Scott's memorable hero—Lord Marmion of Flodden Field—was pure invention and owes nothing but his name to this lovely village. The fifteenth-century Marmion Tower was gatehouse to the family homestead, of which no other trace remains.

The church makes up for this loss with its wonderful array of Marmion tombs; each has its alabaster effigy of some lord or lady of the family who lived when the Yorkshire abbeys were in their prime. Around the tomb of Robert de Marmion and Laura, his wife, there is a strange, tent-like iron framework called a 'herse' or hearse. The spikes fitted at intervals around the crenellated bar on top were intended for candles, which would be lit periodically as prayer tokens for the departed. Very few such hearses have survived. Although this one probably dates from the fourteenth century, it has provided the church with a novel design for some new porch gates. The upright bars on these wrought-iron gates faithfully reproduce the pricket candlesticks from that medieval tomb!

Other modern links with monastic England occur in the choir. Carved in oak, four monks make a joyful noise unto the Lord with fiddle, horn, flute and harp. It is just as though—by some miracle—one of the old village church bands had been requisitioned by a few monks from neighbouring Jervaulx or Fountains.

Britain's finest monastic ruin—that is the unanimous opinion of most architects and archaeologists who have come under the spell of Fountains Abbey. Dr. Pevsner puts the matter categorically: 'There is no other place in the country in which the mind can so readily evoke the picture of thirteenth-century monastic life, and the eye a picture of the vast extent and yet the crispness and freshness of Cistercian architecture in the wild North Country forests.'

The 'wild forests' pertained only to the early centuries. Today, instead of surrounding forest, there is beautiful parkland and good farming country. But when the first monks came here in 1132—twelve stalwarts who had cut themselves adrift from the laxity of St. Mary's, the Benedictine house at York—the prospect that greeted them, here in the valley of the Skell, was indeed stark and forbidding. Brother Hugo of Kirkstall was echoing the words of the aged Serlo, from Fountains, when he described this Skell Valley as having been 'uninhabited for all the centuries back, thick set with thorns, lying between the slopes of mountains and among rocks jutting out on both sides; fit rather, it seemed, to be the lair of wild beasts than the home of human beings'. Allowing for Serlo's fancy about each brooding hill being a 'mountain', the picture seems valid enough. This unpromising piece of land was given to the seceders from York by Archbishop Thurstan.

Thurstan had befriended them and championed their cause from the start—and what a strange start it was, with a riot at St. Mary's over the Archbishop's inspection on their behalf. 'The whole Chapter House', wrote Thurstan, later, 'rang with such tumult and confusion that it seemed more like the seditious uproar of drunken revellers than the humility of monks, of which there was no sign. Many of them rushed up and came upon us with outstretched arms, as if to wrestle with us, and all cried out that they would be roused to fury if I entered.' As official Visitor of St. Mary's, Thurstan *did* enter—and somehow, in the mêlée that followed, he and his retinue managed to cover the escape of the twelve monks whose only desire was to keep faith with conscience and worship God in sincerity.

Thurstan took them with him, first to the shelter of York Minster, and then to Ripon where he had a house and other property. It was a slice of this property which he gave to his protégés as a Christmas gift, in 1132. It was also a *testing* gift, as they soon found after tramping those three miles from Ripon to the Skell wilderness. For some time this new brotherhood, comprising Richard the former Prior of St. Mary's, Richard the former Sacristan, Ranulph, Thomas, Gamel, Hamo, Robert of Subella, Geoffrey, Walter, Gregory, Ralph, Alexander, and Robert from Whitby Abbey, had no church in which to sing their praises, no abode even, except the shade afforded by a large elm-tree.

The ensuing story of Fountains is one of near-starvation, gradual recovery, erection of the first conventual buildings with gritstone quarried on the site—Serlo's 'jutting rocks', extensive damage by fire, growing prestige and wealth, establishment of daughter houses like Newminster and Kirkstall—all threaded by holy charity until, towards the end, there were junketings at the Abbot's overloaded table, and many evidences of personal honour and glory; the very things which the founders had sacrificed so much to renounce.

One of the last abbots, William Thirsk, was accused of stealing abbey property, and conniving with a certain goldsmith over the removal of precious stones from the gold altar cross which the monastery now boasted. Marmaduke Bradley actually *bought* the abbacy, and when the Dissolution deprived him of its emoluments he returned to his comfortable Prebend in Ripon, richer by a pension of £100 per annum as ex-abbot of Fountains.

Huby has already been encountered, at his Nidderdale retreat. He had no qualms about entertaining friends with the very un-Cistercian diet of 'a quarter of a yard of roast beef and a black jack of strong drink'. He may have been guilty of more serious, moral offences, and yet one of the finest features of Fountains Abbey is the tower he built, adjoining the north transept. In his splendid history of the abbey, the late Canon Bell wrote: 'The great tower stands as the magnificent memorial of his (Huby's) abbacy, and also as the outward and visible sign of the repudiation of Cistercian simplicity. The original rule sternly forbade anything in the shape of a lofty tower.' But it was now the late fifteenth century; the Renaissance had dawned. Huby was moving with the times! Pride, prestige, and easy living—before the great fall engineered by an avaricious Henry in 1539!

Nevertheless, so much of the monastery remains, though in stately ruin, that the wonderful story of Fountains can be read, even today, from its weathered stones. Delicate ferns may sprout from the crevices and an occasional thrush build her nest in a crumbling door-socket, but—however fragilely—they do bring a touch of life to the cloister, and the great church, and the Chapel of the Nine Altars—still sublime after seven centuries. One quiet day, some years ago, an elderly couple, while wandering through the ruins, faintly but distinctly heard some singing in the empty choir. The man—a church organist—jotted down the strange, haunting tune, and had it identified later as a piece of medieval plainsong. . . .

Fountains Abbey may mean different things to different visitors. My own fondest memory is of our church choir gathering in the presbytery and giving unstinted voice to 'O Gladsome Light', from Sullivan's *The*

Golden Legend. Never did it sound better! An antiquary, on the other hand, might prefer the silence of the ages, so that he can concentrate on the huge Norman arcades of the nave, the slender shafts of the Nine Altars Chapel, an unexpected water-leaf capital, or the magnificent vaulting of the cellarium—that long, low building partly spanning the Skell and dating back to the earliest days at Fountains.

Floodlighting has given the abbey a new, autumnal popularity, the effect being enhanced by Alan Cuckston's authentic background recordings of *Ave Mundi Rosa* and other music composed here in the Middle Ages. When superseded by newer tunes, the *Mundi Rosa* and other pieces of parchment music were not destroyed but used by the monks as book bindings. That is how the chaste old music—stilled for so long—has come through to this day.*

Fountains Abbey is certainly worth seeing when thus *en fête*, but there is no substitute for an unhurried daylight visit—or many such visits—to the monastery that took its lovely, tuneful name from the numerous surrounding springs.

How those floodlighting amenities would have been welcomed by William Aislabie, who annexed Fountains to his Studley Royal property in the eighteenth century! Marmaduke Huby's Perpendicular tower and the other claustral buildings bathed in a soft pink eerie glow would have crowned the delight of his guests, as they beheld this highly picturesque ruin by night. Yet Aislabie was more fortunate than most gentry of the period. He had no need to build a well-placed ruin 'to improve the view'. The ruin was already there. The improvements he did introduce took the form of a great landscape garden with ornamental lakes fed by the Skell, a Temple of Piety, and various 'coigns of vantage' cunningly devised for giving the excited visitor surprise views of the abbey; other kinds of surprise, too, for one guide would show visitors the classical statuary, solemnly pointing to the 'Venus de *Medicine*' and 'Hercules strangling *Anthony*'.

* Alan Cuckston tells me that two such fragments have survived. The first, containing unique Cistercian music of the early fourteenth century, occupies four leaves of parchment used later as flyleaves in a miscellaneous MS. book long kept at Ripley Castle, but now in the Fountains estate office. The second, containing polyphonic music of the fourteenth and fifteenth centuries, was immured in the binding of a memorandum book recording events at the abbey between 1446 and 1460. This book is at the British Museum. The music from both sources has been transcribed by Mr. Cuckston, and the *Ave Mundi Rosa* has been given a TV broadcast. Mr Cuckston is known for his musical recitals and also plays the harpsichord in Yorkshire country-house concerts.

19   *Fountains Abbey, dominated by Abbot Huby's fifteenth-century tower*

All of this can be enjoyed today, along with the deer park that connects the grounds to Studley Royal village. On the other, western side of the abbey a different outcome of the Dissolution is seen, for the beautiful Fountains Hall was largely built from abbey masonry, about 1611. Amongst many interior features of great appeal, there is a stone stairway which spirals through three floors—much as it once did over at the abbey.

Although it was a Cistercian house, and therefore withdrawn—in theory —from the evils and distractions of town life, Fountains Abbey is only four miles by road from the ancient city of Ripon. Several links between the two places are still noticeable, especially in Ripon Cathedral.

A small altar at one end of the Norman chapter-house may have witnessed Thurstan's final blessing upon that band of resolute monks as they set out for the inhospitable Skell-dale 800 years ago. And then, in the splendid library overhead, there is a fine copy of Anton Koberger's moral repertory and dictionary once in use at Fountains, as clearly shown by a hand-written inscription on the first page—'*liber sce Marie virginis de ffontibus*'. This book seems to have been tucked under his cloak, as a much-coveted prize, by William Thirsk—that penultimate abbot to whom a little thieving was not incompatible with his sacred calling. The moral precepts in the book apparently left him unmoved. But he was soon in trouble. Ejected by the King's Commissioners, he found himself penniless, took refuge at Jervaulx Abbey, became embroiled with the Pilgrimage of Grace, and—probably to his own complete surprise—went in consequence to a martyr's death, being hanged, drawn and quartered with the more virtuous victims.

Another ex-monastic treasure in the library is a thirteenth-century manuscript of the Apocalypse, etc., from Bridlington Priory. Its presence here is unexplained, but a Latin curse on the contents page must have fallen on deaf ears: 'he who takes away this (book) let him be anathema.' It is a relief to turn from religious taboos and execrations to see what Dean Derring has to say about life in early eighteenth-century Ripon. In his diary and account book, preserved here, he records the moneys paid to bell-ringers for celebrating the Culloden victory after the 1745 Rebellion —and, in the same breath, 1s. 8d. to his charwoman for five days' work. A shilling buys the Dean some nasturtium seeds to pickle, and another shilling 'two pound of Rush Lights'. I wonder if he begrudged paying his window-tax?—15s. at Lady Day and 15s. again at Michaelmas.

To one who has known the place all his life Ripon Cathedral is itself

20   *Ripon Cathedral: the Early English West Front*

rather like an old tome, worn and 'well thumbed' but bulging with good things. Here I can only flick over a few of them.

First, by every right, comes the Saxon crypt of St. Wilfrid, dated about 670. It held the holy relics, and although the pilgrims' approach to it has only partially survived, the essential atmosphere remains. The 1,300 intervening years slip easily away. One opens a trap-door in the nave choir, descends a narrow flight of stone steps, gropes through some medieval passages—echoing those in the Pyramids, and suddenly enters this small, crude, barrel-vaulted chamber, where nothing has any validity save Wilfrid and his credulous times. The concealed electric lighting might come from oil lamps; there is practically no furnishing. Yet the place grips. The guide explains all that is necessary, including the strange traditions about St. Wilfrid's Needle. Anybody who can squeeze through this narrow cavity in one wall is thereby assured of Heaven's forgiveness. Originally, however, to thread this Needle was a proof of chastity. When the crypt was fashioned, Fountains Abbey was still in the womb of history.

Another interesting phase of the cathedral's story summons the Ripon School of Woodcarvers from the shades—or rather from the chancel, for it was this famous body of sixteenth-century craftsmen who took a number of well-known Biblical subjects and lavished upon them—as they carved each misericord—much subtle north-country humour. Jonah being swallowed by the whale, below one seat, is matched in vigour by the disobedient prophet's subsequent ejectment on the shores of what appears to be some South Sea atoll. The poppy heads are equally diverting. One is an ape, but the best carving is on the Bishop's Throne and shows an elephant astride a tortoise. This strange combination—an old verger used to tell me—is supposed to illustrate an ancient Indian theory once held to account for the occurrence of earthquakes. The whole earth, it was argued, rested on the back of a huge tortoise. When this creature moved, its burden naturally wobbled—hence our seismic disturbances! The Ripon woodcarver responsible for this little masterpiece probably knew nothing of a spherical earth, so he modelled an elephant instead. Complete with castle-shaped howdah and a few mahouts, the elephant symbolised India for him.

Beyond the choir, several fine monuments help to recall Ripon's social past. In the South Transept the Aislabies of Studley keep company with William Weddell—the latter a lovely piece of work by Nollekens and particularly apt in view of Weddell's renowned sculpture gallery awaiting us at Newby Hall nearby. Over in the North Transept the Markenfields of

Markenfield Hall look sadly worn and battered; 600 years have proved too long a vigil for the guardian angels beside Sir John's lady, though Sir Thomas's splendid collar with its stag medallion is still handsome, if a little frayed.

Hugh Ripley's monument, near the pulpit, shows his be-ruffed self kneeling rather awkwardly. The tablet has little aesthetic appeal, but Ripley was an outstanding figure in seventeenth-century Ripon and one cannot do better, on leaving the cathedral, than follow the trail of events that made him the town's last Wakeman and its first Mayor. . . .

When Ripon hailed its first Mayor in 1604 the town was already ancient, for its original charter was bestowed in 886. The charter took the form of a horn, traditionally presented by Alfred the Great, though this is sometimes disputed. The charter horn was meant for use by the Wakeman, then the town's chief citizen; he or one of his assistants was required to blow a few horn-blasts every night at 9 o'clock in the Market Place to signalise the setting of the watch. All domestic fires must then be quenched. From 9 p.m. until sunrise next day the Wakeman was responsible for the safety of the town. Every householder paid him a small regular sum for this service and was thus assured of recompense should his property be violated during the night hours—a form of burglary insurance.

The nightly horn-blowing ceremony—minus the insurance benefits!— is still observed. It is well worth timing some tour of the neighbourhood so as to witness and hear this survival from Saxon times. Just before nine a strange-looking figure wearing black tricorn hat and fawn skirted tunic steps past all the waiting cars, well equipped—it would seem—to make a sonorous rehearsal for the Last Trump. He is the official horn-blower. The instrument he carries, and proceeds to blow at the four corners of the market cross, is a Scotch bull horn; its dirge-like blast can be heard all over Ripon and deep into the surrounding country.

This is the third horn to sound Ripon's so-called curfew. The original charter horn is in retirement and hangs from the wonderful baldric worn by the sergeant-at-mace. When not needed for official processions, the horn is displayed for all to see—by courtesy of the Council—in the Georgian town hall. The old horn is now covered with purple velvet, and two supporting straps carry silver emblems of Ripon's bygone trades. More of these emblems appear on the broad baldric, each one representing some bygone Wakeman. Among this entertaining pageantry of farriers, woodcutters, foresters and spur-makers, one's gaze fixes at length upon

Hugh Ripley's badge. An inscription states that he was 'Ye Last Wakeman 1603. By Hys goode endeavors ye towne obtained a new Charter of incorporation from Hys Majestie James 1st, 1604'. Only the Corporation minute books reveal that he had to wait five years for the repayment of £64 expenses incurred in going to London and cooling his heels until the Charter materialised!

In 1953 a new baldric was provided to carry all the mayoral badges from 1886 onwards. One recent mayor—a builder by profession—is represented by a modern villa; another—a railway official—displays a railway signal and part of the iron road. What symbols will the nuclear age add to this unique record? The second baldric also has its horn—a splendid specimen from the Chillingham herd of wild cattle. It is normally displayed with the older baldric, in the town hall, and if one is lucky other civic items will be on show, including an historic pair of true Ripon rowels. The rowels, or spurs, are preserved as a reminder of an old town craft and of the tradition that James I, after once staying overnight in Ripon, was given a pair of rowels which he wore on riding away.

Ripon's ancient motto—'Except ye Lord keep ye Cittie, ye Wakeman waketh in vain'—enjoys a banner-spread across the town hall façade. Ripon's daughter city—Ripon, Wisconsin—has adopted the same Biblical motto, and now has a recording of the Wakeman's horn, so that its peculiar wail can be heard, as filially desired, despite the separating distance of 3,000 miles. The mother town built up its fame on rowels—'As trew steel as Rippon Rowels' was an old saying, and the daughter town has learned to do something similar with moccasins. After a visit to Ripon, Yorks., in 1952 a certain American lady sent three pairs of this beautiful Indian-type footwear, in coloured wools, for the personal use of the Mayor, the sergeant-at-mace and the horn-blower. They were made in the other Ripon.

Other Yorkshire towns have their overseas offspring, but Ripon's bond with America is doubly strong, for there is a persistent tradition that the stars in the American flag were derived from the star-shaped rowels produced long ago in the crooked back streets of this homely town. Perhaps the device went over with Ripon's first settlers in the seventeenth century? Anyhow, the town museum, at Thorpe Prebend House, displays a goodly assortment of locally-made spurs from that peak period. Here, also, are some facsimile carvings from Fountains Abbey, and pictures recalling the remote times of St. Wilfrid.

But a stately seventeenth-century house such as this, overshadowed by the cathedral and presenting a picturesque assortment of gables and chimney-stacks towards St. Agnesgate, must have had an interesting life of its own. It was one of the seven houses used by the prebendaries of Ripon. One of the resident clergy would have to bustle around and have a fine polish on his furniture for the arrival of Mary Queen of Scots—if, indeed, it was here that she stayed for the night while on her way south from Bolton Castle, in January 1569. A surer tradition brings her son, James I, to this house on the night of 14 April 1617. He was the guest of a Mr. Dawson. Perhaps it was in this house that James received those presentation spurs ?

One venerable building that cannot easily be missed is the Wakeman's House, facing the Market Place. Being a shop today, full access is not feasible as formerly, but the frontage is attractive with its twin gables and timber-framing. The oldest part of the house recalls the times when the Wakeman was expected to live here faithfully during his term of office. Rule Seven in the Town Book of Ripon, dated 1598, was explicit on the matter :

> It is condescended, concluded, ordered and established . . . that the Wakeman for the time being shall not flit out of the Town to dwell or sojourn elsewhere . . . except God do visit the said Town with pestilence. . . .

The fine for any default was £20. Perhaps Hugh Ripley, the last Wakeman and first Mayor, took this injunction too much to heart. His ghost lingers on and is said to have peered down upon modern Ripon from the topmost window !

eight

Around the Great North Road: 2
from Harrogate and Knaresborough to Roman Aldborough

The Ripon countryside is charming. To the west, little red-roofed villages cluster around the Skell and the Laver. To the east, all roads lead to the A1, three or four miles away, but the lane that winds through Sharow seems untouched by the twentieth century and preserves the base of an old sanctuary cross. South of the old city a web of by-roads spreads on both sides of A61, linking together such delightful spots as Copgrove, Burton Leonard, Bishop Monkton, Markington, and Sawley.

One little-known country house which epitomises much local history is Hollin Hall. Three miles south of Ripon on A61, this fine estate covers one of Yorkshire's lost townships—Aismunderby-cum-Bondgate. A. H. Boynton-Wood, the joint owner, tells me that part of the property, Chapel Garths Farm, occupies the site of a building that was a chapel-of-ease either to Fountains Abbey or to Markenfield parish. 'In the earliest deeds', says Mr. Boynton-Wood, 'the Hall is called Hollin Close, or Hollin Close House, and the first reference we have to it is in a deed dated 1649 bearing Thomas Markenfield's signature.' This indication that some of the Markenfields lived here—within a mile or so of their erstwhile home, the moated Markenfield Hall—is quite intriguing, for it has always been said that the family fled to the Continent eighty years before and remained there, following Sir Thomas Markenfield's participation in the Rising of the North and consequent forfeiture of all their domains.

Of these dissensions there was no audible echo when John Wood of York came along in 1719. A huge contemporary landscape painting—hung in the Dining Room—shows the place as John Wood saw it, with a sublime eastward aspect culminating in the Hambleton Hills. This was the

Hall I had been invited to see—a gracious Queen Anne house with pillared portico framing that same entrancing view.

The portraits here form a fascinating 'who's who', covering many people and events mentioned elsewhere in this book. One portrait, from the early 1600s, depicts a previous John Wood who had refused a knighthood at the Coronation of Charles I—such honours could be very expensive! His wife was a niece of the ill-fated Thomas Wentworth, Earl of Strafford, whose ghost haunts Wentworth Woodhouse. Then there is the John Wood who settled at Hollin in 1719. He became Treasurer of Lincoln's Inn in 1748 and is companioned here by his wife, who had family ties with Temple Newsam during its arcadian period. Another portrait recalls Stephen Croft of Stillington Hall, near York, who rescued the MS. of *Tristram Shandy* when Laurence Sterne, his friend, threw it into the fire in a fit of temper. Yet another turn in this historic parade confronted me with two gay young girls—daughters of Colonel Wood; one of them, Elia Maria, was to learn something of the Luddite rioters through her husband's activities as High Sheriff of Nottinghamshire.

What stories a family portrait gallery can unfold! Documents too. Many old marriage settlements were produced for my inspection. That relating to the marriage of Charlotte Augusta Rothery—Mr. Boynton-Wood's great-grandmother—takes up about twenty large skins of vellum! Quite frequently on these documents some of the parties were stated to be marrying 'by God's permission'. The wax seals attached show several versions of the three woodmen, from the family coat-of-arms, and lists of wedding presents occasionally include a year's supply of wax candles.

A different kind of document is the will forged by Edward Walkington, butler to John Wood Boynton (1707–1778). By this will Walkington and the housekeeper were going to inherit the Hollin estate and together enjoy a rosy future. But on the will cover I read these words: 'This will, forged by Edward Walkington, fell out of that wicked man's pocket'. Brief, but to the point. That little accident was providential for the family. Perhaps he was the butler who drowned himself in the small lake which then existed on the south side of the house.

John Wood Boynton's dinner service—which the 'wicked butler' must often have handled in loving anticipation!—is of outstanding interest. It is a famille rose armorial service of seventy-five pieces, including four punch bowls. Boynton followed prevailing fashion by having the service specially made in China, hence the little woodmen from the family coat-of-arms have Chinese faces.

The family crest is an oak-tree. This naturally derived from the forest lands around Swinsty Hall—medieval home of the Woods—in the Wash-. burn Valley, and is seen most entertainingly on the harness of Henry Richard Wood's coaching outfit. Horse trimmings, coloured braid, coachman's silver buttons—all carry the little forest oak, bearing their own witness to Henry Richard's frequent travels to his father-in-law's beautiful home, Claverton Manor, near Bath. On these journeys Henry Richard was always accompanied by his own household orchestra. The Ripon countryside can have seen few pleasanter sights than the Wood family setting off for Bath early last century, their coach followed closely by the music-makers and all their paraphernalia in a special caravan.

Across the River Ure from Ripon another fine old house appears to view—Newby Hall. It is regularly opened to the public. Although its lovely grounds dip down in floral majesty to the Ure, there is no river approach to Newby; one must take the Boroughbridge road from Ripon, B6265, and after two miles branch right for Skelton village where the park begins.

The first feature to greet one is an equestrian statue—not the best medium for a transformation act, but that is what has happened here. Originally, the figure represented John Sobieski, King of Poland, trampling on a Turk to signify his notable victory at Vienna in 1683. But the plan misfired. As the statue was never paid for, in that exultant capacity, Sir Robert Vyner, the famous London goldsmith, bought it to serve as a vigorous portrayal of Charles II, though Oliver Cromwell sometimes gets the benefit of this remarkable *volte face*. After further adventures and metamorphoses, the statue came north with one of the Vyners in 1883 and settled down at Newby to a peaceful existence. One is only sorry that William Weddell did not live to see it. He had an eye for good sculpture.

Weddell is the man who looks out from that classical portico designed by Nollekens in Ripon Cathedral. It might almost be a portico overlooking his own garden. Resplendent in mellow red brick faced with stone, Newby Hall had been built about 1705 for Sir Edward Blackett. When Weddell bought the property, some sixty years later, he employed Robert Adam to make several changes. This great craftsman must have found particular pleasure in creating the mahogany chamber organ, in the entrance hall. Decorated with Delphic tripods, Ionic columns, and swags, it is crowned by a domed niche of gilded pipes worthy of Arcadia.

Ever resourceful, Adam converted the original entrance hall into a room for the display of a glorious set of Gobelin tapestries illustrating classical subjects. He designed the Library, with large alabaster vases to cast a 'dim religious light' for those who browsed among the great, calf-bound tomes, beneath one of Angelica Kauffmann's rich ceilings. William Weddell's sculpture gallery—for which Adam built a special, single-storey wing—leads directly out of the Library and accommodates the important collection of antique sculpture, Greek and Roman, with which the wealthy connoisseur had returned from Rome about 1765.

It is good to visualise Weddell sitting in the library and entertaining his guests with tales of ancient Athens and Herculaneum as they gazed through the open door along the grand vista beyond. Weddell must have gloried in such occasions. Yet his anecdotes are lost for ever, for he left no record of how he acquired his treasures. Other stories are, however, easily read, from the different statues and busts, by anybody familiar with classical mythology and the early history of Greece and Rome. Caligula is here—the mad Roman emperor who bestowed the consulship on his own horse; Silenus, a tipsy old fellow with bulging wine-skin; Ganymede, whose physical beauty caused Zeus to seize him as his personal cup-bearer; Geta —he whose name was erased throughout the Roman Empire; and Septimus Severus himself—that great Emperor who died in York in A.D. 211, 'worn out by the combined evils of gout, a quarrelsome family, and the British climate'.

Weddell was probably thinking of sunny Italy when he placed a Roman bath in the apse which closes the Sculpture Gallery. This bath also sufficiently recalls the manner of Weddell's tragic death, in 1792. An extremely hot day in London tempted him to enter the large, so-called Roman bath in the Strand—but the water was too cold for his constitution. He expired almost immediately. His identity was discovered by the bath-keeper seeing his name written inside his hat. But for his untimely death, Weddell might have set down in writing, for the benefit of posterity, a full account of where and in what curious circumstances he obtained the remarkable sculptures that people his gallery with so much grace and elegance. It may be, of course, that he *intended* the secret to die with him.

A good companion to have in the neighbourhood just ahead is Celia Fiennes. Though she travelled 'through England on a side-saddle in the time of William and Mary', her diary bearing this title still provides many useful stimuli. At Knaresborough she loiters beside the Dropping Well which 'does turn moss and wood into stone. . . .' At Harrogate she finds the 'Sulphur or Stinking spaw not Improperly term'd, for the Smell being so strong and offensive that I could not force my horse Near the Well'. But at Copgrove—where St. Mungo's Well and its guest-house gained fashionable popularity—she immerses herself in the waters: 'I used my bath Garments and so pulled them off and put on fflanell when I came out to go into bed. . . .' Despite this rather fuzzy description, the treatment was effective, for it 'Eased a great pain I used to have in my head'. One looks in vain for Copgrove 'spaw' today, though its memory is preserved in the Norman church by a window portrait of St. Mungo blessing two youngsters beside the old, village well.

Celia Fiennes's other objectives in this district call for more detailed comment.

Knaresborough, about ten miles south of Ripon, is calculated to delight the eager child that lurks in most adults. I am not thinking primarily of the zoo that has lately brought wild beasts on the scene, but rather of the remarkable geological structure of the old town and its legacy of caves, rock terraces, towering crags, a fine sweep of the River Nidd and—as if that were not enough—the renowned Dropping Well.

St. Robert's cave-chapel, hewn from a lofty, beetling crag of magnesian limestone overlooking the river, is pleasantly described by Celia Fiennes as 'a little Chapple cut out of the Rock and arch'd and carved with ffigures of Saints . . . his (St. Robert's) Effigee is Carved at the Entrance, there is an alter yt was decked with flowers and the Ground with Rushes for ye devout that did frequent it'. After she wrote, at the end of the seventeenth century, the chapel fell into neglect, but in recent times loving hands have restored it to proper use. Sixpence is a small price to pay for the privilege of peeping inside the tiny oratory; one's gaze joins with that of a few monks' faces, carved perhaps to represent some of the former Knaresborough Priory community. The altar is now adorned with a modern Madonna and Child inscribed 'Our Lady of the Crag'.

Celia was mistaken about the 'effigee' at the entrance. The larger-than-life-size figure handling his sword-hilt was somebody's idea of a Crusader, presumably guarding the little shrine.

As noted elsewhere, magnesian limestone is often pitted with cavities. At Knaresborough, centuries ago, a few of these were enlarged into dens and used for human habitation. Some buildings in the market place have cave-like cellars of great age, suggesting that Knaresborough's earliest dwellers were troglodytes. It was a great advance when somebody thought of building a house *into* the accommodating rock. The best surviving example is Fort Montague, a few yards from St. Robert's Chapel.

Fashioned about 200 years ago, the castellated house suggests an outsize tallboy wedged in the crag!

Thomas Hill was a poor weaver when he started work on it. A natural shelf in the great cliff-face gave him the initial idea. For twelve years the house grew inwards and upwards from that challenging shelf, with the rock providing three of its four walls. Hill died before seeing the job complete, but his son continued—and eventually came out, literally and triumphantly, on the crag top.

Once, on entering by the original bedroom floor, at the basement, I began to hear the owner's strange account of the place, then traversed a rock passage, climbed two stone stairways, and—somewhat bewildered—left the house via the kitchen near the top of the crag. Lewis Carroll could hardly have imagined a 'curiouser' dwelling.

Bizarre—that's what this corner of Knaresborough is, and long may it remain so. The Dropping Well is a contributory factor. Leland tells us that the calcium-charged water falling over the lip of limestone rock— which provides the spectacle—was once valued for its medicinal qualities and conveyed by conduit to the neighbouring Priory. As the Priory has since vanished, his remarks on the well itself are more pertinent.

In his delightfully naïve Elizabethan manner, Leland wrote: 'This water is so could, and of such a nature, that what thing soever faullith oute of the Rokkes ynto this pitte, or ys caste in, or growith about the Rokkes and is touchid of this water, growith ynto stone'. In the prosaic language of to-day, such objects are said to be *petrified*. An odd assortment, including toys, old hats, stockings, and gloves is usually suspended below the falling curtain of water. At first sight it looks as though some second-hand dealer were having a washing-day, but the impression is corrected after persuading the proprietor of the neighbouring 'Mother Shipton' Inn to show his remarkable collection of petrified objects, some dating back to the eighteenth century. The fashion was evidently set when Sir Charles Slingsby brought hat and riding gloves here to be 'treated'. Reduced in colour by the water's action to a nice clerical grey, they are—or were— accompanied in the inn-keeper's museum by a pair of gloves surrendered for the disguising process by Prince Christian of Sweden, a half-knitted sock with the needles in correct working position, a glengarry, and—of all things—a wedding bouquet. On his Yorkshire map Michael Drayton excels himself by indicating the Dropping Well with one of his nymphs reclining there like a petrified Venus. The encrusting process may take anything from three to eighteen months.

Mother Shipton's Cave—her reputed birthplace—shares the same fantastic side-scene. In 1486 she made her compact with the Devil. She also foretold the closure of the monasteries, using her satanic insight, one supposes. Other prophecies included the following:

> Carriages without horses shall go
> And accidents fill the world with woe.
> Iron in the water shall float
> As easily as does a wooden boat.
> A house of glass shall come to pass
> In England, but, alas!
> War will follow with the work
> In the land of the Pagan and the Turk.
> Gold shall be found, and found
> In a land that's not now known.

Of course, in the fullness of time, the 'house of glass' was identified as Paxton's Crystal Palace, the war as the Crimean War, and the land of gold as Klondike.

One thing that even Mother Shipton would hardly foresee, as she looked out from her cave, was that her 'carriages without horses'—motor-cars, naturally—would find their champion in a man who spent his later years in a riverside cottage only a few yards away. I refer to the motoring pioneer, Rowland Winn. His name became a byword in Yorkshire, though there are few who can now recall his determined struggle to popularise the new-fangled contraptions, around 1900. Hearing his daughter talk about those early, pioneering days, while gazing across the Nidd, seems a strange fulfilment. And what days they were, with 'Rowly' taking his 'horseless carriage' all over Yorkshire and beyond to give driving lessons to dukes and gentry; enthroning his bride and himself in an open car with fringed awning for their wedding—the first such wedding outfit in Leeds; and once even driving his car up Leeds Town Hall steps and down again, for a wager.

They talk much about Eugene Aram along this stretch of the river, and point with misplaced pride to the cave where he buried his victim. But that was a foul thing from long ago. I would far rather visualise the youthful Rowland Winn, whether dressed—as for some polar expedition—in his ankle-length, fur-lined coat: for even the regulation 12 m.p.h. could be rigorous in an open car! Or coasting through town and country, years later, in a smart limousine that gave out cheerful little tunes from the self-made organ he operated from the dash-board. It was exhilarating to know 'Rowly', as I did for several years.

The Long Walk, a fine avenue of trees bordering the river near the Dropping Well and continuing to High Bridge, was laid out and planted by Sir Henry Slingsby between 1738 and 1740. It affords many good views of the Nidd and of the almost-vertical face of the limestone escarpment as both accomplish their dramatic S-bend. At the water's edge there is an old flax mill. Houses of many shapes and sizes cling to the crag at seemingly precarious levels. Winding amongst them are narrow cobbled alleys, like Water Bag Lane, up which the town's water supply—from the peat-laden Nidd—was formerly carried by donkeys, in leather bags, pannier-wise. Steps wind up the cliff-face to the battered keep—meagre relic of the castle built during Henry I's reign, which later imprisoned Richard II. However, the Tudor court-house just opposite is fairly intact and shoulders the castle's connection with the old Forest of Knaresborough.

The court house staged the Sheriff Torne, or civil court, to which offenders in the Manor and Forest of Knaresborough were duly summoned for trial. One can still see the rough-hewn oak benches, superintended at the far end of the main chamber by a great baulk of timber where the Justice and his clerk would sit, or perhaps squirm, for there is no degree of comfort. It would be interesting if one could draw time's curtain aside to see a few deer stealers being tried here by the ancient procedure, or listen to the foresters disputing with the monks of Fountains Abbey over certain forest boundaries, or hear the Prior of Bolton explain away his alleged 'riotous trespass' on certain valuable lead-mines in 'Knaresburge Forest'.

Beyond the court house, Knaresborough the market town opens up as an almost separate entity. A few Georgian houses and shops have fortunately survived, with the market place boasting the 'oldest chemist's shop in England'. In appearance this shop is the very embodiment of eighteenth-century balsams and elixirs; a bearded apothecary should really be in charge, though the actual wares are as modern as the latest capsule.

If one is interested in old-time nostrums and cures, the Parish Church will have an appeal even additional to that of its Early English and Perpendicular features—for here, in the Slingsby Chapel, two men are commemorated who had much experience along these lines.

The first of them was Sir Henry Slingsby, who in 1658 paid the supreme penalty for backing the royalist cause. He lies here beneath a black marble slab which is supposed to have been placed, originally, over the remains of

St. Robert the hermit, at Knaresborough Priory. But at his home—Red House, Moor Monkton, near York—Slingsby had kept a diary of all his family affairs—'a thing pleasant to read', he says in his introduction, 'when time began to wear out the Rememberance. . . .'

If sickness and ill health are remembered too frequently, in this record, Slingsby's accompanying comments provoke some—unintended—mirth. Peter Clark, his gardener, had long complained of having 'a great worm in his gutts that did knaw and torment him, which made me when he dy'd send for a chirurgeon from York to embowell him; but no such thing appear'd'. Another servant 'sickn'd upon a cold he took . . . and by a surfeit of eating Plumbs'.

But Slingsby's constantly ailing wife naturally gets the fullest due. Most of the doctors prove useless. One, summoned to treat Lady Slingsby for the 'spleen' 'doth not a little brag of . . . his £50 and £100 cures'. Another 'professeth to cure all manner of diseases, and his practice is but his tryall, he never attains it. . . .' In desperation, a woman who 'practised chimistry' is called in, but despite the concoctions she applies to the patient 'in a taffity bag', the cure miscarries. Eventually, the sun breaks through. Sir Henry takes his wife to see Dr. Mayerne of London who 'seldom went to any for he was corpulent and unwieldy; and again he was rich, and the King's phycitian, and a Knight, which made him more costly to deal with'. Perhaps these social qualifications had some therapeutic value, for from Mayerne, wrote a jubilant Slingsby later, 'she hath reap'd the most benefit for her health'.

Occupying a niche overlooking Henry Slingsby's tomb a figure wearing broad-brimmed hat and armour stands at ease. He might be contemplating some bygone military engagement, though I prefer to think of him as looking back to the day, in 1571, when he first noticed a certain spring in the neighbourhood. Similar medicinal waters on the Continent made him realise its value. William Slingsby's discovery led to the foundation of Harrogate as a spa.

That at any rate is the old tradition, and—in Harrogate—anybody who airs doubts on the matter may have a brimming glass of sulphur water, neat, forced upon him! Tewit Well on the South Stray—supplying chalybeate water—was the one Slingsby spotlighted, but in time Harrogate spa came to depend chiefly on its sulphur well. This can still be seen—and tasted ?—in the basement of the old Pump Room, now the Town Museum.

There is a world of entertainment in this museum. Many curious pictures and mementoes call forth the folk who once forgathered to take the waters at this place, before the present handsome stone octagon was built, in 1842. Laurence Sterne, William Wordsworth, and Charles Dickens are of the company. Celia Fiennes has already been heard on her experiences at the well, but she should have realised—as most other visitors did—that the taste and smell were nasty enough to cure anybody.

Long after her day the well was still without any superstructure, save the simplest of stone covers. In a fine drawing recently given to the town, Thomas Rowlandson depicts the Sulphur Well in this primitive, unadorned state, and even introduces his stock character, Dr. Syntax. One of the attendant nymphs—as they were called—hands him a tumbler of the potent fluid, while local gentry stand about in fashionable languor, having either sipped their own daily portion, or summoning enough courage to do so.

In this parade of bygone times, Betty Lupton cuts a commanding figure with her lace bonnet and crinoline. She became the chief nymph here—or 'Queen of the Harrogate Well'—and is seen with her long-handled ladle and horn tumbler. Thus equipped, and with a lantern to light her way down the dark steps to the enclosed well, she ministered to the ailing public for fifty-six years. She 'came to life' again in a local pageant not long ago, still brandishing her symbols of office.

One reminder of Betty Lupton has unfortunately vanished. It was a piece of racy doggerel that formerly decorated the Pump Room frieze:

> As Satan was flying o'er the Harrogate Well,
> His senses were charmed with the heat and the smell;
> Says he, 'I don't know what region I roam,
> But I guess from the smell that I'm not far from home.'

> Then Old Betty called after him, 'Satan, I say',
> You seem mighty pleased with your journey today;
> Pray stay till I've done, and we'll both go together,
> For I'm heartily tired of this changeable weather.'

> But Satan well knew if for Betty he stayed,
> His going back home would long be delayed.
> For Harrogate Waters such wonders can do,
> That the Devil himself is oft robbed of his due!

The fine range of later buildings known as the Royal Baths, nearby, embody a Lounge Hall and Fountain Court. All the modern treatments are dispensed around this nucleus—and thousands of rheumatic and other sufferers have reason to bless those responsible. But one who saw the funny side of things, at the Baths, was Louis Wain. After taking the recognised cure he presented the management with a drawing he had done showing some of his beloved cats taking the waters at dainty little tables to the accompaniment of a feline orchestra. In the general manager's office, Wain's drawing hangs near one by Ernest H. Sheppard of *Punch*; this shows Neville Chamberlain deliberating over what must be—judging by his wry expression—a glass of Harrogate's noblest vintage.

In the eighteenth century those who flocked to Harrogate for the cure were apt to cancel any benefit by feasting at night 'on the best substantial things, such as hot shoulders of mutton, rump steaks, hot pigeon pies, veal cutlets, and the like', plus 'what wine, punch and ale every one chuses' from the selected inn's tempting cellar.

Today, Harrogate has other allurements. Two hundred acres of common land form the Stray, which enfolds the town with a quiet, natural beauty on three sides—and woe betide anybody who dares to encroach! Here retired colonels walk their spaniels before breakfast, and children frolic on the soft green turf under their nursemaid's watchful eye. Here the Scorton Archers sometimes forgather for their annual meet. Christ Church confronts the Knaresborough road as this crosses the Stray. Not far away was the 'Green Dragon' Inn where the famous Victorian artist, William Powell Frith, lived for several years, while his father was landlord. There is an inscription to Frith's memory in Christ Church. Although born at Aldfield, near Fountains Abbey, his youth is best recalled in this district, where he would journey to and from school at Knaresborough, forever sketching different people he knew. Later he was to achieve renown with his 'Derby Day' and the well-known 'Railway Station' study; but those early impressions of Harrogate Stray were indelibly etched in his mind.

For many people today the Harrogate cure means nothing more demanding than a seasonal visit to this undulating Stray—for 'a breath of really fresh air'; to the Valley Gardens, the adjoining Pine Woods, and—maybe—Birk Crag beyond. The town is *reared* on flowers, beginning with the snowdrops and crocuses bordering the Stray, and the almond and cherry blossom of early spring, to the roses and dahlias and herbaceous borders that transform the Valley Gardens, challenging every passing

21   The River Nidd from the Long Walk, Knaresborough

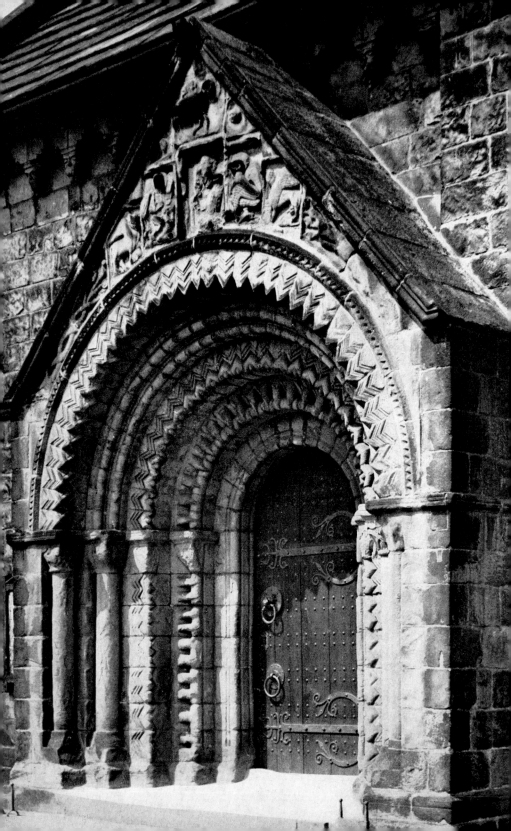

photographer. For the connoisseur there are the magnificent Harlow Carr Gardens, to the west of the town. They are one great nursery of floral beauty and charm.

Harrogate is also fortunate in its wider setting. Southwards there is good country on both sides of A61, almost as far as Leeds, with the small Norman church at Adel—cited earlier—now clamouring for more than passing attention. An exterior 'string' of corbels is fiendishly alive with grinning faces and grotesque animals. More animals adorn the receding orders of a glorious south porch, while the bronze closing-ring—also Norman—hangs from a boss representing a monster's jaws clamping upon its little human victim. On the chancel arch, within, Norman burlesque finds further expression—dragons in combat, an imp playing a fiddle, a centaur using bow and arrow, and a 'menagerie' of strange beasts, all as backdrop for the Baptism of Christ, and the Crucifixion.

Harewood, three or four miles north-east of Adel, is roughly half-way between Leeds and Harrogate. Harewood House has already been mentioned, but perhaps few people realise that the attendant model village was also designed by John Carr. Edwin Lascelles had first set his team of craftsmen to work on Harewood House; the village scheme followed, affording much quiet grace for his tenants. There is something of the Cotswold character about the cottages, but a noticeable omission from the well-ordered symmetry of the village is a church. Eventually, after passing down a lane flanked by two of Carr's elegant pavilions, one finds the church—in the grounds of Harewood House. Villagers assemble for worship in this fine Gothic building, sharing the lustre of bygone lords and ladies of Harewood who recline here in alabaster. Ever since his death, in 1426, one of those lords—Sir Richard Redman—has been resting his booted feet against a recumbent lion, and on the lion's neck Sir Richard's bedesman, or chaplain, sits with his rosary, fast asleep.

The magnificent dales country opens up to the west of Harrogate. Within a few miles, eastwards, one comes to the old coaching town of Wetherby, on the A1, and a fine cluster of satellite villages: Kirkby Overblow, Collingham, Boston Spa, Bramham, Kirk Deighton, Spofforth, Cowthorpe, Little Ribston, Follifoot. Who could possibly neglect these and other old-world villages, once he knew they existed, here in this little 'outback' watered by the now quiescent Wharfe and Nidd? Country houses abound in this favoured lowland area. Bramham Park is

22 *Norman Porch, Adel Church, near Leeds*

famous for its gardens, with towering beech hedges and enchanting vistas laid out during the eighteenth century in the French manner. Ribston Hall preserves the apple-tree—or its vestigial stump—that produced the first Ribston pippins. Of Plumpton Towers, near Knaresborough, nothing unfortunately remains except Daniel Lascelles's six-acre lake, created about 1760; as this mirrors a group of fantastically shaped gritstone rocks, resembling those at Brimham, one can sense the family's loss—and that of potential guests—when Lascelles suddenly dropped the Plumpton scheme and made his home at neighbouring Goldsborough Hall.

It was the first impact of the Industrial Revolution that caused Sir Joseph Radcliffe to change his abode. He moved from Milnsbridge House, near Huddersfield, to a little pocket of the old Forest of Knaresborough that included the quizzically named Follifoot. He proceeded to build Rudding Park—a mansion of honey-coloured stone and pronounced Regency bows. From its spacious grounds, York Minster is seen pricking the eastern skyline, with the Wolds rising beyond, forty miles away.

Many fascinating things are shown to visitors, but here a few of the heir-looms must take precedence.

In the Tapestry Hall one's attention is at length diverted from the curious sight of Nebuchadnezzar eating the grass of humiliation—illustrated with other Bible subjects on some fine sixteenth-century Brussels tapestries—to a showcase whose contents recall the romance, tragedy and humiliation of the Stuarts. Several of the small objects belonged to the last of the Stuarts—Henry, Cardinal of York, son of the Old Pretender and brother of the 'Bonnie' prince who set so many hearts aflame. One can perhaps visualise the Cardinal wearing this sixteenth-century jewel, which contains a minute figure of St. Sebastian, or this reliquary holding a few threads from the hair shirt worn by Sir Thomas More. . . .

How often do these Yorkshire country houses supplement each other in the stories their treasures relate! At Nostell Priory, for example, Thomas More is happily surrounded by his family in a magnificent Holbein painting; here in the reliquary at Rudding Park is the obverse of the picture—Henry VIII's chancellor in secret, self-imposed torment. Likewise, at Everingham Park, near Market Weighton, I have seen the mother-of-pearl lantern which Louis XVI took with him to the Temple prison before his execution; Rudding Park shows the toy silver tea-service which Louis's young son played with in the same prison before he, too, died. At Everingham again, amongst much else concerning the 1715 Jacobite rebellion, there was a thrilling hand-written account of how Lord

Nithsdale, one of the chief rebels, was smuggled out of the Tower of London by his determined wife; Rudding portrays a Jacobite leader for whom there was no escape—James Radcliffe, Earl of Derwentwater.

The Dauphin's tea-set and the Derwentwater portrait were shown to me by the Earl's descendant, Captain Everard Radcliffe, in the Blue Drawing Room, along with another portrait. This depicts Prince Charles Edward himself—a gay, debonair figure wearing the white cockade that rallied to his cause adventurous men from the Yorkshire dales, like Basil Woodd of Oughtershaw, beyond Buckden, and maybe a Metcalfe or two from Wensleydale. I wonder how much they would understand of rousing Gaelic songs such as 'Hi ri ri, tha e tighinn' ('He comes'), or 'Sound, sound the Pibroch loud on high', which the Highlanders sang around them on that ill-fated march.

Did the Yorkshire contingent strike up answering choruses in their own expressive dialects? Very probably. Which makes it all the more stirring to see the Prince's cockade—faded now and worn—mounted in the frame of this romantic portrait at Rudding Park. The cockade vividly recalls the hero of the Skye Boat Song and many another old ballad; also the disillusioned prince, some of whose followers, after the Retreat from Derby, took refuge in the Yorkshire dales and married where their proud Gaelic hearts found solace. . . .

Yet another fine residence is Ripley Castle, two miles north of Harrogate. The public enter by the original gateway where, in the fourteenth century, a Swiss guard may have been on duty; 'Parlez au Suisse', states a notice over the porter's door. I have attempted to describe the Castle in another book, but the last word has never been written about an old dwelling, least of all Ripley, for 700 years the home of the Ingilby family.

In the tower block (1555)—the oldest part of the present house—Library, Tower Room and Knight's Chamber occur in that ascending order. There are strange echoes in these evocative rooms—Roman echoes stirred by a pig of lead bearing the stamp of Domitian and the date, A.D. 88; monastic echoes from Mount Grace Priory, a Carthusian house near Northallerton founded in 1396 by John Ingilby; Cromwellian echoes, already distinct but somewhat amplified since the discovery, in 1963, of a secret hide behind the oak panelling that lines the Knight's Chamber.

Sir Joslan Ingilby, present owner of the Castle, likes to speculate as to which of his ancestors might have found this retreat particularly opportune. A likely candidate would be Francis Ingilby, whose portrait hangs below in the Library. After being ordained to the Catholic priesthood in

1583, he was subjected to the usual cat-and-mouse treatment and eventually went to a martyr's death at York. Another whose shadowy figure might have vanished through that concealed door was Sir William Ingilby, the royalist.

Oliver Cromwell is supposed to have spent the night at Ripley Castle, after the battle of Marston Moor—not in some comfortable four-poster, but sitting beside a table and confronted by a brace of pistols levelled at him by the lady of the house to ensure his good conduct.

Some versions of this story say that Sir William was still away, fighting for the King and accompanied by his sister whose garb as a trooper won her the title, ever after, of Trooper Jane. Another version has it that Ingilby was home again, when Cromwell's men entered the village and their leader demanded hospitality at the Castle. Discretion being the better part of valour, Sir William—it was suggested—spirited himself out of sight.

Does this newly discovered priest-hole explain how and where?

The Ingilby monuments are in the fourteenth-century church, opposite the Castle gateway. The antiquity of the place is also suggested by a remarkable weeping-cross, in the churchyard. Hewn in stone to cylindrical form, it is equipped round the base with niches for penitents to kneel in as they bewailed their sinful plight. Totally different was the outlook which banished the ill-kempt cottages that had housed Cromwell's bedraggled troops, and produced an eighteenth-century model village. This charms everybody with its pleasant mixture of Gothic and Tudor styles. It cannot be accidental that a few cottage doors virtually reproduce one of those in the Castle's secretive tower.

Despite its many other interests, this area bordering the Great North Road would be infinitely the poorer were a certain quiet little village near Boroughbridge to be obliterated. This could easily have happened if the new Boroughbridge section of the A1 had swung round to the east of the former coaching town instead of a few furlongs to the west. For here, barely a mile away from the old 'Borobrigg' which the Devil once tried to 'ding down' with his monolithic Arrows, stands the much older Aldborough.

Incidentally, one used to see the Devil's Arrows—all three of them—spaced out over adjacent fields and in line with an ancient ford across the River Ure. This arrangement, which has prompted a guide-post theory for their original purpose, has been obscured by housing development. But nothing seems to have changed at Aldborough since the eighteenth century.

In 1534 Leland had remarked upon the 'tesselata pavimenta', or tessellated pavements he saw here, but it was the excavations initiated by Andrew Lawson, local squire and M.P., early last century, that really focused scholarly attention on the Roman and even pre-Roman significance of Aldborough. This place began as Iseur, headquarters of that powerful tribe, the Brigantes. Later the Romans established a camp here for the Ninth Legion, and as *Isurium Brigantum* it became an important Romano-British town. It was served by a road linking *Eboracum*, or York —seventeen miles to the south, with Catterick, and with Hadrian's Wall in far Northumberland.

Stretches of Aldborough's own wall—a defensive one built around the Roman town—are still to be seen in some lovely grounds behind the village museum. The small quarry which gave the builders their red sandstone eventually made an unusual rock garden for the Lawson family, whose eighteenth-century house, Aldborough Manor, straddles an unexcavated portion of the enclosing wall.

This is one of the choicest corners I know in Yorkshire. Somebody will one day chance upon it by accident, and then write a fine historical novel about *Isurium* and the people who first used these altars and querns and mosaic pavements, now bordered in season with daffodils, violets and forget-me-nots. The little idol cut into one face of the quarry was probably due to misplaced antiquarian zeal last century. It was doubtless intended to heighten the witchery of the place. A magnolia-tree in full bloom and an eagle-clawed maple—survivals of the rock garden— achieved this witchery for me quite adequately on my last visit, presiding as they did over a jungle of ferns and trailing creepers.

The pavements Leland reported have gone the way of most unprotected treasures, but others have been found. Two fine specimens, showing respectively an eight-pointed star and a leopard beneath a palm-tree, are preserved in the garden of the 'Aldeburgh Arms' Inn and can be seen on request. Perhaps Aldborough's greatest surprise for visitors is in the beautiful fifteenth-century church, where a figure of Mercury—from a Roman temple—accompanies a list of bygone vicars! The pulpit follows suit, having been made in the seventeenth century—so they say—from the pile of a Roman bridge. Did this bridge stand somewhere along the great historic highway through Yorkshire? Imagination and surmise have much to feed upon in Roman Aldborough.

nine

The City of York

In praising York as the county's 'most-lov'd City', Michael Drayton, who keeps popping up like a wayfarer's jester in these pages, pens many comic word-pictures of the rivers that help to swell the mighty Ouse, particularly Swale, Ure and Nidd. His accompanying map is equally diverting, Swale with its nymphs and shepherds, Ure its episcopal dame and attendant hound, Nidd its wise woman with finger upraised in warning—perhaps Mother Shipton. Ouse itself is presided over by 'that great Forest-Nymph, fair Gautresse'—a personification of the old Forest of Galtres that once enclosed York's northern boundaries.

Drayton's star-turn on the map is the hefty wench who balances York Minster on her head, and then spreads out two brawny arms as if to say, 'It's really quite simple'.

Tourists' reactions on beholding York Minster have often been curious and entertaining. A few years after the Civil Wars John Evelyn, the diarist, saw it as the cathedral 'which of all the greate churches in England had been best preserv'd from ye furie of ye sacrilegious . . . it is a most intire magnificent piece of Gotic architecture . . .'. Two centuries later, Mrs. Hughes of Uffington travelled to within a few miles of York by the newly macadamised Great North Road—which she greatly admired—and then, on reaching the old city, became quite poetic about the Minster: '. . . it seems as if Giants had built it, and employed the fairies to finish it, so exquisite and minute are the carvings. . . .'

To Hugh Miller, in 1846, the Minster's grey loftiness in 'the thickening twilight' gave two very strange feelings. 'The impression more resembled what I have sometimes experienced on some solitary ocean shore, o'erhung by dizzy precipices, and lashed high by the foaming surf; or beneath the craggy brow of some vast mountain. . . .' What occult vision!

One could go on quoting such delightful eulogies, but the cutest modern remark I have heard was that of an American, who pulled up beside the south door in his sleek car, gazed around for a few moments, and then decided. 'I'll do the inside,' said the man to his wife, 'you do the outside, and we'll meet here in half an hour.' I hope both were late—very late—for their rendezvous! American tourists are, of course, generally amongst the Minster's most appreciative visitors. And how varied is the list of subscribers to any restoration scheme here! When a fabric appeal was launched some years ago one unknown man responded by sending half-a-crown—all he could afford—because he had proposed to his lady-love (and was accepted!) half a century before, on top of the central tower.

It would be a grand thing if somebody would do what has been done so well for King's College Chapel, Cambridge—compile a list of tributes paid at various times to this wonderful building in the heart of York, with an addendum on incidental matters. The latter record would include some strange episodes—Beau Nash appearing at the Minster door clothed solely in a blanket, for a wager; Martin Lister, the seventeenth-century naturalist, observing the habits of rare spiders from the central tower: some of the floating webs which 'fell and were entangled upon the pinnacles, I took and found them to be 'lupi'—which suggested a paper he read later before the Royal Society. Another memorable occurrence that has lost nothing in the telling was the Great Fire of 1829.

The fire was first noticed by a choir boy who, while sliding on the early morning ice, fell on his back. Looking up he was amazed to see smoke pouring from the Minster roof. Scrambling to his feet, he quickly gave the alarm. But the fire had already caused considerable damage, destroying the choir woodwork and bringing down part of the roof.

Eventually the fire was found to have been the work of an incendiary—one Jonathan Martin. Due to some long-standing, though wrong-headed, quarrel with the clergy, he had hidden himself in the Minster overnight, and started the mischief by making a bonfire of Bibles and prayer-books and cushions which he first slashed to ribbons. All this in fulfilment of his previous warnings: 'Hear the word of the Lord, O you dark and lost clargymen, you desevers of the people'; and 'Your gret churches and minstairs will come rattling down on your giltey heads'.

When finally arrested, Martin's only regret was that the damage to the Minster—estimated around £70,000—was not greater. His judges found him guilty but insane.

Today it is odd to think of a man having to gallop horseback to Leeds, twenty-five miles away, to summon further help in fighting that fire. When at length a Leeds fire engine did reach the Minster—about 2 p.m.— the fire was under control, and onlookers were already salvaging bits of scarred wood. One occasionally comes across curious mementoes into which those fragments were carved.

Covering a span of nearly thirteen centuries—far too long a period for description here—the splendid architecture of York Minster must be left to make its own cumulative impact on each visitor. An excellent book-stall in the South Transept provides ample stimulus and, nearby, the large Graphic Chart designed twenty years ago by Miss Isabel Saul is so com-pelling in its appeal that—as the late Dean once remarked—'Some visitors look at it longer than at the Minster itself!'

The personalities depicted on this chart are sufficient to evoke the long line of those who have held the See of York since the earliest days. They make a very mixed company, for some were avaricious and worldly; others, like Walter de Gray and Thoresby, achieved fame as builders of the Minster; several won almost saintly renown.

The company is led by a few pioneers of the Christian faith who, as yet, could only enjoy the title *Bishop* of York. First comes Paulinus himself, who—after the remarkable Council of Northumbria—baptises the newly converted King Edwin at York on Easter Day, A.D. 627. The present Minster stands on the site of the wooden chapel where that event took place. A well in the crypt is usually regarded as that of the royal baptism and decorated accordingly, but a surer link with Paulinus and his mission-ary zeal is the fine old church at Goodmanham, near Market Weighton, where a modern stained-glass window shows Coifi, the high priest of Woden, trampling on the idols that Edwin has renounced and brandishing the torch with which he—also caught up in the shining tide of conversion —sets fire to the old pagan temple. I should like to see another window inserted at Goodmanham, one illustrating the equally dramatic sequel— Paulinus and his royal convert galloping off to York for that touching little ceremony at the well. . . .

Jostling for attention, now, are the quarrelsome Wilfrid (664–78) who stifles the influence of the Iona church and eventually builds the early minsters at Hexham and Ripon; and Wilfrid II (718–32), who is said to have started the age-old dispute between York and Canterbury for ecclesiastical precedence. Wulfstan (931–56) appears as one of the scholar bishops. A curious portrait in St. William's College, nearby, shows him at his desk with the tools of a scribe—a goose-quill and a knife for scraping the parchment. His loud check socks are not as modern as they look! Diplomacy and guile characterise Aldred (1061–9): has he not bribed his way to the See of York? Although having lately crowned Harold as King of England he has no compunction about performing the same service, shortly after, for William of Normandy.

One figure that all who love their Yorkshire would eagerly seek, in this shadowy parade, is Thurstan (1114–40). Though somewhat imperious, it is he who has befriended the handful of seceding monks from St. Mary's Abbey and given them—as described earlier—that Christmas present of a plot of land where they built Fountains Abbey. One of the men who accompanied Thurstan on that epoch-making visitation of St. Mary's is here too—William Fitzherbert, then Minster treasurer. He succeeds Thurstan as archbishop—and triggers off an amazing series of miracles, which increase after his death.

He is usually known as St. William of York; one window in the Minster depicts many of the miracles. Renewed interest in St. William was aroused a few years ago by the discovery of some medieval alabaster panels in Hungate, near the Shambles. One, dealing with his birth, shows the baby being fondled by the nurse while a posset is prepared for the mother; in another, William has become archbishop and rescues from drowning many people thrown into the river by the collapse of Ouse Bridge; a third panel illustrates one of the posthumous miracles—Edward I being saved from disaster on falling down a Welsh mountain-side. These alabasters are now displayed, with many other treasures, in the Yorkshire Museum—near the ruins of St. Mary's Abbey.

Close behind Fitzherbert, in our imaginary procession, is Roger de Pont l'Évêque (1154–81). He looks around in vain for the Norman choir he built; it was superseded by the present, fifteenth-century choir, though the western crypt retains some of Roger's magnificent pillars, reduced by necessity to much dwarfed proportions. A proud man, Roger, and inordinately jealous of his rank. At the Council of Westminster in 1176, when the Archbishop of Canterbury places himself on the honoured *right-hand* side of the papal legate, Roger—not to be out-manœuvred—actually sits on Robert of Canterbury's lap! For his effrontery he is seized and beaten.

The whole episode seems incredible in these days, but no more so than William de Melton's (1317–40) *army of clergy* which waged a battle against the Scots. This occurred at Myton-on-Swale and came to be known, contemptuously, as the Chapter of Myton.

Always, however, there have been men who deplored such negations of Christianity. Here comes one of them—John de Thoresby (1352–73). His Perpendicular work in the Nave and Lady Chapel still inspires awe. Reform against all kinds of abuses, including immorality among the clergy, marks his episcopacy, during which the old wrangle between York and Canterbury is resolved. Through some hair-splitting diplomacy it was agreed that henceforth the Archbishop of Canterbury should be styled Primate of All England, and the Archbishop of York, Primate of England!

Alexander Neville, Thomas Fitzalan, Robert Waldby—so the roll might continue, until Richard Scrope (1398–1405) comes into view. For conspiring against Henry IV he was condemned to death at Bishopthorpe and beheaded. Gent, the York historian, describes the scene vividly:

> Scrope was 'put upon a horse, about the value of forty pence, with a halter about its neck, but without a saddle on its back. And the Archbishop gave thanks to God, saying, 'I never liked horse better than I like this.' Twice he sang the Psalm *Exaudi*, being habited in a sky-coloured loose garment . . . but they would not permit him to wear the linen vesture used by bishops. At the place of execution he laid his hood and tunic on the ground, offered himself and his cause to heaven, and desired the executioner to give him five strokes in token of the five wounds of our Saviour, which was done accordingly.'

Scrope's plain, table tomb is in the north choir aisle. Crowds once came with their gifts and prayers to the good man's last resting place. So fervid was their loyalty to his memory that an embarrassed government attempted to keep the people away by barricading Scrope's tomb with timber and stones. But his memory is still green. Only a few years ago I watched Harry J. Stammers, the York glass-painter, prepare a beautiful set of windows commemorating 'Saint Richard Scrope' for Bishopthorpe Church.

To single out each remaining personage would be wearying, but some of them cannot be overlooked. Here is George Neville (1465–76), brother of Warwick the King-maker, still looking replete after celebrating his elevation to the See of York by giving what may have been the biggest banquet England has ever known. It was held at Cawood, near

Selby, former residence of the York archbishops; 2,000 cooks were hired to prepare the food, which included over 1,000 sheep, 500 deer and 100 oxen!

But who is this now approaching, with the rolling gait of a sailor? Surely none other than Lancelot Blackburne (1724–43). Horace Walpole referred to him as 'the jolly old Archbishop of York, who had all the manners of a man of quality, though he had been a buccaneer. . . .' His youthful exploits on a pirate ship would surely embarrass those who later conferred episcopal honours upon him! Visitors who are inquisitive will find the Fiddler statue in the crypt helpful—but only up to a certain point. Here Blackburne, wearing tam o' shanter, plays the violin 'borrowed' from his college tutor before sailing off for the high seas. His subsequent taking of Holy orders provides no greater contrast than that only too noticeable between the smiling Fiddler carving and its neighbour—a horrifying piece of sculpture known as the Hell Cauldron. Probably a relic of Archbishop Roger's Minster, it portrays the damned being boiled in a huge cauldron, with imps and demons stoking the fire and contributing every kind of torment. What a good thing this hideous travesty lay buried for many years. Today it is 'safe'; only a depraved mind could take such medieval notions seriously.

Miss Saul's colourful chart prompts many other quests. It directs one, for example, to the Zouche Chapel in the south choir aisle, where many besides John Evelyn have stopped to admire St. Peter's Well in the 'hollow wall'. Evelyn failed to record that this 'well of sweet spring water' frequently cured the sick. Lime absorbed from the walls evidently gave the water some medicinal value; it was sometimes carried to needy folk in the town. Many years ago this chapel was the meeting place for York Convocation, and some wag declared that when the proceedings were dry the water—'christyl and pleasant'—was freely drawn upon.

A fascinating tour is also suggested by Miss Saul's reference to those who first 'put glass in the windows which excluded the birds and rain and yet admitted the light'. Of these craftsmen the most famous was John Thornton of Coventry. Between 1405 and 1408 he designed and made the Great East Window. Along with the other priceless stained glass here, this enormous window was removed for safety during the last war, but in the following years—before the window was re-inserted—Dean Milner-White and the present-day Minster glaziers set to work on it, rectifying the mistakes of earlier generations and repairing where necessary. Jonathan Martin's fire had inflicted much of the damage.

The final restoration of this East Window has brought meaning and sequence back to Thornton's wonderful scheme, which covers many Scriptural subjects, notably the Creation. Binoculars are necessary to appreciate the detail of this latter series, though an illuminated chart nearby reproduces the subjects in facsimile. One of the best—and least affected by previous mis-handling—is that illustrating the Creation of Birds and Fishes. On the other hand, the panel devoted to the Creation of the Firmament had reverted to something like primeval chaos. In the glaziers' shed, opposite the Minster, I watched some of these and other panels being pieced together—slowly, thoughtfully, experimentally, like part of an immense jigsaw puzzle, some problems being posed by disconnected bits of blue sky, saints minus their heads, a crown wanting a king, and so on.

In this skilful, though laborious manner, the Garden of Eden has been reconstructed with Adam once more in pristine command; Noah's Ark breasting the flood waters, though the sole survivors of the animal cargo are a whippet and a red cow; and the Tower of Babel. For the glaziers, and the indefatigable Dean, it must have been like starting humanity's story all over again!

Modern life is leaving its own imprint upon the Minster, however. John Thornton's conception of Sun, Moon and Stars glows afresh in his East Window, but a very different one is represented on the tall Astronomical Clock, unveiled in the north transept as a memorial to fallen airmen during the 1939–45 war. To quote from the explanatory booklet on sale: 'The Clock has two main dials: the 'Astral' one on the east side and the 'Zodiacal' one on the west. On the Zodiacal side, the edge of the large convex disc represents the horizon as seen by a navigator flying just over York and facing south. The Clock's 'sun' rises from behind this horizon in the mornings, and sets behind it again in the evenings, at the actual times of sunrise and sunset for York, all round the year. . . .' Harry Stammers—the artist who could so imaginatively present Archbishop Scrope's trial of 500 years ago—also helped to decorate this sublime token of twentieth-century sacrifice.

To relegate York's many other fine buildings to a mere list for quick consultation seems impious. Nearly all the older churches are worth seeing, particularly Holy Trinity, Goodramgate, for its undulating set of box pews; St. Margaret's, Walmgate, for its Norman doorway; and St. Mary's, Castlegate, for its inscribed Saxon dedication stone. All Saints', Pavement, has a remarkable bronze closing-ring—like that at Adel—showing a woman being swallowed by a dragon, a scene reminiscent of one of York's medieval Mystery Plays. Another All Saints' Church, in North Street, shows the End of the World in a rather terrifying window based on the fourteenth-century poem, 'The Pricke of Conscience'. In one panel a sea-monster rears up in protest, for in the all-embracing terrestial fire the ocean itself has burst uncomfortably into flame!

Another kind of fire, caused during the blitz, partially destroyed St. Martin's Church, Coney Street. I remember walking next morning on the heat-softened tarmac, just outside; it had become a mosaic of coloured glass blown from the east window. The church has since been restored by George G. Pace of York, and should be seen in its new rôle as centrepiece for a Garden of Rest. The fine bracket clock that reached over the pavement from this church was another victim of the fire. Its surmounting figure of an eighteenth-century naval officer reading his sextant was part of its charm. Fortunately, I was able to supply the architect with pre-war photographs of clock and figure. It is good to welcome the officer back to his post once more.

In recent years St. Mary's Abbey has gained fresh prominence as the venue of the York Mystery Plays, performed as background tapestry for the city's triennial Festival. It is a thrilling experience to sit here through the descending darkness of a June evening and watch as Heaven takes translucent form around the nave's Gothic window-spaces, and Earth enacts its pitiful dramas on the sward below. The Plays are a Biblical coverage of Man's life-story *sub specie aeternitatis*—against the background of eternity, and could have been written by a monk or monks of St. Mary's, about 600 years ago. Originally, the Plays were performed from street wagons, or pageants, by the different trade guilds. Delicious bits of buffoonery animate the Plays, therefore, and much homely speech. In the Harrowing of Hell scene, performed by the town's saddlers, Jesus confronts the Mouth of Hades and calls out, first in Latin—

Attollite portas principes—

then, using language every Yorkshireman understands, 'Oppen uppe . . .'.

The version of the Plays now in use is that written by Canon J. S. Purvis. For the 1963 Festival he transcribed another play—Abraham's sacrifice of Isaac as originally given by the 'bokebynders', who traded in Minster Gates, that lovely little alley opposite the south door of the Minster.

York is amazingly rich in ancient halls. The town's medieval Guildhall was gutted during the 'Baedeker' raid in 1942 but has since been restored. Its forest of oak pillars, spars and purlins—populated as before with carved angels, musicians, and horrid little devils—is much better lighted than formerly. In Aldwark a rather plain building contains the impressive, open-timbered hall of the Merchant Taylors, and a room lit by one of Henry Gyles's colourful windows. Before achieving fame in Oxford and Cambridge, Gyles of York did some good secular work in his own county —a sundial window at Tong Hall, near Bradford; another one, dated 1670, at Nun Appleton, near Tadcaster; and here at the Merchant Taylors' Hall this more ambitious window portraying Queen Anne and the Arms of the Merchant Taylors of London. Probably Gyles was not responsible for the erroneous statement, in this glowing panel, about the Company 'haveing in their Fraternity eight Kings, eleven Dukes, thirty Earles, and forty-four Lords'. A rather too formidable line-up, despite the York Company being entrusted with the Ascension in the annual Mystery Plays.

York's finest open-timber roof—perhaps the finest in England—graces the main chamber of the Merchant Adventurers' Hall, in Fossgate. The old Forest of Galtres furnished its soaring timbers at a time when Galtres was a real hazard to wayfarers, because of lurking robbers and wolves. In a chapel at one end of the oak-pillared undercroft, below the main hall, services are still held periodically by this ancient Company. The members also celebrate, here, with venison feasts partaken in candlelight. When the Hall drops back into its silences the public are admitted—but far too few take advantage!

St. William's College, to the east of the Minster, also deserves better of visitors. From a college for chantry priests, erected in the fifteenth century, it has evolved into the present-day meeting-place for York Convocation. But its cobbled courtyard survives, also its great timbered halls— and the small Painted Chamber where, not long ago, a lady visitor inadvertently saw deep into the past. A medieval priest was sitting there; a ghost to be sure, but unconcernedly reading his book.

Treasurers' House, a few yards away, should be full of ghosts but apparently claims none. Its noble façade looks across Dean's Park to the Five Sisters Window and the Chapter House—the two nearest features of the Minster, which had its Treasurers until the Reformation. Those bygone worthies were even more decorative than the people who succeeded them here as private tenants, through Jacobean and later times. In my own mind, however, I like to pair some of them off—for example,

Martin Collins, one of the Tudor Treasurers, with William Gray, the Victorian amateur astronomer. They had nothing in common save *panache*. Martin achieved his by riding forth in magnificent scarlet gowns lined with miniver or squirrel fur and bequeathing all his serving gentry with a well-equipped nag; Gray, by inviting friends to see his observatory in the garden here, though the invitations were usually phrased in the grand manner, viz., 'to Tea and the Heavenly Bodies'. What an amazing slice of history, human as well as architectural, has here come into the guardianship of the National Trust!

But York—if one can overlook a few of today's shoddy reproductions and excrescences—is rampant with Time's endless pageantry. To zestful archaeologists Roman *Eboracum* is continually yielding tokens of its hey-day; the Yorkshire Museum has a fine section devoted to that period, while the Multangular Tower nearby testifies to the staying power of Roman building methods. Medieval York has been mentioned at some length. Of Georgian York—the city of glittering county balls, link-boys and street-criers—much also remains. Some streets are still more suited to sedan chairs than motor-cars. And to have lunch in the great marble-pillared hall of Lord Burlington's Assembly Rooms is to share, in imagination, the company of such luminaries as the Rockinghams and the Fairfaxes and to hear all the latest social gossip, from the doings of the town's Jacobite suspects, to some highwaymen's audacious attack on Lord Downe's coach. The nineteenth century did not lack its occasions, either. At a fancy-dress ball held here in March 1842, Charles Waterton, the naturalist, dazzled the ladies in the capacity of Montezuma, his outfit being 'composed of feathers and ornaments obtained during his travels in America'.

Lord Burlington also designed the Mansion House. It was to have been nothing more than a 'proper Repository for the Records, Books and Papers belonging to the City'. But Burlington the magnificent could not be so 'contained'. The archive idea was strangulated in favour of a City House which should serve as the Lord Mayor's official residence—and that is still its main purpose.

By arrangement, the interior is occasionally shown to visitors. I cannot think of a more entertaining way of taking the civic pulse of York. John Carr's rubicund visage, in one prominent portrait, is enough to tell us that he has not only 'arrived', as a fashionable architect, but has twice been made Lord Mayor of England's 'second city'. His Horbury days seem far behind as one beholds the silver tea-urn he presented in 1796, to enrich a display of civic plate second to none in the country. Knowing his humble background, there is a special thrill in visualising him drinking the King's health in a priceless gold loving-cup of 1672, and addressing the assembled guests while Emperor Sigismund's sword—another treasure —flaunts its red dragons nearby.

Here in this gracious building, which achieves a dizzy flamboyance in the State Room overhead, one can also see and hear something about George Hudson—already encountered at Croft Spa; it was he who begged George Stephenson to 'mak all t' railways cum to York'. How the present-day rail closures would have galled him! His eventual disgrace, through unwise financial speculations, should not blind one to the fact that he had helped to switch England over from stage-coaches to railway transport. As a three-times-appointed Lord Mayor of his adopted city he still has a right to look on from the soft shadows when the present-day civic parties dine here—by candle-glow. Remembering the fortunes he made for some people, let his advocate be the little figure which decorates a lovely eighteenth-century epergne—the figure of Justice, balancing her scales. The epergne was presented in 1796 as a table centrepiece for use whenever the Lord Mayor should give a banquet, or the Judges meet for York Assizes.

John Carr designed the Assize Courts, in the Castle Yard, but the Judges' Lodging in Lendal, very near the Mansion House, recalls a piece of macabre humour worth knowing. It is a house of beautifully panelled rooms, graced by an elegant staircase. Dr. Clifford Wintringham, a physician who 'practised in York with the highest reputation and success for thirty-five years' lived here at first—but did he realise that the site was still littered with human bones, from the former St. Wilfrid's churchyard? Its tombstones had even been requisitioned to line the kitchen oven, so that a loaf would sometimes bear upon its crust some Latin reference to the mortality of Man! Perhaps that suited the outlook of an eighteenth-century doctor?

In 1746 Wintringham succeeded the renowned Dr. Burton as physician to York County Hospital. Laurence Sterne lampooned Dr. Burton as Dr. Slop in *Tristram Shandy*, and some of Burton's 'cures' are amusingly represented in the apothecary's shop in York Castle Museum.

Today the term 'York Castle' is something of a misnomer. All that remains of the Norman castle is Clifford's Tower—a small stone keep that presides over the area from the summit of its lofty green mound. It con-

23　*York Minster from the medieval city wall*

fronts three much larger buildings which, together with the keep, form a spacious quadrangle—the Castle Yard. When the prison inside Clifford's Tower proved too small, it was decided to erect a bigger one—the middle building of those just mentioned, and known thereafter as the Debtors' Prison. It was completed in 1705 and is sometimes attributed to Vanbrugh. The companion building facing south is the Assize Courts (1777). Its architect, John Carr, also designed the Female Prison (1780) immediately opposite. The two ex-prisons now accommodate the world-famous Castle Museum.

I can recall some of the grim features encountered by Dr. J. L. Kirk and his team as they tackled the museum's first venue—the old Female Prison—away back in 1937. Some of those features have been preserved and are only too eloquent of their former purpose. Several of my early talks with Dr. Kirk were in the condemned cell, and the narrow passage leading to it was inscribed with prisoners' comments and sketches: *graffiti* tinged occasionally with ribald humour.

Two larger cells contribute to the transformation that brought Kirkgate into being, for they accommodate the fire station, and a tallow-dip factory from Pickering. Although the flagstones that border the cobbled carriage-way once echoed to the dull tramp of unfortunates at exercise, they now give a touch of refinement—and foot comfort—to this delightful street. One padded cell is preserved, for old times' sake!

The architectural highlight of Kirkgate is the Elizabethan timbered house, rescued from Stamford, Lincolnshire. On either side there are shops that display the appropriate wares of a pewterer, a coppersmith, the afore-mentioned apothecary, a barber, a toy dealer, and a glass dealer. Each awakens the past in its own peculiar manner. Hanging from the barber's pole, for example, there is a bleeding-bowl as once used by the barber-surgeons; and G. Pomfret's glass-shop contains witch balls and smugglers' bottles that remind one of certain nefarious practices lurking behind the Georgian social niceties.

Alderman's Walk, branching from Kirkgate, commemorates the late Alderman J. B. Morrell, one of York's outstanding personalities. At one corner an eighteenth-century doorway—fitted with flambeau extinguisher —bears the name-plate of John Carr, who designed this building at a time when streets were dark and dangerous. A link-boy would escort his patron home and then quench his flambeau or torch by thrusting it into the cone-shaped snuffer beside the door. York still has three such extinguishers *in situ*; one is in High Petergate, near the Minster.

24   Overstepping gables in the restored Shambles, York

Better lighting conditions are simulated at the farther end of Kirkgate, where a Victorian post office is snugly ensconced within a tiny court. The post office was opened on 6 May 1960—the double diamond-jubilee of the Penny Black postage stamp. To mark the occasion, facsimiles of this pioneer adhesive stamp were issued here, and they have since sold by the thousand. I wonder what visitors' friends think on receiving a card bearing one of these 'penny blacks' ? And franked 'Kirkgate' ? Mail is collected here regularly—but of course current stamps must also be affixed.

From here a little shopping arcade leads to Princess Mary Court, opened by the Princess Royal in 1950. In almost every instance its Georgian and Regency shops represent traders of bygone York. The company includes Joseph Terry, confectioner, Henry Hindley, clock-maker, William Hornby, cordwainer, James Brown, saddler, Elias Wolstenholme, weaver, Thomas Cook, optical-instrument maker, and William Alexander, publisher and bookseller. A good story is told about this Quaker publisher and Sir Walter Scott. Having admired the way in which Alexander had produced Hargrove's *History of York*, Scott asked if he would tender for the printing of his own book, the newly finished *Ivanhoe*. 'Friend,' came the measured reply, 'I value the friendship which has caused thee to make this offer, but I fear that thy books are too worldly for me to print.'

The Parish of York Castle—as it is now euphemistically called—was further expanded, in 1951, by the transformation of the Debtors' Prison. Its ground-floor cells are very small, but they do serve to indicate the cramped working conditions of many bygone craftsmen whose workshops they now accommodate. Blacksmith, wheelwright, cutler, brush-maker, gunsmith, comb-maker—these and others forgather here, and their several tools and appliances look as though they had only just been put down. The blacksmith's forge is a replica of one used for estate work at Ness Hall, North Riding, until 1951. The clay-pipe maker's outfit is still capable of producing 'churchwardens' and 'aldermen' in bold, sweeping lines; it was given to the museum by a Leeds clay-pipe maker whose grandfather practised the trade on an itinerant basis. As for the cutler's forge and stiddy, they represent the day-to-day work of one of Sheffield's 'little mesters' of whom so few now remain. As in the Female Prison, one cell has here been kept intact. It is Pompey's Parlour—the vernacular name for the condemned cell, where Dick Turpin, Eugene Aram and several Jacobite rebels spent their last days.

The latest development is Half Moon Court. This is reached via the cell corridor in the Debtors' Prison, and banishes the gloom of its former usage as a prisoners' exercise yard by presenting a microcosm of York-shire town life about the beginning of the present century. The inevitable 'pub' is the 'King William Hotel', brought here from Walmgate in York. 'Good Beds for Cyclists' are blatantly advertised on the exterior; gas burners flicker seductively just inside the windows; and drawn up at the entrance—ready to provide anything from 'Charley's Aunt' to the 'Blue Bells of Scotland'—there is a smart barrel organ.

The publican's neighbours are an attractive lot, offering for sale the latest thing in hip baths, peggy sticks, and telephones, but motorists will pause longest before the garage that fills one end of Half Moon Court. The garage was actually brought here from Whip-ma-whop-ma-gate, nearby, and bears the name of the original proprietors, who loaned a special state coach—now standing at one side—to the Sheriff of York as required. Temptingly on view at the garage door, as though ready for hire, are two veteran cars—a Grout steam car of 1899, and a Colibri petrol-driven car of 1909. All the accessories for such a trip, plus petrol at 1s. 4d. a gallon, are 'available', and for anyone who would know more about those adventurous days there is a side window that displays various cups and medals won by Dr. Kirk in motor races between 1909 and 1912.

Incidentally, this garage recalls that other phase of the good doctor's activities. So great was his antiquarian zeal that for years he crammed his Pickering residence with bygones, filled his coach-house with ancient vehicles, and slept perforce in his study. The Castle Museum, with all its later ramifications and wide educational appeal, really stems from his idiosyncrasies.

Even now, only part of York's immense drama has been suggested—the larger and more important part, I hope, though I am conscious of having said too little about the old streets and some of the quaint houses they half conceal.

It is known that Guy Fawkes was baptised in St. Michael-le-Belfry Church, opposite the south-west corner of the Minster, and that he was educated not far away at the original St. Peter's School. Three old houses contend for the kudos of being his actual birthplace—all within the small area bounded by High Petergate and Stonegate. Unlike most antiquaries, the proprietors of one small Petergate hotel are in no doubt. To strengthen somebody's claim that their rear building—outwardly decorated with odd little white figures—is the one in question, they provide all their dining-tables with menu cards slotted in small barrels marked 'gun-powder'!

Even in its post-war, over-restored condition, the Shambles is irresistible. Most peculiar are some crooked medieval gables that lean towards each other across the narrow street, like a couple of bonneted gossips, each straining to hear what the other is saying. There was much to whisper about when Margaret Clitherow lived lower down the street. She was accused of harbouring priests there, and helping them to escape. Her penalty was the horrible one of being literally pressed to death. To commemorate this youthful martyr of 1586, a beautiful shrine has lately been constructed in the lower room of her old timbered house. Professor Maugsch, a Hungarian refugee sculptor, has made for it a life-size statue that reflects Margaret Clitherow's tranquillity of soul.

ten

The York Countryside

Most of the older buildings of York, including the city walls and gateways, have a creamy white appearance. This is due to the building material—magnesian limestone. The walls, mostly thirteenth century, form a gleaming girdle around the old town and are enhanced in springtime by daffodils nodding all over the supporting, grassy ramparts. Strangers frequently ask who has the colossal task of washing the walls, to keep them so white. The answer is, of course, only the rain; it is the weather, also, which—after hardening the exposed stone—gives it that attractive pearly gloss.

Much of this stone was quarried in the Tadcaster area, about ten miles south-west of York. All down the centuries one particular quarry has yielded stone for the Minster. It is known today as Jackdaw Crag Quarry, but its former name, Peter's Post, is a more telling link with the Cathedral, or Minster, dedicated to St. Peter.

Peter's Post and its adjoining quarries belonged to the Vavasour family of Hazlewood Castle, nearby. The following tribute to their generosity was penned by a visitor in Tudor times:

> Out of a little pece of a Quarry within ye Mannor of Haslewood hath been taken ye Cathedrall church of Yorke, ye Minsters of Howden, Selby and Beverley, ye Abbey of St. Mary's in Yorke, Thornton Colledge in Linkolnshire and divers other Churches.

For freely granting their stone in this way the Catholic family of Vavasour enjoyed a rare privilege during the Protestant reign of Elizabeth I: they were allowed to celebrate Mass in their private chapel without hindrance or censure. What a pity Margaret Clitherow's husband was a mere butcher. Now if he had only owned a quarry . . . !

It is regrettable that Hazlewood Castle—another impressive product of the Vavasour quarries—no longer welcomes visitors. I once went there by a former owner's invitation, and saw how a Tudor building could effectively put on Georgian airs and graces, chiefly in the Great Hall. I was shown the exonerated chapel, too, and heard for the first time about Mistress Ann Vavasour, Queen Elizabeth's favourite maid-of-honour. In a contemporary portrait, now owned by the Company of Armourers and Braziers, a very pensive Ann is as regally robed as her Queen.

Some of the Vavasours believed that their family's immunity, at Hazlewood, was due to Ann's influence at Court. Of her Sir John Stanhope wrote to Lord Talbot, 'our new mayd Mrs. Vavasour flourisheth like the lily and the rose'. She seems to have exerted some influence elsewhere, too, if one can accept the tradition that she was the Dark Lady of Shakespeare's sonnets. Others of the family gave the credit for their being unmolested, as Catholics, to Sir Thomas Vavasour, who commanded the *Foresight* during the Armada conflict.

But the 'stone' theory has most advocates, and to support it William Vavasour stands in a niche beside the west door of York Minster, holding a sizeable sample from Peter's Post.

Other important quarries that helped to embellish the older buildings of York are situated at Huddlestone, a few miles south. This Huddlestone limestone also modelled the neighbouring village of Sherburn-in-Elmet, whose fine medieval church stands like a white sentinel on the only hill. To the east, along B1222, one can still follow the Bishop's Dyke which floated the stone down to the River Ouse at Cawood. I like to think of those times when so many buildings that are now famous were still in embryo, and dependent on this little centre of the ancient British kingdom of Elmet. Boatloads of limestone went up-river to York and beyond; others were sent south, by way of the Humber, for the construction of Eton College Chapel, King's College Chapel at Cambridge, and so on.

Cawood, where the River Wharfe finally merges with the Ouse, still seems to be listening for the return of its archbishops. Little but the white gatehouse of their palace now remains, however; one beautiful oriel window looks up-river towards York, symbolising the achievements of so many—not forgetting the unfortunate George Mountain.

While yet a choirboy at Cawood Church, Mountain had determined to become Archbishop of York one day. Eventually, he took the first few steps, becoming in turn Bishop of Lincoln, of London, and of Durham. When the See of York fell vacant Charles I asked him whom he should appoint. Prompted perhaps by thoughts of Neville's gargantuan feast, and the days when Cawood was reckoned the Windsor of the North, the Bishop's answer came pat: 'Your Majesty, hadst thou faith as a grain of mustard seed thou wouldst say to this Mountain, Be removed and cast into the See'. Charles, greatly titillated, gave Mountain his reward. But within a month the new Archbishop had died. In Cawood's riverside church a forlorn sculptured figure gives him a modicum of immortality.

Cawood was but one of York's former archiepiscopal residences. Another stood in the shadow of the Minster. This later became one of Sir Arthur Ingram's collection of desirable homes; its Early English chapel has since become the Minster Library. It must have been a grand place, especially when Ingram introduced an organ costing £500 and added some ornamental gardens. One visitor borrowed a description even then becoming rather threadbare and called it 'a second paradise'.

Nothing could be much fairer, however, than the one surviving palace, at Bishopthorpe—three miles south of York and about six miles north of Cawood. Archbishop Walter de Gray bought the place, then known as the manor of Thorpe St. Andrew, from the monks of Kirkstall in 1226. Gray, one of the chief builders of the Minster, knew well how to tackle this property and bring it into line with primatial standards. The present thirteenth-century chapel here is his work, but many alterations have occurred that would dismay him. In the eighteenth century Archbishop Drummond threw a Gothick 'curtain' of stone across the main frontage. Thomas Atkinson of York, his architect, then built the detached entrance gateway as a Gothick fantasy—an elaboration of the surviving gatehouse at Cawood, using some stone from the Cawood ruins as a nice, nostalgic gesture.

Indoors, some lovely seventeenth-century plaster ceilings escaped Drummond's remodelling scheme, and how the older archbishops seem to appreciate them as they gaze around, meditatively, from their gilded frames. Yet Drummond did introduce lightness and many a touch of holy joy, especially in the Drawing Room ceiling, and the Entrance Hall's prettily arched canopies.

On reaching Bishopthorpe by road, or from an old landing-stage on the Ouse, it is difficult for a stranger to sense anything here, from the past, apart from high church affairs. The road used to bring the Archbishops along in their sumptuous coaches, while the river took them down to

York in a state barge. All seems straightforward if somewhat grandiose. But, as we have seen in the case of Richard Scrope, politics sometimes went hand in glove with religion. And that meant plotting.

There was great cause for alarm when Prince Charles Edward swept down from Scotland. Archbishop Thomas Herring wrote anxiously to a friend, 'God grant that I may feed my swans in peace'. Bishopthorpe, however, buzzed with excitement during the Forty-Five Rebellion, for Herring—jeopardising his beloved swans—plunged deeply into politics. Over the river in York there were several Jacobite suspects—the ubiquitous Dr. John Burton, for example, and Henry Hindley who harboured dangerous ideas—it was thought—as he went around making and fixing clocks for the Corporation, the Minster and local gentry. It was therefore safer for loyalists to meet and make their plans some little distance away, within the sacrosanct walls of Bishopthorpe Palace. Herring's campaign here raised £40,000 in support of the Government. Two years later he received his accolade—the See of Canterbury.

Another 'plotting house' stands in the fork of the Wharfe and Ouse, roughly five miles south-east of Tadcaster, via Bolton Percy. It is Nun Appleton Hall. Few people go that way today, for the large brick mansion stands in a cul-de-sac and is not normally open to visitors. The Restoration of Charles II was virtually hatched in this remote place; General Fairfax—then crippled with gout—and others of his family, were amongst the chief plotters.

I recounted this story at some length in *North Country Profile*. Here it is perhaps sufficient to think of Brian Fairfax, disguised as a 'young country clown', leaving Nun Appleton secretly with a message for General Monk at Coldstream. This 'touched off' the coup. And out of the five men deputed to meet Charles at Breda, his Continental exile, and offer him the throne of his fathers, three were of the Nun Appleton plotters. An interesting group, those three. One was the irrepressible Brian; another, Edward Bowles, the Presbyterian divine from York who had once tutored General Fairfax's daughter, Mary; and the third, the Rev. Henry Fairfax, Rector of Bolton Percy.

The quiet village of Bolton Percy is worthy of its fine fifteenth-century church, where so many Fairfaxes rest from their labours. Henry Fairfax had previously held the living at Newton Kyme, a good mile on the other side of Tadcaster. Here, in an even quieter church, the Fairfax nimbus has a Norman and Early English setting of rare charm.

Cawood may have lost much of its former glory, but the surrounding countryside pulsates with unexpected interest. It is flat, meandering country, rich in crops. The River Derwent wriggles through, to join the Ouse at Barmby-on-the-Marsh; one of the country houses it passes—Thorganby Hall—hid the fourteenth-century glass from All Saints' Church, York, during the last war. Not many people can claim to have had a sea-serpent lurking in their cellar! The villages are mostly worth seeing. There are splendid churches at Riccall, Skipwith, Stillingfleet, and Wilberfoss, but one cannot travel far in this area before realising its intimate connection with the battle of Stamford Bridge, fought on 25 September of that pivotal year, 1066.

Personally, I rarely look upon the Humber and the Ouse without seeing, in imagination, that flotilla of dragon-prowed ships as they pressed inland prior to battle. Near Goole the Humber narrows and becomes the Ouse, and although the Ouse would have taken the Northmen as far as York, they chose to disembark at Riccall, near Cawood, leaving their sailing craft under a strong guard. They marched the remaining nine miles to York and there defeated Edwin and Morkere. Playing for safety, the people of York greeted the victorious Hardrada and his ally Tostig and gave them provisions and hostages as a guarantee of continuing loyalty. But a different fate awaited them a few miles away, at Stamford Bridge. There they were overtaken by the newly crowned Harold of England, and the opposing forces ranged themselves on either side of the Derwent.

The only turbulent feature at Stamford Bridge today is the river, which is liable to flood the low-lying banks—as if to erase all sign and memory of that long, bloody combat. Yet Stamford Bridge—on A166—is only a small village and one can never be far from the spot where that preliminary parley—recorded by Snorri Sturlason, the Icelandic saga collector—supposedly occurred between Harold of England and his brother, Tostig. Offered his pardon and restitution of his Northumbrian earldom if he calls off the invasion, Tostig asks, 'What then shall be given to King Harald of Norway?' The answer rings clear: 'Seven feet of English earth, or perhaps a little more as he is something tall.'

During the battle that ensued a giant Norseman held the narrow bridge against all comers, swinging his axe to deadly effect. Eventually, an Englishman slipped quietly into a boat and, guiding this beneath the bridge, disposed of the Norseman by spearing him through some chinks in the bridge timbers. This familiar story is given in the *Anglo-Saxon Chronicle*, but the people of Stamford Bridge kept it alive until about forty years ago by holding an annual feast at which quantities of spear pies were consumed. Boat-shaped and bearing an impress of the fatal spear, the traditional pies were reintroduced by the villagers for their 900th anniversary celebrations of the battle, in 1966.

Folk memories are strong hereabouts, despite population changes. The older folk 'know', for instance, that the boat represented by the pies was actually a *swill-tub*. What of the man who so skilfully handled this curious craft? The late Sir Harold Wilberforce-Bell of Portington Hall, near Howden, once assured me that the hero was an ancestor of his—William of Eggleston—and that his victim was none other than the mighty Hardrada. This same ancestor accompanied King Harold on that precipitate march to Hastings and there accounted 'for eight Normans with his own sword'. On returning north he married Margaret de Kyme, whose dowry included the manor of Wilberfoss and a plot of land bounded, rather significantly, by the old Stamford Bridge itself. This was probably sited about a hundred yards upstream from the present graceful structure of 1727.

A striking commentary upon this last victory of the Saxons—achieved despite Hardrada's hastily summoned reinforcements from Riccall—occurs on the church door at Stillingfleet. Its ancient wrought-iron emblems include a Viking ship. The serpent prow and the paddle are unmistakable. And the serpent motif is repeated on the door-hinges as if some peculiar gaiety had possessed the craftsman responsible. According to local tradition, this wrought-iron vessel was fashioned in gleeful celebration of the victory at Stamford Bridge, for of the large fleet of 300 ships that had arrogantly sailed up to neighbouring Riccall a few days before, only twenty-four were left to limp back home with the remnants of Hardrada's army.

The aftermath of 1066, around here as in other parts of Yorkshire, is visually recorded in some splendid Norman architecture. Selby Abbey—a superb building, still in regular use—was founded in 1069 by Royal Charter of William the Conqueror, and was the first monastery to be built after the Conquest. In due time both Riccall and Stillingfleet succumbed to the new ecclesiastical style. Each church has a fine Norman porch, that at Stillingfleet 'framing' the Viking boat with an impressive arch of five orders.

Any jaded schoolmaster here must find relief in this one thing, when history lessons pall. The church doorway can always be relied upon to pro-

vide the children with both prologue and epilogue to the 1066 debacle—
in novel fashion.

The most important thing that has happened at York in recent times is the
establishment of its University. It is not mere loyalty to the county of one's
birth that prompted many of us to say that 'old sacerdotal York' should
have had its university long ago. Clutton Brock's standard guide to York
Minster actually does refer to a university being in existence here in the
eighth century A.D. He was thinking of the famous School of York headed
at one time by the great scholar, Alcuin. But the Harrying of the North by
a vengeful William, after the Conquest, destroyed Alcuin's magnificent
Library and prevented the School from developing later to full university
status. Many subsequent efforts to emulate Oxford and Cambridge proved
fruitless. Petitions for a university had been made to James I in 1617 and
again to Parliament in 1652. 'We in the North', argued the petitioners,
'have been looked upon as a rude and barbarous people, and a University
would be a special means of washing from us the stain of rudeness and
incivility.' Surely a weak-kneed plea, for northerners!

To secure these 'advantages' York had to wait another 300 years. Meanwhile, all hope of finding an adequate site *within* the old city had vanished.
When the university idea became vocal again, in the 1950s, Heslington
Hall came into focus. The late J. B. Morrell had a wonderful plan to make
this old home of the Deramores into a Folk Park, to which visitors could
travel the intervening two miles by stage-coach from the Castle Museum.
The Folk Park may yet materialise—though not at Heslington Hall,
which was eventually acquired for the University of York.

The first students to take up residence, in 1963, saw this Elizabethan
mansion pretty much as that noted wit the Rev. Sydney Smith would see
it a hundred years before, when he lodged in the village and caricatured
the owners. His great days as the exhilarating parson of Foston, near
Castle Howard, were still ahead. Meanwhile, he found scope for his gifts
in this lordly place. The squire's lady, he wrote, 'looked as if she had
walked right out of the Ark, or had been the wife of Enoch', while the
Squire himself 'was a perfect specimen of the Trullibers of old. . . .'
Soon, however, they all became good friends. I wonder what absurdities
Smith invented for their delectation about the fantastic topiary work in
the grounds? This Yorkshire cleric who had poked fun at Brighton Pavilion by saying that 'the Dome of St. Paul's must have come down to
Brighton and pupped', would hardly be tongue-tied on seeing these yews,

shaped like gargantuan chessmen! Most if not all these freaks have by now made way for the watercourts that separate the different colleges grouped around the old hall. It was hoped, however, that a few of them would be spared, along with an eighteenth-century gazebo overlooking the kitchen garden and lake.

The creation of York University has also solved the problem of the King's Manor. This rambling building in the city centre began as a private dwelling for the Abbot of St. Mary's. After serving successively as head-quarters of the Council of the North, royal mint, range of private dwellings—with John Camidge, the Minster organist, entertaining Charles Dickens in one of them, after the *Nicholas Nickleby* trip to Teesdale—the King's Manor was let early this century to the Yorkshire School for the Blind. I have watched the boys play cricket here. They played remarkably well, in one of the spacious courtyards, using a specially-made cricket ball that enclosed a bell.

And now this fine building—a delightful pastiche of plum-coloured brick and Yorkshire's 'white stone'—has graduated afresh as part of the University undertaking. No longer does it seem unwieldy.

The Vale of York is threaded by innumerable roads with interesting places clinging to them, like so many acorns on the crooked boughs of Galtres oaks. Some of the villages still bear etymological witness to this old forest, which Shakespeare mentions in *Henry IV*. Sutton-on-the-Forest, wedged in a crinkle of B1363, was surrounded by Galtres. A few oaks in the grounds of Sutton Hall are old enough to be survivors of the forest, which was finally cleared about 200 years ago. The present Georgian hall contains some exquisite plasterwork, reputedly the work of the Italian craftsmen who had been busy decorating Castle Howard, and in the Dining Room there is a 'cloud' ceiling copied for the late owner from the famous one in G. F. Handel's London house.

This quiet village never gave birth to any stranger character than Tristram Shandy. It was the Vicar's literary progeny—his gift to the dilettanti of Georgian society. We have seen how Stephen Croft of Stillington rescued part of the MS. when Sterne peevishly threw it on to the flames. Croft, indeed, grew quite accustomed to his Vicar's foibles, as when Mrs. Sterne—imagining herself to be the Queen of Bohemia—had to be driven in a single horse-chaise through a stubble field with as much rattle and din as would exorcise a dozen Bohemians. This piece of tom-foolery was devised by the master mind that produced *Tristram Shandy*, the novel which made its author so famous that a letter addressed to 'Tristram Shandy, Europe' would readily find him—it is said—at the Sutton vicarage. He served the joint parishes of Sutton and Stillington for over twenty years. Then came the better-known Coxwold period—but this must wait until we are out of the Forest area.

Another Forest village is Sheriff Hutton, three miles east of Sutton. The chief attractions here are the old castle—now alas in ruin, the church, and the beautiful hall known as Sheriff Hutton Park.

It is sad to see the fourteenth-century fortress of the Nevilles tacked on to a farm. Much of English history—ringing with names like Warwick the King-maker, Richard III, Anthony Woodville the poet, and the captive Princess Elizabeth of York—reduced to a stamping ground for cows!

Some years ago a lady visitor with clairvoyant powers actually 'saw' the Castle in its heyday—peopled with figures in resplendent gowns and robes. Earlier still a village boy, while playing around the castle moat, found a gold Posy Ring which the British Museum identified as of late fifteenth-century workmanship. It bears two inscriptions in Old French—*bon core de core* (good heart of heart) and *le tout vôtre* (I am all yours). Whose was the fair hand that once wore this love token? Perhaps it is enough to know that there *was* a little romance here, as well as scheming and treachery. . . .

The great days of the Castle have left their touch upon the church, notably with a small alabaster figure reclining in the north aisle. In the belief that it represents Edward, Prince of Wales—son of Richard III and Anne Neville—this pathetic effigy, long neglected, was restored a few years ago. By making a contribution to the cost of the work, the late Queen Mary bestowed her motherly smile—as it were—upon this lonely little prince who had died during his parents' absence.

Sheriff Hutton Park began its career as a forest lodge and was built by Sir Arthur Ingram, in 1621, although he had those forty other Yorkshire houses to boast about, with Temple Newsam at the head of the list. The Temple Newsam papers, preserved in Leeds City Library, have much to say about the bad characters who once lived in Sheriff Hutton village—but in some contemporary letters preserved at the hall it is Ingram himself who receives censure. He *would* enrich this new house of his with panelling and doors and other fittings purloined from the Castle—which was still partly occupied! The protests, addressed from Whitehall, were voiced by Thomas Lumsden, Keeper of Galtres Forest. But Ingram evidently treated them with disdain. In reducing Sheriff Hutton Castle to its present state, the processes of time were accelerated, therefore, by this astute financier. His grinning face on the Oak Room chimneypiece, at Sheriff Hutton Park, is only too eloquent; a ringleted visage sharing that glee, nearby, is presumably that of his lady wife.

Crayke, the hill-top village six miles to the north-west, once marked the northern limit of Galtres. Stretching away to the south is the vast Plain or Vale of York; to the north—forming a wide arc of variegated country—the Vale of Mowbray unfolds, rimmed in the distance by the Hambleton Hills. Crayke is worth visiting for its views alone, but here one also walks in the footsteps of St. Cuthbert. In A.D. 685 Crayke and a three-mile fringe was given to him as a resting place while journeying between Lindisfarne and York. Cuthbert was eventually laid to rest in Durham Cathedral, of course. Yet because of its former association with Cuthbert, Crayke was for centuries regarded as part of County Durham— which meant, amongst other things, that malefactors could pop in and out of 'Durham' and Yorkshire and evade the law with roguish impunity. Only when Crayke reverted to Yorkshire about a hundred years ago did these facilities cease.

Crayke Castle, now a private house, owes something of its structure to the Prince Bishops of Durham. Sharing the same ridge, St. Cuthbert's Church presides over the village with medieval graces that are well sustained indoors, though I have a particular liking for the Jacobean pulpit— fitted with contemporary angle-poise candle-brackets!

William Ralph Inge was born at The Cottage, below the church. In one of his books, *Assessments and Anticipations*, he recalled his own youth in the very clerical household here. 'Sunday', he wrote, 'was a mitigated Puritan Sabbath'; but one is given, nevertheless, an impish vignette of the future Dean of St. Paul's gloating with a cousin over the ingenious tortures illustrated in Neale's graphic work on the Christian Martyrs—'the only amusing book we were allowed to read' on that holy day. The barrel organ in the church gallery recalls an earlier, portable barrel organ which, Dean Inge relates, had to be carried into the churchyard once, during divine service, because it would not stop playing the Old Hundredth!

Superlatives are difficult to avoid when describing the Hambleton Hills and the Vale of Coxwold they cherish. Elsewhere in Yorkshire even the finest areas may have bad patches—due perhaps to so-called development or ill-considered planning, but here an unseen agency seems to have been at work, preserving all that is best and demanding a like quality from each succeeding generation. Perhaps the monastic influence did not stop with the Reformation?

Certainly, this neighbourhood was thick with abbeys and priories. To a Yorkshireman their names are music—Rievaulx, Byland, Newburgh, with outliers like Kirkham near Malton, Mount Grace near Northallerton, and, for good measure, the modern Benedictine Abbey and School at Ampleforth.

The late Robert Thompson of Kilburn first made me aware of this influence from the past. While helping in his father's carpentry shop, early this century, he would think of the glorious work once fashioned by devoted craftsmen for the surrounding abbeys, and great churches like those at Ripon and York. Later, he opened a workshop of his own, making by hand such articles as refectory tables, altar pieces, faldstools, and carving upon them his tiny 'mouse' signature. Some of his finest work was done for Ampleforth Abbey, four miles away, but by now several modern abbeys all over Britain have drawn upon this same 'field of inspiration'.

The seed planted in Bob Thompson's fertile mind is still bearing fruit, as anybody may see by visiting the busy workshop in Kilburn village, six miles north of Crayke. But the heritage does not stop there. In Brandsby and other neighbouring villages, small, unobtrusive ateliers have sprung up with similar aims—inspiration from the past, without slavish copying. And if one seeks the reason for the carved Gothic-style furniture and fittings, probably adze-shaped and oak-pegged, which bring admirers from far and near, one has only to look once again at the Yorkshire abbeys that cream the surrounding landscape, and at one or two secluded old churches —like Leake, near Thirsk—where some of the old monastic woodwork escaped the notice of Henry VIII's despoilers.

Rievaulx Abbey must be sought deliberately. There is no direct approach. One splendid route leaves the A19 four miles north of Thirsk and romps over the moors via Kepwick and Hawnby, passing Arden Hall. Mary Queen of Scots' overnight stay at Arden was barely long enough for her to be shown the lovely abbey falling to ruin at the end of this lonely trail. Perhaps her sympathies were mainly with the poverty-stricken nuns who had once lived here, when the place was known as Nun Arden and the Archbishop of York had to rebuke them for various shortcomings.

Another fine route to Rievaulx branches left at the top of Sutton Bank— east of Thirsk, then right at Old Byland. The advantages of this upland route along the crest of Hambleton's oolitic ridge are the glorious views, especially to the south, where Kilburn and Coxwold and Byland Abbey nestle among the cornfields. Gliders soar overhead, and the White Horse of Kilburn leans back against the steep slope of Sutton Bank, along White-stonecliff, so that all may see it for miles around.

The more usual way to Rievaulx Abbey is via the attractive market town of Helmsley. This route, and the one through Hawnby, converge at the top of Rievaulx Bank—three miles west of Helmsley, on the Bilsdale road, B1257. Even then, the final winding descent to the elusive abbey should be delayed, so that one's curiosity may be satisfied on seeing a signpost marked The Terrace. A car can be driven along the little track here indicated.

Those who ignore this sign miss one of the best views in North York-shire, for The Terrace was designed by the Duncombe family in the eighteenth century to provide an elegant promenade, studded with classi-cal temples. The nearest temple, of Ionic design, was painted inside with mythological subjects by Burnice, an Italian artist, but—for once—Andromeda being sacrificed to the sea-monster and other spicy episodes loose their full impact. Out there, from the long crescent of green sward, Rievaulx Abbey rivets one's attention. It is glimpsed, far below, through the tree-gaps, looking as though it had just dropped from heaven: roofless today, of course, but so lovingly cupped in this loop of the Rye Valley—and over-arched with glorious moorland and banks of trees—that the fell hand of the Reformation is barely noticeable, until one surrenders the artifices of The Terrace for the realities that come by closer inspection.

Even in semi-ruin, Rievaulx Abbey is a noble building. A descriptive leaflet by the Ministry of Public Building and Works gives the main out-lines of its history and architecture, typically Cistercian, but a few details must colour my own narrative.

Near the Chapter House there is an impressive two-storeyed shrine erected in honour of the first Abbot, William. As former amanuensis and secretary to Bernard of Clairvaux, William would have handled those beautiful 'Flowers of St. Bernard' now sung as hymns in most Christian churches. After his greatly lamented death, Abbot William is said to have formed the pleasant habit of reappearing to Waldef during the afternoon siesta allowed by the Rule and conversing with him. William's shrine is finely carved in stone, with a key-block—now in the abbey museum—representing the Agnus Dei.

In 1131 William had seen the inception of this first Cistercian house in Yorkshire. Under Aelred, the third Abbot, Rievaulx became the chief centre of Cistercian influence in England. Yet Aelred remained humble

25   *Roofless arcades and rubble: legacy of the*
     dissolution at .Rievaulx Abbey

and lovable. His personal qualities have come down to us in the writings of a contemporary monk, Walter Daniel. Monastic scribes were not always complimentary to their superiors, but Daniel is full of praise for Aelred and for the 'holy mansion' he governed with such understanding.

Although Aelred won some renown as a spiritual healer, he could not cure his own arthritis, which got so bad that occasionally he had to be carried about on a linen sheet held at the four corners by monks. This affliction is hardly surprising when one reads that Aelred in earlier years would frequently retire to a hidden well, there immersing 'his whole body in the icy cold water, and so quench the heat in himself of every vice'.

Some twelfth-century sculptured stones from the abbey infirmary—where at length Aelred ate and slept so as to enjoy a little warmth—are kept in the museum. One shows a horse delivering corn to be ground at a windmill. In another, a couple who have stolen a tigress's cubs divert the attention of the enraged beast by throwing a mirror in her path. The ruse succeeds, for the carving clearly shows the tigress pausing to admire her reflection in the mirror while the interlopers escape. Did the suffering Aelred find any amusement in this subject—or see only the warning against Vanity it was meant to convey?

When the Ministry of Works started operations here, in 1921, the Nave was 'ten feet deep in fallen masonry and soil'. This debris could have dated from the closure of the Abbey in 1539, for the heap was found to conceal some pigs of lead melted down from the roofs. Perhaps the local people, angry at the turn of events, had deliberately pushed a wall over to cover these aggravating ingots—each already stamped with Henry's seal—and thus cheated the King's men of their booty. Whatever the reason, this valuable cache of lead remained there, hidden and unsuspected, for almost 400 years. When finally brought to light, the ingots were carefully distributed—one went to the British Museum, one was retained for the Rievaulx Abbey museum, and the remaining five were sent to York Minster for the much-needed re-leading of the Five Sisters Window.

In an area so wonderfully blessed repeated visits are necessary to extract even a modicum of its interest and natural beauty. Castle Howard, Vanbrugh's huge masterpiece and its grounds, near Malton, really demand several days—and a book to themselves. Even Horace Walpole felt somewhat daunted when first confronted by Castle Howard. 'Nobody had informed me', he wrote, 'that at one view I should see a palace, a town, a fortified city, temples on high places, woods worthy of being each a metro-

26 *Castle Howard—Vanbrugh's colossal masterpiece*

polis of the Druids, the noblest lawn in the world fenced by half the horizon, and a mausoleum that would tempt one to be buried alive.' Laugh as
one may, at this eulogy, yet the same lucid pen could dip in fire to expose
the iniquity of slavery years before Hull gave birth to Wilberforce. . . .

The villages of Hovingham, Nunnington and Gilling, clustering around
the Malton-Helmsley road, B1257, have each a fine historic home to be
enjoyed. But my closing words, in this chapter, must be reserved for a
much smaller home, Shandy Hall at Coxwold, between Kilburn and
Byland. This house is to be opened as a Laurence Sterne museum.

Two hundred years ago every literary fan knew his *Tristram Shandy* inside out. The novel had taken English society by storm, raising its author
from the ranks of the poor country clergy to such a position that he could
soon afford to ride about in his own carriage. The Coxwold parsonage
where he wrote the last seven volumes of this most unparsonlike novel—
followed by *A Sentimental Journey* and *The Journal to Eliza*—might well have
come to be known as Sterne Cottage. Shandy Hall is much more appropriate. It suggests, truly, that the real Sterne became vocal through the
odd creatures of his off-beat mind.

Sterne came to live at Shandy Hall in 1760 when Lord Fauconberg of
neighbouring Newburgh Priory conferred on him the affluent Coxwold
living. In one of his letters he refers thus to his new home:

> 'Tis within a mile of his Lordship's seat and park. 'Tis a very agree-
> able ride out in the chaise I purchased for my wife. Lyd (his daughter)
> has a pony which she delights in. Whilst they take these diversions I am
> scribbling away at my *Tristram*. . . . My Lydia helps to copy for me, and
> my wife knits and listens as I read her chapters. . . .

Presumably, Mrs. Sterne no longer humoured herself as Queen of Bohemia.

Probably Tudor in origin, the house has several peculiarities, one being
a tiny, eye-like window in the huge chimney-stack. Sterne's study, to the
right of the entrance, remains the cosy, box-shaped room where one day
its owner would prepare a sermon, and the next a rollicking chapter or
two of *The Life and Opinions of Tristram Shandy*. Actually, both kinds of
writing had much in common. 'Sorrow is better than laughter—for a
crack'd brained order of Carthusian monks, I grant, but not for men of the
world.' That is how he began one of his sermons. If his congregation were
in his mind when he wrote the words, Uncle Toby was surely tugging at
his sleeve.

Personally, I can best visualise Sterne in the spacious kitchen. Here his long, lean frame had liberty to expand before a roaring fire, with all his characters about him. In *Tristram*, Sterne lavished most of his corkscrew wit on Uncle Toby—the old, pensioned-off soldier, and his faithful 'shadow' Corporal Trim who prepared military maps and designed imaginary fortifications for himself and his master to elaborate later. Here too, perhaps, Sterne planned that 'siege to the citadel of my Uncle Toby's heart' by the amorous Widow Wadman—and threw another squib at his *bête noire*, Dr. John Burton of York, caricatured in the novel as Dr. Slop.

The bedrooms are reached by a squat wooden staircase with queerly-shaped balusters that remind me, forcibly, of some of the curious scrawls and flourishes which punctuate Sterne's writings; notably, the blandishments of Trim's whip, which flicks down the full length of one page in the first edition of *Tristram*. Sterne's bedroom, a small chamber on the right, is fitted with a powder-closet. For his morning wash, Yorick (his nickname) stretched through a hatch in the wall of the powder-closet and drew a pail of water by pulling on an old well-rope in the adjoining room. On my last visit parts of this Heath Robinson contrivance were still to be seen.

Shandy Hall has other interesting features, but the beautiful old church over the way—a church with octagonal Perpendicular tower, three-decker pulpit, and the Fauconberg family tombs—shares the picture.

A letter of September 1761 preserved at Newburgh Priory refers to 'a new scheme of Mr. Sterne's' regarding the seating in the church. The scheme provided that those who approved of the Vicar 'can face him, and those who don't can face the other way'. I do not know how many parishioners switched their pews around, in consequence, but the whimsy illustrates perhaps better than anything else the personality of the curious individual whose eight years at Shandy Hall lifted the village from humble obscurity.

The peculiar merriment which animates a few of the ancient roof bosses in the church might have suited Sterne's outlook, but even he—with all his resources—could hardly have improved upon the situation suggested on a floor-brass in the nave. The brass records the death of Sir John Manston in 1464. His wife's name, Elizabeth, is added and a space is encouragingly left for the date of her death. The space is still blank after 500 years! John must be tired of waiting for her.

eleven

Holderness and the Wolds

'East Riding looketh to the Sunn-rising and the Ocean . . .'. So wrote William Camden, and 300 years have not blunted the poetry of his re-mark. John Evelyn was impressed by the rich 'fenny' country around Hull, while Michael Drayton—never at a loss—rhapsodised about Humber's 'fair-enamouréd Flood'. Drayton elaborates the theme on his companionable map. Rather ungallantly he plumps one of his shepherd-esses into a 'fenny' patch, to indicate its swampy nature, has a few cows grazing the cliff-top pastures, and then shows a rather surprised Neptune surfacing in the wide Humber estuary.

The time has come to let some sea breezes blow over the Yorkshire scene, but as the one hundred-mile-long coastline includes a few stretches of dis-tinctly limited appeal, the better places will be approached in a number of sorties from the hinterland.

On travelling from Selby to Hull, especially by train, one may get a geological thrill in the region of Hessle. Hereabouts, fragments of chalk cliff are to be seen—nearly twenty miles inland! They are relics of the original coastline, which ran north and north-east from this point via Beverley and Driffield to Sewerby, near Bridlington. The vast alluvial area designated Holderness—an area now embracing Hull and a host of inter-esting villages—was formulated and joined to the rest of Yorkshire by glacial action at the end of the Great Ice Age. 'Against these cliffs', wrote Frank Elgee, 'glaciers discharged their cargoes of clay and boulders, sand and gravel, and thus built up a new land of morainic mounds and ridges enclosing lakes and meres . . .' Hornsea Mere—Yorkshire's largest lake and a yachters' delight—is the only one of these lagoons to have survived. But another strange legacy of that embryonic period is Spurn Head.

Now a bird sanctuary under the control of the Yorkshire Naturalists' Trust, Spurn juts far out to sea and still oscillates with tides and current. The sea tries to push this narrow, shingly bar across Humber Mouth, but the Humber—mighty with the combined strength of most of the Dales' rivers—pushes in a contrary direction. Spurn is a strange, desolate region of sand-dunes and flats, where the tides may throw up old boots, a bit of tarpaulin, or a foundered box of oranges. None but lifeboatmen and their families, and the lighthouse crew, live here. It is a much more natural place of sojourn for beautiful wading birds like dunlin and turnstone, and the many other migrants.

Beverley is the best centre for this corner of Yorkshire, and its own attractions are many. For one thing it is almost surrounded by common pastures—a green belt of ancient origin. Conferred by Archbishop Neville in the time of Richard II, the Westwood-Hurn pasture comprises 640 acres and borders the roads from York, A1079, and Walkington, B1230, with delightful thickets and copses. Beverley's portion of the prehistoric range of low chalk cliffs runs somewhere beneath Westwood's billowing contours.

Of the medieval town little remains but the picturesque North Bar, and its two fine churches. Most of the traffic to and from the west and north has to filter, single-file, through the low brick arch of North Bar—and for years nobody has seemed to mind. Even the double-decker buses were equipped with a specially domed roof to negotiate that medieval arch. Doubtless, if one lived on the spot and heard some of the drivers' imprecations, the new by-pass that is planned would seem thoroughly justified.

This ancient gateway, which cost the town exactly £96 9s. 11½d. when rebuilt in 1409, leads into North Bar Within—a street of gracious Georgian houses tastefully aligned with the eighteenth-century Market Cross beyond and, gleaming afar, the venerable Minster. The late Fred W. Elwell, R.A., used to say, 'Where will you find a lovelier street in all England?' A few modern intrusions would have saddened him. He frequently received me into his old house adjoining North Bar and talked to such purpose that I began to observe Beverley through his eyes. Much of the town explains itself, given time and enthusiasm, but meeting a man who had lived most of his life with Beverley and its people, in and through his paintings, was like meeting an oracle.

Many of his local paintings were bequeathed to the town and can be enjoyed in the Public Art Gallery. One subject shows Beverley's 'last cabby' in North Bar Within. A fine study in its own right, it also recalls an incident about Elwell's father—a gifted woodcarver whose *magnum opus* was the organ screen in Beverley Minster. This old cabby was always called upon to take any of the Elwells to the railway station. One day, old James Elwell had a companion—the Archbishop of York. They were still discussing some projected piece of church work after being trundled in the cab to the station. Taking a bit of chalk from his pocket, the bearded woodcarver—who resembled one of Michelangelo's Sistine prophets—knelt on the platform and made some rough sketches on the flagstones, while his gaitered listener bent over in complete absorption. They apparently stayed thus until His Grace's train arrived.

James Elwell appeared in many of his son's paintings, now as Mayor of this ancient town, now as magistrate in a trial scene in Beverley's seventeenth-century Guildhall—a benevolent magistrate bestowing comfort on one in distress. Other studies include the old Mace Bearer, and the eighteenth-century kitchen in the 'Beverley Arms' Hotel with the maids at their 'elevenses'. Few if any aspects of Beverley can have escaped his brush and palette. To follow his leading, even today, brings much reward.

Beverley Minster is easily the finest Gothic church we have in Yorkshire. Sir Gilbert Scott, while once discussing the organ screen with James Elwell, went further, claiming that it was the finest in the world. In designing the Elwell screen, Scott the architect certainly entered into his kingdom, providing a goodly array of clustered columns, fan vaulting, and delicate vine trails, all surmounted by a galaxy of regal figures occupying crocketed niches. The design was based on the early sixteenth-century tabernacle work of the choir stalls, whose sixty-eight misericords run the whole gamut of burlesque and quaint homely fun.

Another lovely piece of Gothic is the canopy adorning the Percy tomb nearby. Lady Eleanor Percy would have no idea that her memory was to be garnished with such a hierarchy of angels and saints and knights in combat. She made little stir in her own generation; just a brief earthly sojourn of forty-two years, ending quietly in 1314. But she has created a sensation, almost ever since, because of this massive canopy with its impressive escort for her passage to Heaven.

A surprisingly harmonious progression, from Early English to Decorated and then to Perpendicular, characterises the Minster's sublime interior. Nowhere, perhaps, does the magnesian limestone glow with such purity as in the tall, Decorated nave. But every niche and statue benefits, too, so that—especially in the drifting sunlight—strange carvings are apt to 'leap' from the walls: the wimpled head of a queen, a man about to liberate his falcon, another man playing bagpipes. One set of label-stops in the north aisle can hardly be said to 'leap' into view, however; known as the medical set they represent all the anguish suggested by Stomach Ache, Toothache, Sciatica, and Lumbago.

One almost unique possession is the tread-wheel crane, in the roof. About fifteen feet diameter and three-and-a-half feet wide, it is operated by workmen walking on the inner circumference, on the principle of the old dog spit. The 'Catherine Wheel'—to use its local name—was introduced here early in the eighteenth century and still hoists building materials, as required, through a dummy boss in the crossing vault. Permission to view this curiosity is sometimes given. It is approached by a spiral stair in the south transept, and one then steps along some staging flanked on both sides by ancient buttresses—as odd in their way as the tread-wheel beyond, for they are contrived, not from stone, but from twisted tree-branches which in their bleached condition look quite ghostly in the comparative gloom.

Yet another curiosity is the sanctuary chair, or Frith Stool. It is cut out of the solid stone and may originally have been John of Beverley's episcopal seat, early in the eighth century. Two other such chairs exist—one at Hexham Priory, Northumberland, and one already noticed at Sprotborough Church, near Doncaster. The Beverley chair is the plainest of the three—a paragon of austerity. Could that be why King Athelstan, about the year 937, made it over for use as the sanctuary chair?

Anybody fleeing from justice could hardly object to sitting in this cold, unyielding seat while the church authorities decided what to do with him. He was usually given board and lodging for thirty days, then safe escort to the county boundary or the nearest place where he could find a boat to take him overseas. In any event, once reached, the chair guaranteed safety from pursuers. Placed near the high altar, it occupied the innermost sanctuary circle, which none dare violate. In 1877 a well discovered beside the chair was found to contain a number of items presumably dropped in, long before, by those claiming sanctuary, or by pilgrims. Shown in a glass case nearby, the votive offerings include a rowel, a crab's claw, four gold pins, some rosary beads, and a silver coin of Plantagenet times.

If the Minster had never been built, Beverley could still command high regard with St. Mary's—a very lovely church whose minarets and Perpendicular west window bring a foretaste of King's College Chapel to North Bar Within. Here again the magnesian limestone is seen to full advantage. It gives a soft radiance to the great Gothic interior. The creamy whiteness of the stone seems particularly apt in one of the animal carvings, for this little creature—in the north choir aisle—is supposed to have suggested the *White* Rabbit to Lewis Carroll during one of his visits to Beverley.

Another pleasant diversion is the group of five medieval minstrels carved high up on one nave pillar, near the pulpit. They represent the old Beverley Guild of Minstrels; three of their silver chains of office are now worn by the Mayor and Mayoress of this endlessly fascinating town.

With their passing, the waits or minstrels left a gap in the musical life of Beverley. Latterly, even bell-ringers have been in short supply—which explains why, only a few years ago, a taxi was kept in readiness to take the few available ringers with great speed across the town from the Minster to St. Mary's for their service a little later, on Sunday mornings. It was a typically Yorkshire way out of a difficulty.

To north and west the Yorkshire Wolds sweep back invitingly from Beverley, but there is still much to see in the flatter country bordering the Humber and the adjacent coast. Bishop Burton, two miles west of Beverley, centres upon a small mere that should—but does not quite—reflect its fine old church. As though bygone theological differences are forgotten this church now gives some prominence to a life-like bust, in elm-wood, of John Wesley in the act of preaching. The carving was originally set up, however, in the Wesleyan Chapel nearby. Subsequently, during renovations, it was found to be worm-eaten and propped temporarily beside the entrance door. When passing, later, the Vicar took pity on the outcast and offered thirty shillings for it. Afterwards he always twitted the 'Ranters' for having sold their master for thirty pieces of silver. A Beverley craftsman improved the occasion when submitting his bill to the Vicar for 'treating' the worm-ridden carving with oils, etc. His charge included a few shillings for 're-baptising John Wesley'.

The humour so often bound up with genuine devotion in these East Riding chapels is embodied again in a true story recalled not long ago by an old Methodist minister. During a rather protracted prayer-meeting one farmer got up and beseeched the Almighty's support for the Government, in these words: 'Lord, bless 'em. An' may they hang together in accord—and in concord—and in . . .'. During that fatal pause a fellow member of

27   The fourteenth-century Percy Tomb, Beverley Minster

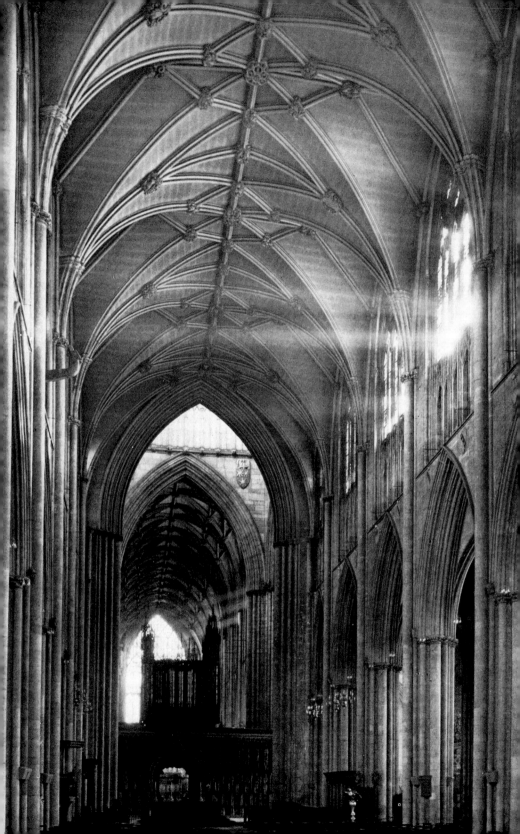

different political persuasion interjected, ' . . . onny sort o' cord, Lord, as long as Thoo dost 'ang 'em'.

Rowley, five miles south-west of Beverley, via Little Weighton, is a vestigial village; its church and the former rectory are the only visual reminders of the Rev. Ezekiel Rogers who migrated with his entire flock to America. They sailed from Hull in 1638, resolved to stand no more of the King's interference in religious matters and to start life afresh overseas—which they did, employing all their accustomed ways of building and agriculture. An American friend of mine who lives near Rowley, Mass., tells me that some of the first settlers' timber houses—equipped with oak beams, and open fireplaces with brick ovens—survived there until a few years ago. They faithfully reproduced the homes deserted for conscience' sake in the mother country.

Another of the East Riding's splendid churches is at Cottingham. Some good Georgian houses, notably Kingtree House, add their prestige nearby. Then, barely four miles away, the port of Hull looms into view. Some tourists profess to scorn Hull, but they must be ignorant of a manifold appeal that overrides industry. The docks—seven miles of them—are always of compelling interest, and the town itself has lovely public gardens, several buildings of exceptional worth, and some first-rate museums covering an amazing span of interest, from the Northern Whale Fishery to the work of Hull's bygone silversmiths.

Trinity House occupies a large, central site and fortunate are they who gain access to its fine range of buildings, mainly of the eighteenth and early nineteenth century. Because of its strong associations with Thomas Ferres, Trinity House is a place to keep firmly in mind until the Whitby countryside is reached.

Most of the town's eighteenth-century houses have been turned into offices; at several in High Street—once the opulent preserve of merchant princes—ledgers and bills of lading only half conceal the Adamesque swags and scrolls of a former day. During the last war I photographed dozens of these survivals for the National Buildings Record. The blitz had already destroyed much High Street property, but in one commercial building*—formerly owned by the Maister family—it was and still is possible to mount a glorious Palladian staircase and be gazed upon by a sculptured figure of Ceres, the work of Sir Henry Cheere. She is gazed upon, in turn, by the philosopher, Locke, for a plaque bears his meditative image on the landing, just opposite.

* Acquired by the National Trust in 1966.

28 *The Gothic nave, York Minster*

Hull has long been a touchstone in the realms of culture and ideas, as well as commerce. In the person of William Wilberforce it played a momentous part in the abolition of slavery. The impressive Elizabethan house that bears the Wilberforce name, in High Street, was his birthplace. Today it is a museum devoted—as was the great-hearted though rather foppish statesman it chiefly commemorates—to the Abolition cause. Nowhere else in England can the full weight of the evil he and his supporters overcame be properly gauged. Wilberforce House registers the conscience of mankind.

It would have been fitting had Wilberforce's private carriage come to rest here, along with his books and his diary and his favourite Chippendale chair. But the *period* of such elegant travel is abundantly represented in the Transport Museum, a few yards farther along High Street. There are resplendent coaches once used by local families, and many curiosities—from the kind of Velocipede or bicycle Charles Dickens used, to an early steam car bonneted like an old lady and described as an *Automobile à Vapeur*.

For sheer bravura, however, the laurel must go to a remarkable sleigh from Nunburnholme, on the western slope of the Wolds. The Nunburnholme estate has witnessed many notable events, but surely nothing half as spectacular as Lady Chesterfield tucked into the shell-seat of this sleigh, with its ornamental swan and unicorn reared up in front of her as if to augment the efforts of a gaily caparisoned horse still further in front. Bells jingled all around as she thus glided over the snow. This Russian outfit was actually seen in Hull market—twenty miles away—early in the present century. It must have seemed like a visit from Fairyland.

Holderness may be flat and its cliffs of the dull, boulder-clay variety, but the eastward road from Hull, A1033, provides compensations like Hedon, one of the oldest boroughs in England with a church—the 'King of Holderness'—to match its antiquity. Close by, on Humberside, the tiny village of Paull should be seen; it looks across the great, glistening path of maritime romance to Lincolnshire and has a short promenade. Amongst some quaint Dutch cottages, Patrington—seven or eight miles beyond— enthrones a fourteenth-century church of such beauty that one readily defers to it as the 'Queen of Holderness'. This 'queen' gets far too few admirers. The tower and spire are superb; so are the nave arcades, the south transept, and the Easter Sepulchre.

The sea is continually encroaching hereabouts. It would be a major calamity if the thieving waves ever attacked Patrington. Three miles separate the village from the coast, however, and the average rate of erosion locally is two yards per year. By this reckoning Patrington would seem to be safe for 2,000 years at least. But the sea is under no obligation to abide by statistics. My old acquaintance, Tom Sheppard of Hull, once wrote a grimly factual book entitled *The Lost Towns of the Yorkshire Coast*. Ravenserodd was one of them. In 1350 it was a flourishing port. By 1400 the sea had removed almost every trace, along with Ravenspurn. One survival was a sculptured cross that had been erected nearby to mark the landing of Henry Bolingbroke in 1399. It now stands in the grounds of Holyrood House, at Hedon—an object of wonder, perhaps, for the old people who have come to spend their last years beside this 'waif' of the seas.

All flotsam and jetsam along the Holderness coast belongs by ancient right to the Constable family of Burton Constable. In practice, this means little today; the late Brigadier Chichester-Constable—forty-sixth Lord Paramount of the Seigniory of Holderness—once told me that, in fact, his high-sounding rank had its disadvantages. 'I have to pay', he said somewhat ruefully, 'for burying or otherwise disposing of any whale grounded on the Holderness shore—and it costs about £20 a time!' One whale washed up in 1821 was carted along to Burton Constable and displayed in the grounds. In *Moby Dick* Herman Melville relates that visitors made such sport of the skeleton that locks had to be affixed to the articulated parts; afterwards people could only step inside its cavernous jaws when the footman was in attendance with his keys.

The whale's skeleton offers no scope for would-be Jonahs today, but much else demands an audience at this magnificent place, so recently opened to the public. The great brick mansion stands well back from the coast and is most easily reached via Hedon and Sproatley.

Tradition assigns part of the hall to the reign of King Stephen (1135–1154). Stephen's Tower, overlooking the east forecourt, echoes the tradition without supplying any real architectural evidence of such an early origin. Medieval work there may be, in this antiquated corner, yet even the Tudor building attributed to Sir John Constable, about 1570, was effectively masked in the eighteenth century when the entire house was re-modelled on Jacobean lines. Despite this seeming anachronism, the owners kept abreast of their times by employing eminent Georgian architects and craftsmen. The result is wholly satisfying.

'Capability' Brown laid out the spacious grounds with fine clumps of trees, seventeen acres of lake—and a pantheon of statuary presumably inspired by that at Versailles. Indoors, there is a range of state rooms,

splendid and awesome, yet calculated to set off a number of social 'hares'
—the legitimist King of France, Louis XVIII, living here in exile after
the Revolution, for example, or young Roger Tichborne, who spent
Christmas at Burton Constable in 1847.

One can readily imagine this observant youth—heir to a baronetcy and
a fortune—taking breakfast with Sir Clifford Constable among the French
Empire furniture of the Blue Drawing Room; basking in the splendour of
the Red Drawing Room, with its overmantel from the Doge's Palace at
Venice; peering up by candlelight at the portraits in the Long Gallery—
wonderful portraits including Zucchero's Mary Queen of Scots, and two
Holbeins—Thomas Cromwell and Chancellor Thomas More. The odd
thing is that when the Tichborne Claimant turned up, years later, his
detailed 'memories' of Burton Constable and its family life convinced Sir
Clifford Constable, at first, that he was indeed the Roger whom he had
once entertained—the pleasant, friendly youth lost soon after at sea. . . .
Subsequently appearing from Australia, as the missing heir, the Claimant
touched off one of the most famous lawsuits of Victorian times. Its repercussions, here, are as unexpected—as the dragons!

These dragons have the run of the Chinese Room. Hung with hand-
painted Chinese paper, the walls reach up to a dainty cornice fringed with
real bells to simulate oriental eaves. For contrast, a Chinese lantern is held
from the ceiling by a nightmarish dragon gleaming like polished steel.
Equally ferocious dragons claw the window jambs, and all around baby
dragons glower in mock hostility. Challenged by this grotesque decoration—which antedates the Prince Regent's corresponding extravaganza
in Brighton Pavilion—Thomas Chippendale had a holiday from the furniture ordered for the Long Gallery and designed a Dragon Chair for this
Chinese Room. Evil-looking monsters are its dominant motif. The chair
would have suited a Ming emperor.

Driffield has a picturesque waterway that links the town with 'the coun-
tery of Holderness', as Leland called it, via the River Hull. Being a chalk
stream in these upper reaches the Hull is also renowned for its trout, as
amusingly testified by the waterside inn at Wansford Bridge; the inn sign
is a nice fat trout served up on a platter.

But the chalk Wolds may well exercise a greater pull. Their highest
point, at the top of Garrowby Hill, is only 808 feet, yet the contours are
often dramatic, as where the Driffield-Pocklington road, B1246, sweeps
grandly past Warter Priory, or where the northbound road from Sled-

mere, B1253, plunges past some fine tree-clad slopes towards the Derwent Valley above Malton. The moods of the Wold country change swiftly too. One February day at the foot of Garrowby, some friends and I saw no sign of winter, save the swollen river. But the upland lane to Thixendale, four or five miles to the north-east, was practically snow-bound, and the views were Alpine in quality if not in immensity.

On driving through the Wolds, in any direction, one suddenly comes upon little villages cupped in natural hollows, and mysterious entrench-ments carved out by tribesfolk of long ago. A westering sun enhances the sometimes eerie effect of these depressions. Winifred Holtby loved them. In a letter to Vera Brittain, her friend and future biographer, she wrote of the old familiar roads around Rudston, her birthplace: 'Part of me seems to fit into their hills and hollows as one does into a familiar and well-hollowed bed.'

The very names of these Wold villages ring with invitation. Bishop Wilton, Great Givendale, Warter, Thixendale, and Kirby Underdale are just a few near Garrowby Hall, which hides among the trees beside A166. Farther south, Middleton-on-the-Wolds groups its cottages around a thirteenth-century church. But I have a special fondness for the Wold country rising and dipping like a bird, around Sledmere, to the north of Driffield.

Before 1771 the Wolds generally were a barren tract of country only lately delivered from wolves and supporting little but sheep. During the next thirty years, however, Sir Christopher Sykes of Sledmere and his son, Tatton, transformed vast areas of the Wolds into 'one of the most produc-tive and best cultivated districts in the County of York'. The quotation is taken from a memorial in Sledmere village, but testimonies to this remark-able family are legion hereabouts. Several of the Wolds churches were built or restored by them. Some of the trees they planted now ride like argosies over the hill-tops. Rudston House, with its farming estate of 940 acres, is a result of the policy of improvement and cultivation which the Sykes family initiated and inspired amongst other landowners. It was the Rudston countryside that Winifred Holtby knew best.

Before looking any closer at Rudston, however, one should visit this elevated village of Sledmere—B1252 from near Driffield—and enjoy its urbane atmosphere. If Sledmere seems to have dropped more or less whole from some classical sky, it is because different generations of the Sykes family have cooperated to make it their elysium. Tritons blowing their horns—obviously on parole from the family crest—provide a curious fanfare from gates, pillars and village inn. An elegant domed rotunda covers the village well. A remarkably fine copy of an Eleanor Cross, designed and executed by Temple Moore, stands opposite the church gates. The church itself shifts the time-scale somewhat, for it was the 5th Baronet's attempt —nobly carried through by Temple Moore—to reproduce the building as it had been in the fourteenth century.

And then, across the Park, Sledmere House comes into view—a fine Georgian mansion thoroughly fulfilling the good wishes expressed by Lord Robert Manners, M.P. for Hull, when he wrote to Richard Sykes in the 1750s: 'Till Sledmere is quite completed, the delight you take in that pretty place, I dare, say, will not let you stop your hand, but afford you daily employment and the most delightful amusement. . . .'

The 'pretty place' was to be improved, in 1776, by Christopher Sykes. A beautiful Romney of Sir Christopher and his wife, Elizabeth Tatton, takes pride of venue in the Music Room.

But how can anybody briefly convey the magic of Sledmere House and its far-flung grounds? Great names echo around the place—'Capability' Brown who landscaped the Park, for example, and, indoors, Joseph Rose, the stuccoist, who provided some glorious ceilings and friezes. One frieze—in the Staircase Hall—is a comical procession of tritons and elephants. Much of the furniture was made by John Robbins, the London cabinet-maker, but Chippendale is here, too, with an impressive set of chairs in his Chinese style and a 'Chinese' bed with little carved parasols above the cresting. In the book-lined Library, one hundred feet long, even a devoted bibliophile could hardly keep his gaze from roaming over the sumptuous furnishings and the great domed roof.

Other great names are family ones. Sir Christopher has already been mentioned. His son, the first Sir Tatton, now 'retires' to a shadowy corner of the Drawing Room, but this fine portrait by Sir Francis Grant shows him on one of his beloved horses; a memorable, stately figure who caused one admirer to say that the three things most worth seeing in the county were 'York Minster, Fountains Abbey—and t' owd Squire o' Sledmere'.

Sir Mark Sykes, 6th Baronet, carried the heritage forward into the present century, though his 'memorial', here, takes the astonishing form of a Turkish Room. Its strange, tiled decoration in exotic colourings signifies his reputation as an orientalist—a reputation freely drawn upon by the British Government during the 1914–18 War. In this room there is a tin box containing the 'Sledmere Papers' relating to many of his missions to the Middle East. One document shows that he was the moving spirit behind the negotiations which turned an obscure T. E. Lawrence into Lawrence of Arabia.

When Sir Richard Sykes, the current owner, plays classical pieces on the eighteenth-century organ for Sunday afternoon visitors, Sledmere comes fully into its own; past and present are fused into a gracious, satisfying harmony.

A white riband of road that crests the Wolds as they billow towards the coast provides the best, the most tuneful approach to Rudston. 'Wod Yat' the natives call this soaring track. There is nothing to drown the bird song from its teeming hedges. A whole day might pass without the intrusion of a single car, for Wold Gate—first cut into the chalk by the Romans—is a deserted highway. It is joined just outside Bridlington or, inland, at Kilham.

Rudston has spelt home for Briton, Dane and Roman. The megalith known as the Rud Stone in the churchyard testifies to its extremely ancient lineage. Most of the village spreads out below the church, and on the western edge—backed by a glorious flourish of Wold country— stands the detached villa where Winifred Holtby was born on 23 June 1898.

Here, as time went on, she would surreptitiously pore over *Jane Eyre*, hiding it under her pillow at night, as the book was then considered 'dangerous' for a young girl. She and her sister wrote excoriating tragedies, such as *Griselda's Vow*, *The Highwayman's Curse*, and *A Living Lie*, and then performed them in the great farm kitchen, always contriving 'to strew the stage plentifully with corpses. . . .'

In the garden there is a small, fairy-like dell with a bubbling spring— one of the feeders of the Gypsey Race which flows through the village. For generations superstitious villagers have called this stream and its tributaries the Woe Waters, for when they appear in spate some national disaster is said to be imminent. Winifred Holtby was in the Upper Fifth at St. Margaret's School, Scarborough, when her mother noticed the garden spring gush forth after a long period of quiescence. The First World War began later that year! The spring became active again just prior to the General Strike of 1926. But so many national crises have occurred since then that even the Woe Waters must find it difficult to keep pace!

At Burton Fleming, three miles north of Rudston, children formerly went out with gifts to placate the Gypsey Race as it flowed by. Daughter of a later age, Winifred Holtby used her gifts to better purpose, as her books and other writings show. The Woe Waters thread and sometimes swamp her native countryside, as strife and calamity raise their heads in *South Riding* and *The Land of Green Ginger*. Yet the Wolds always gave her unbounded joy, and doubtless she found impish pleasure—as others have done—when the Gypsey Race appeared in flood without *any* dire consequences.

The Gypsey Race takes a serpentine course through the Thorpe Hall estate—Rudston home of the Macdonalds of the Isles, then through the grounds of Boynton Hall, eventually flowing into the sea at Bridlington—the 'Hardrascliffe' of *South Riding*. Other places in this story, which crowned her all too brief career, are Hornsea and Withernsea as 'Kiplington', Hull as 'Kingsport', the River Humber as the 'Leame', and Beverley as 'Flintonbridge'. Hull had already given her the title, *Land of Green Ginger;* it is a street-name, off Whitefriargate, signifying the place where a bygone tradeswoman plied her customers with a sweetmeat called green ginger.

Rudston became the 'Anderby' of so many of her stories. It is always a pleasure to meet somebody in the neighbourhood who knew David and Alice Holtby's 'golden-haired lass'. For me one such encounter came when I had cycled over to see the Roman villa. This was unearthed at Breeze Farm in 1933, causing a special flutter amongst archaeologists as such villas were comparatively rare in the north.

Henry Robson, a friend of the Holtbys and then owner of Breeze Farm, told me that he had intended sowing some late wheat that April afternoon, but when his ploughshare uncovered a few tesserae he abandoned the plough for a spade. His workmen cast contemptuous eyes on the 'bits o' chalk' he was eagerly disclosing, but Robson knew the historical significance of those small coloured cubes.

At length, two tessellated pavements—one showing a none-too-modest Venus—lay revealed, and the remains of a hypocaust. Other discoveries followed, notably a little workshop-floor still heaped with tesserae for future use. Winifred Holtby had often raced over the surrounding country on one of her father's mares. By 1933, however, she was no longer the tomboy of Robson's early remembrance, but an imaginative writer. Robson turned his Roman villa into a showplace; the authoress came over and made it the basis of an exciting story, *Pavements at Anderby*, with old Henry Robson as Ted Burroughs.

In 1963 the pavements were rolled up like carpets—after appropriate

29   A Georgian facade at Sledmere House, on the Wolds

fixative treatment—and transferred to Hull Transport Museum, where they re-tell their ancient tale near a similar pavement from Harpham, five miles south of Rudston.

Only two years after *Pavements at Anderby* appeared, friends, villagers and literary celebrities gathered to see Winifred Holtby laid to rest in Rudston churchyard. At the head of her grave there is a marble book— only half its pages turned—bearing the inscription:

> *God give me work till my life shall end*
> *And life till my work is done.*

She had lived thirty-seven years—an even shorter span than Charlotte Brontë's, over at Haworth—yet Winifred, too, had found time to write immortal stories, and also to champion the causes of 'black' Africa and World Peace.

At first sight Bridlington may seem to offer little but the popular forms of seaside amusement. The Old Town, however, is a place almost apart, with its splendid Priory Church, approached through the picturesque Bayle Gate, and a lovely sweep of Georgian houses and shops in High Street, though these are slowly being ousted by modern, tasteless anachronisms.

Bridlington has also suffered badly from that other kind of onslaught— coast erosion, the annual loss increasing from two yards in the early nineteenth century to as much as five yards by 1872! And yet, within a couple of miles of Bridlington harbour, the friable coastal clays suddenly give place to the durable chalk. Flamborough headland is the chalk's first dramatic gesture.

The whole Flamborough peninsula is worth exploring, but North Landing and Silex Bay are of outstanding merit. Along the entire Yorkshire coast there is nothing to equal the thrill of visiting the North Landing caves by fisherman's coble. It is another world, down here at the foot of lofty chalk cliffs—the world of bygone smugglers, and wreckers and just ordinary seamen, but how the boatmen make their various exploits ring in return for the few shillings spent on the trip!

Because of ancient Scandinavian associations, Flamborough was long known as Little Denmark; a philologist would still find pleasure in the old place-names. Several years ago some 'furriners' who came to live in new houses erected near the lighthouse objected to Stottle Bink being part of their address. Couldn't it be changed to something more pleasing? But

30. Late-Elizabethan architecture: Burton Agnes Hall, near Driffield

Stottle Bink has survived the little rumpus, as befits the old name for a rock-shelf supporting a Danish look-out station.

One could hardly expect to see a country house along these rather bleak, wind-swept chalk cliffs. Now Burton Agnes Hall, with its carvings in wood, stone and alabaster, would satisfy the most fastidious person, but that Elizabethan mansion is five miles inland, along the Driffield road. There is one cliff-top house, however, which does arrest the eye while driving between Bempton and Speeton, along B1229. It is Buckton Hall. Seventy-year-old John Robinson evidently wished his house to be an architectural 'echo' of the tall Buckton cliffs, so he built it of the very same material. And there it has stood since 1745, not large but very impressive because its white walls soar above the flat adjacent fields as the cliffs themselves do above the rolling expanse of sea. Robinson also echoed the sea indoors, with shells, fish and other marine motifs, but a disastrous fire in 1922 destroyed the whole interior.

Camping sites and rashes of selfishly sited bungalows are gradually spoiling parts of this otherwise glorious coastline. In their pursuit of natural beauty, many people are destroying the very boon they seek. Let us hope the National Trust can acquire, while there is yet time, many of the bays and headlands that have made the north Yorkshire coast memorable for so long.

I should imagine Filey Brigg to be proof against despoilers. An outcrop of oolitic rock forming a natural pier that is awash at high tide could hardly 'invite' a row of villas, or a holiday camp. But no kind of erection should be allowed to encroach upon Carr Naze either. This bold cliff leads steeply down to the Brigg and—round the corner—to a set of coves whose whimsical names convey no idea of their real fascination.

Here as elsewhere in Britain, only constant vigilance and a ready outspokenness will preserve our national heritage. This particular area had one great stalwart in Canon A. N. Cooper, the Walking Parson. He was Vicar of Filey's lovely old church in the 1920s. With knapsack on his broad shoulders, he tramped for miles through his beloved countryside, talked to its people, delved into its history—and then wrote several informative books that should shame anybody who might have thoughtless or selfish designs on some treasured part of the East Riding landscape. We could do with more parsons of the same breed. It was not to this situation at all, however, that one of the Filey church gravestones refers. Of the woman buried there one reads this epitaph: 'She being dead yet speaketh'. Her name, oddly enough, was Susannah Naggs.

twelve

North-east Moors and Coast

Beyond Filey one enters the North Riding, famous for its oolitic hills and cliffs, and its glorious heather moors.

With Pickering as a centre, delightful countryside opens out in most directions. The southbound road to Malton, A169, is flat and featureless because it crosses the old Lake of Pickering, formed in glacial times. At Kirby Misperton, however, the lake area has found new aquatic life in the flamingoes and pelicans and other water-loving birds which offset a goodly collection of wild animals at Flamingo Park. The nucleus of this zoo is Kirby Misperton Hall, a late eighteenth-century house which overlooks a rectory—now part of the same estate—built about the corresponding time with stone from Rievaulx Abbey.

The Lake, or Vale of Pickering—once about three times the size of Windermere—is encircled today by the main roads linking Scarborough, Pickering, Helmsley, Malton, Ganton and Filey—a great elongated loop reaching from the eastern flanks of the Hambleton Hills to the coast. Most of the vale lies less than one hundred feet above sea-level, and its own hills—mere humps some 130–230 feet high—carry several little villages that recall the lake-dwellings of remote times. Even today any flooding of this vast agricultural arena tends to make places like Great Edstone and Normanby into islands.

Any tour of the vale rightly begins at Pickering itself—a small market town that has weathered 1,200 years of recorded history and has something to show from Norman times onwards. The oldest existing monument is the castle, whose broken walls command fine views over the vale's sweeping carpet of spangled green. A little ground mist, however, can make the whole area resemble the lake it once cradled. There is Norman work, also, in the Parish Church, but the chief attraction here is the remarkably fine set of medieval wall-paintings. Of the various saints and martyrs they graphically portray, the larger-than-life-size figure of St. Christopher seems particularly appropriate. He is carrying the Christ child through some waters that readily suggest the neighbouring lake of olden times.

Two miles east of Pickering along the old lake margin, via A170, Thornton Beck prattles through the village streets of Thornton-le-dale. This place has long endured the consequences—in terms of coach-loads of trippers and ice-cream vans—of being acclaimed Yorkshire's prettiest village. Its undoubted charm is mostly reserved for quiet days. At Ebberston, four miles farther east, a small beck tumbling through a steep limestone gorge determined the character of Ebberston Hall. This Lilliputian house—a pocket edition of Castle Howard—was designed by Colin Campbell in 1718 as a hunting lodge for William Thompson, M.P. for Scarborough. After cascading through an ornamental canal, the beck was directed beneath the house and thence, via a double canal, through the rest of the grounds. Because of damp chills that threatened rheumatism to everybody concerned, the scheme had to be modified later. Squire Osbaldeston had his own way of explaining the situation. Even the trout, he averred, found the water here too cold for them to reach a plumpness that would tempt his angling friends.

Osbaldeston, a renowned sportsman of the nineteenth century, was the odd individual who called himself the 'Squire of England', yet while he lived here he frittered away his fortune and would often take some of his furniture to the village inn to raise a 'fiver'. Something of his oddity was reflected in the names of his famous hunters; among them were Georgius Sidus—a neat reference to his penchant for hunting by moonlight, and the Devil Among the Tailors. He claimed that his black-and-white hound, Vaulter, was well behaved because it had once swallowed his wife's prayer-book. I like to think of the hound and his master peering inside the coach-house, where the half-crown visitors now take tea.

Another rewarding place at this eastern extremity of the vale is Brompton village, where Sir George Cayley (1773–1857) experimented with his pioneer aircraft. In 1928 his notebook and other biographical matter turned up at Brompton Hall, the family's ancestral home. Now preserved in Scarborough Public Library, they are an invaluable guide to the section devoted to Cayley and his discoveries in Scarborough Museum. But

Cayley's experiments inevitably bring one back to this village, and in particular to a square, detached workshop that still stands corner-wise to the main road. It was here that Squire Cayley made his 'ornithopter' and other aerial contraptions. In a steeply sloping field nearby—Cayley's trial ground—his coachman once stepped from the wreckage of the world's first glider, and expostulated, 'Please, Sir George, I wish to give notice; I was hired to *drive*, not to *fly*.' Obviously, he did not relish acting as 'guinea pig', and had no wish to qualify for such a poem as the versatile Cayley once wrote, entitled 'Epitaph to an Old Servant'.

A few days before Christmas 1857 the man now generally acclaimed as the 'father of aviation' was buried in Brompton Church—the same village sanctuary which had witnessed the marriage of William Wordsworth to Mary Hutchinson, of Gallows Hill nearby, fifty-five years earlier.

West of Pickering the vale broadens considerably, and the encroaching limestone hills emphasise its flat, alluvial character. Kirkby Moorside is suitably ancient, but history assumes a very different pattern at Kirkdale, one mile away, for in this thickly wooded ravine—by-passed by the main road—two narrow slits in a quarry face mark the cave accidentally discovered in 1821 and excavated the same year, with startling scientific results, by Professor Buckland of Oxford.

Beneath twelve inches of alluvium from the old lake he found the bones of several creatures, including elephant, rhinoceros, lion, tiger, wild boar, deer, bear and hippopotamus, together with the remains of nearly 300 hyenas. Although the cave is about a hundred feet long, its entrance is no more than three feet high, proving that no large animal could have gone in or out. Dr. Buckland concluded that it was a den where the hyenas dragged their spoil. It is an eerie spot—despite the dancing anemones nearby.

After crossing Hodge Beck one sees, in the same wooded setting, the small St. Gregory's Minster. It evokes a picture of some hermit voluntarily immured in the wilderness, for the church stands entirely alone. Not even a cottage is in sight. Harry Stammers's window showing St. Cuthbert with some of his animal friends—his horse, and the otters that dried his feet after his long, prayerful vigils standing in water—seems peculiarly apt in this withdrawn place, where no sound breaks the silence but bird song and the soughing of the trees.

When Bede referred to Cedd's founding of a monastery 'among craggy and distant mountains, which looked more like . . . retreats for wild beasts, than habitations for men', he little knew how well his description fitted the vicinity of Kirkdale Cave—that is, if he really meant this place. Historians still differ as to whether Cedd's monastery was indeed established here, or at Lastingham nearby. Whichever it was, the monastery in question is thought to have been erected to commemorate the degree of Christian unity achieved at the famous Synod of Whitby in A.D. 664, when—amongst other matters—the date of Easter was fixed. One suggested solution to the location puzzle is that the original site of the monastery placed by Bede at 'Lestingau', might have been here at Kirkdale, but that because of subsequent Danish raids the monks took their place-name with them and moved into the comparative safety of the neighbouring hills, building afresh at Lastingham. Both of the two existing churches—Lastingham and Kirkdale—possess architectural features that excite the imagination. Lastingham's apsidal crypt—built in 1088 and therefore older than Rievaulx and Fountains—is a complete church in itself, with chancel, nave and two rudimentary aisles, providing an atmosphere like that of the catacombs for its occasional services. Its Norman vault inspired the lovely nineteenth-century one, by J. L. Pearson, in the main sanctuary above.

The outstanding attraction at St. Gregory's Minster is the Saxon sundial over the south door. 'Tosti'—in the sundial's long inscription—was Tostig, who became Earl of Northumberland in 1055 and fell at the Battle of Stamford Bridge eleven years later. This sundial therefore dates the church fairly precisely and supplies an incidental link with the battle fought out around the River Derwent—at Stamford Bridge—after its emergence from the Vale of Pickering via Old Malton and Kirkham Abbey.

The western and southern margins of the vale link together a succession of attractive villages, including Oswaldkirk, Stonegrave, Nunnington, Hovingham and Slingsby. Some of them were mentioned in a previous chapter, but the northern margin—between Helmsley and Pickering—opens up fresh country, wilder country scoured by dales that reach back into the Cleveland Hills.

From Helmsley—where there is a fine, spacious market place—Bilsdale takes the Stokesley road, B1257, through twenty miles of grand moorland once pestered with boggarts and witches. From Kirkby Moorside there is a choice of good by-roads—and footpaths—into Farndale, the valley that is clothed every spring with daffodils. It is an incredibly lovely sight—five miles of daffodils following every caprice of the River Dove and reaching up the steep banks in nodding, golden cohorts. A temporary one-way traffic system has to be organised for visitors. Yet Farndale is a threatened valley. As Hull's supply of water from natural underground reservoirs in the surrounding chalk falls short of modern requirements, Farndale—fifty miles away—seems doomed to pay the penalty and become another impounded area. Or will some alternative scheme be found in time? The threat has been hanging over the valley for many years. Need it fall? The cost of one or two Early Warning Stations—like that on Fyling-dales Moor, not far ahead—would go a long way towards financing some determined effort to desalinate our bountiful supplies of sea-water, on a national scale. Incidentally, some of the men famous in Whitby's maritime story discovered methods of converting salt water into fresh, drinking water nearly 200 years ago!

The finest view of lower Farndale—gained from the hill-top beside Gillamoor Church—caused somebody to inscribe on the churchyard wall one of John Keble's verses:

> Thou who hast given me eyes to see
> And love this sight so fair,
> Give me a heart to find out Thee,
> And read Thee everywhere.

It is impossible to stand at this corner and remain unaffected. Every season paints its own glory; and down amongst the overlapping hills to the right, Hutton-le-Hole and Lastingham await discovery. I cannot imagine anything mean or sordid surviving the beauty and quiet joy of these two villages—one a piece of moorland 'tamed' by tiny bridges and flower-decked cottages, the other with all the profundity of its thousand years. And yet, even as I write, a very real bogy has appeared—a plan that would violate National Park principles and every fine feeling by making Hutton-le-Hole's charming thoroughfare into part of a commercial highway for heavy lorries. Oh, for a dozen vociferous Ruskins!

Lastingham offers a convenient road link with Rosedale, whose small river, the Seven, rises on Westerdale Moor, near White Cross, and joins the Vale of Pickering twelve miles south at Sinnington. Rosedale Abbey, founded by Robert de Stuteville about 1190 for Benedictine nuns, was savagely attacked by the Scots in 1322, and the nuns fled. The Abbey buildings were also dispersed, gradually. Today, one's best chance of re-capturing the past here is to step into the present village church which occupies the site of the nuns' church, and to search amongst the surrounding cottages for evidence of that dispersal in fragments of carved masonry.

Near the churchyard a newel stairway, ending abruptly, stands isolated and forlorn. A different monastic memory is recalled by Rosedale Chimney, 1,000 feet above sea-level on Bank Top. The chimney is not particularly old, being a survival of a nineteenth-century iron-mining enterprise, but the iron itself was once worked by the monks of Byland Abbey.

Yet another of the valleys whose rivers once fed the Lake of Pickering is Newton Dale. The Pickering-Whitby railway line runs through the dale's long succession of deep, twisting gorges—but alas, the service which provided one of the best train rides in England, and a vital link with Whitby, has been withdrawn for the sake of a national policy which has here sacrificed human need to one-sided economy.

Newton Dale is flanked by two roads—one skirting a Roman road known as Wade's Causeway, near Wheeldale Lodge, over to the west; the other being the main Pickering-Whitby highway, A169—grand, exhilarating, elemental. Only the sheep that perpetually graze the verges remain un-impressed. Its chief natural landmark, the Hole of Horcum, looks as though it had been scooped out of the oolite by some superhuman agency. According to one of the legends that take on a certain persuasiveness around this fantastic place, the Hole of Horcum was fashioned, single-handed, by Giant Wade. If anybody casts doubt on the notion, they should be reminded that carving Horcum out of the hillside was only one of the giant's triumphs, though he sometimes had assistance. Did not he and his equally resourceful wife build Pickering Castle and Mulgrave Castle, near Whitby, between them—he in one place and she in the other, tossing their one and only hammer as required over the intervening twenty miles?

A future generation might even invent tales about the Early Warning Station nearby, pointing to its great radomes as Giant Wade's golf-balls! Conversely, the huge white spheres—which many people already regard as White Elephants—look like something dropped from Outer Space.

Even at Saltergate Inn, a short way beyond Horcum, there is an air of fantasy—due, in part, to its turf fire kept burning over 200 years lest a certain ghost 'imprisoned' beneath the hearth be set free to plague the household again. The smugglers who once consorted here were, how-ever, solid enough—except when they had to 'evaporate' for safety reasons. They chiefly plied across the lonely peat moors between Salter-gate and Robin Hood's Bay, but other moorland paths now beckon— paths heading south-east from the Saltergate area and linking up with a lovely network of miniature dales around Hackness, Silpho and Broxa.

Monks and nuns from St. Hilda's Abbey at Whitby once trod those same

31   Lastingham: the nineteenth-century church

moors, doubtless using some of the wayside crosses that still stand among the heather to guide them aright to their small daughter monastery at Hackness. The monastery's only survival is an Anglian cross in Hackness Church.

By car, one can reach the same beautiful area via the Forest Ride that penetrates the Allerston conifer plantations, north of Ebberston on A170; or by continuing along the same main road to West Ayton, here turning left for Forge Valley. From Hackness village a road through steep, hanging woods brings one in fine style to the threshold of Scarborough.

Scarborough's great appeal as a holiday resort—one of the finest in Britain—is due very largely to its geological character, formulated millions of years ago, almost as if in anticipation of future events. Huge knobbly cliffs, with a central oolitic headland that separates two wide bays—out of this matrix has come the Scarborough to which so many admirers return for their holidays year after year.

Dinosaurs left their imprints hereabouts. In the local Natural History Museum at Wood End, a geological relief map shows just where they have been found, mostly in recent years. Succeeding sessions of Time planted a Roman signal station, then a Norman castle on that bulky headland; developed a picturesque harbour in the cruck of the south bay; clothed the cliffs with magnificent public gardens—and created an annual Cricket Festival, in September, which brings some of the world's best players to a sports ground almost within hitting distance of the crisp, curling waves of the north bay.

Thorgils, the Scandinavian prince who settled here about A.D. 966; Richard III, who nourished a 'special affection' for the old port of Scardeburgh; Ann Farrow, whose discovery of the town's spa waters in 1626 first attracted the *élite*; Mr. Aislabie, Mayor in 1688, who was publicly tossed in a blanket for having 'caned' the minister of St. Mary's Church during divine service; Sir John Coade battling with the sea in an attempt to build the Marine Drive round the base of Castle Hill; Len Hutton or Brian Close belting some weary bowler for six after six. Add a few pirates and smugglers for colour; George Fox suffering gladly in the castle dungeon; the Sitwell family amongst their exotic birds in the house that has become the Natural History Museum; a few early twentieth-century bathing zealots entering the waves from cumbrous, horse-drawn vans; music-lovers torn between Scarlatti and the thundering sea at the spa concert hall; children playing Treasure Island at the Mere, with a

32   Runswick Bay: the sea wall

three-masted schooner for their imaginary voyages; old, guernsey-clad fishermen basking reminiscently in the sun. . . .

Such is the Scarborough I know and love.

Yet some of the old narrow streets beside the harbour are doomed. If these were among the streets that a certain Georgian letter-writer had in mind when he declared them to be 'very spacious, so that Coaches pass and re-pass without any Difficulty or Inconvenience', he must have been akin to Sydney Smith's York acquaintance; when somebody growled at the narrowness of one street, this coachman retorted, 'Why, there's plenty of room to pass—at least an inch to spare on each side.'

I shall be sorry for the eclipse of Quay Street, once beloved of smugglers—and artists, but future town development will probably leave untouched that clandestine back-water known as Church Steps—a cobbled way charged with memories of seamen having moored some *Isabella* or *Good Intent* at low water to trudge up between the rows of gravestones to a resounding service at St. Mary's.

It is a fine old parish church, with its own Fishermen's Aisle, though not as picturesque with box-pews and strange, overhanging galleries as when Charlotte and Anne Brontë visited Scarborough in 1849. Anne was desperately ill, and not even the beloved sights and sounds of the resort could revive her. She lies buried in this churchyard, with a signpost to direct the many who come to pay their respects to her memory.

The east window which she and Charlotte would glimpse while enjoying a last sunset from Castle Hill, nearby, was destroyed during the last war. In 1958 a fresh window, by H. J. Stammers, was inserted. His treatment of an old subject, the Benedicite, evokes such a glorious company of creatures—ostrich, dromedary, heron, penguin, stag, monkey, mouse, butterfly, and many others, all presented beautifully 'new' before the Angels of the Lord—that one thinks instinctively of some lines written by the seventeenth-century poet, George Herbert:

> *Wherefore with my utmost art*
> *I will sing Thee,*
> *And the cream of all my heart*
> *I will bring Thee . . .*

Incidentally, few people realise that George Herbert—though not himself a Yorkshireman by birth—was closely related to Sir Thomas Herbert of York who befriended Charles I during his last days. Only a few years ago, the poet's latter-day namesake—George Herbert of Gate Helmsley, near York—became Governor of the York Merchant Adventurers. . . .

The 'splendid chariots and towering phaetons' that once jostled through Scarborough's streets anticipated present-day pleasures by taking their owners, for a change, into the surrounding countryside. They went to Flamborough Head and watched the egg-climbers at work on the lofty cliffs, to the same screeching protests from kittiwake and guillemot that greet any marauder today. They rumbled along to Forge Valley and Hackness, and doubtless waxed poetic about the sylvan paradise. Robin Hood's Bay, sixteen miles north of Scarborough, was then considered much too far for a lady, but I cannot imagine any modern miss being deprived of one bit of this fine, rocky seaboard which—after Scarborough—includes Hayburn Wyke, Staintondale, Ravenscar, and the fisherfolk's labyrinthine alleys of Robin Hood's Bay, as a preamble for Whitby itself.

Whitby is the springboard for a wide arc of attractive country. This reaches as far west as Mount Grace Priory, near Osmotherley, at the foot of the Cleveland Hills, and covers a multitude of small dales, some of whose streams feed Whitby's own river, the Esk.

An outlying spur of the Clevelands provides just the right setting for Mount Grace Priory. From the Thirsk–Stockton road, A19, the steep scarp looks inhospitable, but one soon applauds the site chosen for his Carthusian foundation by Thomas de Holland, Duke of Surrey, in 1396. The site, yes, but the Carthusian Order offered no comforts—only stark austerity and unbroken silence.

Some of the monks' cells are still grouped, abject and solitary, around the great cloister. Each cell had its private garden-plot; it was tended by the hair-shirted inmate who received his meals through a hatch that gave no friendly glimpse of the server.

After the Reformation part of the Priory guest-house became a goodly dwelling for Thomas Lascelles. Eventually, the Bells of Rounton made it their home, which explains why Gertrude Bell—'scholar, poet, historian, antiquarian, gardener, mountaineer, explorer, lover of Nature', etc.—often sought repose amongst the flowers, trees and quietude of Mount Grace. One sad day she laid her beloved little Samoyed, Tundra, to rest in the same tranquil shades.

George Bickham's 'Yarum', seven or eight miles north, is still—outwardly—the Yarm of the old beast fairs, which caused the main street to be lined with almost as many Georgian inns as dwellings and shops. Behind one side of the long street, odd little alleys lead down to equally odd mills; their eighteenth-century brick chimneys, now smokeless, form zigzag patterns in the River Tees.

A curious, 'lost' sort of a place, Yarm—forever wondering where its brisk, noisy, aromatic trade has gone. Even the Parish Church—begun in Norman times—seems about to slide into the Tees, which has looped around to make of Yarm almost an island. But I like this small town. So far it has kept its little dignities intact, and links up with County Durham by spanning the Tees with a splendid bridge first built about 1400 by Walter Skirlaw, Bishop of Durham.

Other gracious little towns in this area are Stokesley and Guisborough. Both are somewhat distantly seen from Roseberry Topping (1,057 feet), a cone-shaped hill—Lias capped with sandstone—which has yielded much archaeological evidence of bygone tribesfolk and their habits. Drayton, aware only of his decorative theme, calls Guisborough a 'second paradise'—a term now losing its intended savour—and seats a shepherd on the Topping.

A more stimulating figure to visualise, up there, would be James Cook, whose exploratory voyages were to chart a new continent. During his early schooldays at Great Ayton, young James must often have climbed this hill, also Easby Moor—to the east of the village—now crowned with an obelisk to his memory.

Mercifully, the 'goodly prospecte' awaiting him from either summit would not yet include the pall of smoke around Middlesbrough and its vast shipyards! The shipyards that were to lure him were those at Whitby, where staunch wooden vessels were made for the whaling crews.

Before following this lure it is pleasant to linger awhile in Great Ayton, where the chatter of the tiny River Leven vies with that of today's children playing around James Cook's little school, built in 1704. Idyllic!

One of the celebrities who might well have coloured a local history lesson here, in Cook's time, was Sir William Turner, a woollen draper and Lord Mayor of London who had founded the wonderful almshouses at Kirkleatham, near Redcar, only forty years earlier. The almshouses are built in the Wren manner and should certainly be seen; also the village church, which has an echo of Sir William's generosity in a silver almsdish. This lovely dish was washed up on the coast nearby about 1740. Whether it came from a wrecked Armada galleon—as believed hereabouts—or not, there is something very apt in its richly embossed design of luscious fruits and cornucopias being turned to a charitable cause.

Marton, Cook's actual birthplace, is a few miles nearer Middlesbrough, along A172. The two-roomed thatched cottage which heralded him into the world, on 27 October 1728, was later demolished. Even so, one is not allowed to forget Cook in this village. With an eye to future greatness, perhaps, the new County Infants School is challengingly named after the local boy who discovered Australia.

After leaving Great Ayton, Cook went first to Staithes, where the yards of cloth and packets of sugar he served over his master's shop-counter can only have sharpened his appreciation of local fishermen and their families, and quickened his own desire to go to sea. Staithes lies roughly midway along the coast between Saltburn and Whitby. Except for the sea's inroads—which at length engulfed 'Cook's shop' and much of the 'Cod and Lobster' Inn—the essential Staithes has barely changed since the thirteen-year-old lad from Great Ayton gazed with wonder at the massive enclosing cliffs and listened to the fishermen's talk. He would also see the women's peculiar bonnets—perhaps even sell them for his master.

At one time it was possible to walk through Staithes and tell at a glance, by the colour of her print bonnet, whether a woman of the village was single, married or widowed. Today, the women wear non-committal bonnets, except widows, who use black ones, though on Sundays most of them will go to church wearing white bonnets. In the men's camp, too, there is a striking individuality. The fishermen wear distinctive guernseys, sharing with their opposite numbers in Runswick Bay a Rig and Fur pattern. In fact, all along the Yorkshire coast—as Mrs. Gladys Thompson has shown in her delightful book, *Guernsey and Jersey Patterns*—there are different traditional guernsey patterns for each fishing community. At Filey, for example, there is a zigzag pattern derived from the steep, winding cliff paths; Robin Hood's Bay favours the Herring Mask, and Whitby the Betty Martin and the Flag.

The coast-wise route to Whitby provides yet another precipitous plunge—this time to Runswick Bay. This delightful village has completely outlived some of its old customs, like sacrificing a cat to herald the safe return of the fishing cobles, and getting the local children to dance and make strange incantations round beacon fires specially lit on the cliffs, during bad sea-weather. But the sea still takes its toll. Recent evidence of this occurs in the tiny Methodist Chapel—a square building wedged amongst colourful old cottages now bearing names like Poop and Capstan. Peering between their pantile roofs the chapel contrives a vignette of the sea—where Robert Patton, lifeboat coxswain, 'died to save another' in February 1934. The organ in the chapel commemorates him and his sacrifice.

Some of us are jealous of this coastline's every bay and headland, all the way down from Huntcliffe and Cat Nab at Saltburn to Filey Brigg. Then, besides other places already mentioned, there are Kettleness, Mulgrave, and Sandsend—all worth knowing, and reached from the coast road. At the top of Lythe Bank, near Mulgrave, Whitby comes into sight—easily recognised by its cliff-top abbey which a westering sun turns into gold.

A fine alternative approach to Whitby is via the Esk Valley. Beginning as a tiny lyric on Westerdale Moor, the river acquires fresh accents of beauty as it flows through Castleton, Danby, Lealholm, and Glaisdale. At Glaisdale it is spanned by Beggar's Bridge, which Tom Ferres built in 1619.

Ferres once fell into the river here and declared that he would one day erect a bridge at that dangerous spot. Local tradition adorns this account by stating that Tom had got his wetting while crossing the Esk to meet his sweetheart in secret. When her father heard of the love affair he sent Tom away, though with the understanding that he might resume his wooing when his prospects had improved.

Ferres went to sea, first on a Whitby boat that joined the fleet against the Armada, then as an apprentice to a Hull shipowner. Later he was able to outfit a vessel of his own, became wealthy, and joined Hull Trinity House, first as a Younger Brother, then as an Elder Brother. In his year of Mayoralty (1620)—an honour which made him Admiral of the Humber— he bought the site of the old Carmelite Friary at Hull for '1,200 broad pieces' and presented it to Trinity House for the erection of new premises. He also gave this ancient corporation an Elizabethan salt engraved with a shell design, and a curious silver-gilt cup. Both are still treasured there.

But that brief Eskdale romance also came to fruition. Ferres married his old sweetheart, built the bridge which he had promised while yet little more than a 'beggar', and bequeathed money to the little Glaisdale chapel where he was probably christened. While standing on the high arch of Beggar's Bridge I often salute the loyalty that survived fame and fortune to keep troth with a village girl. Alice Richardson—or was it *Agnes*?— must have felt mightily pleased!

From Egton Bridge, two miles east of Glaisdale village, several roads climb on to the moors which in autumn are decked for miles in the glowing purple of heather and ling. People who have never been to the Italian Riviera often say the sea cannot possibly be as rich a blue as the postcard views suggest. Similarly, those whose only experience of heather is the little withered bunches sometimes offered for sale on a town pavement can have no idea of the glory that autumn unfolds on these apparently endless moors.

Goathland village is in the heart of it all, but countryfolk are not content to look; they commonly scatter their beehives over the moors, hoping for a rich harvest of heather honey. Even off season the moors have their attraction, being dotted at times with 'pools' of silky cotton-grass, while sheep's wool clings to the heather sprigs to be whipped by the wind into scores of wayside 'distaffs'.

Also there are meandering becks and waterfalls to be followed, and many ancient tracks first trodden by the Whitby monks, perhaps, or the wayfaring folk who set up those mute stone crosses which the moorland sheep now use as rubbing-posts. Ralph Cross on Castleton Rigg, White Cross or Fat Betty above Rosedale, Mauley Cross near Wade's Causeway —all signify good walking country, amongst heather, bracken, bilberry— and of course patches of bog.

Some of the best waterfalls are near Goathland, reached either from Egton in the Esk Valley, or after branching left a few miles north of Saltergate Inn on the Pickering-Whitby road. Another good waterfall, Falling Foss, adds something fairy-like to the Littlebeck Valley.

This small, secluded valley runs back from Sleights—at the foot of Blue Bank on the Whitby road. Its steep slopes once grew oak-trees in abundance for the Whitby shipyards. Earlier still the abbey fraternity ran a small hospitium chapel at Littlebeck. This chapel eventually became an inn, and is now the home of Thomas Whittaker, a well-known wood-carver, and his wife. Their drawing-room—originally the stable where the monks up from Whitby tethered their nags—is the fulcrum of an enterprise that would have delighted William Morris.

The room is furnished with Whittaker's own beautiful handiwork in English oak—wainscoting, doors, refectory table, credence cupboard, figurines, etc., mostly rippling with adze marks and half concealing within a tiny Gothic niche the craftsman's 'signature', a *gnome*. This device comes from an old Norwegian legend averring that a gnome is born with every acorn to act as guardian through all the processes of its becoming a mighty oak-tree. Mr. Whittaker has extended the guardianship to cover his own oaken wares. His workshop is always a fascinating medley, but I still think his drawing-room is pivotal. It is the place where he becomes expansive about his work and his dreams—and where, on occasion, he has to decline some too-generous American offer to buy the entire atrium as it stands, gnomes and all!

These merry little fellows have 'colonised' the neighbourhood, to say nothing of countries like Italy, Spain, and Australia to which Mr. Whittaker's work has gone. Through the furnishings they adorn, the gnomes have helped to transform the Old Mill at Littlebeck. They have appeared in Whitby, too, most appropriately on a screen in the museum that displays some fine pieces of fourteenth-century stained glass from St. Hilda's Abbey.

This long perambulation of Yorkshire could have no better climax than among the old streets and alleys and waterways that Captain Cook knew at Whitby. Since his day there have been many changes—not all of them to the visual improvement of the town, yet one can still see the house in Grape Lane where he was apprenticed for three years to John Walker, Quaker shipowner. Amongst the old shops in neighbouring Church Street there is one that might well have reminded him of Staithes; it then sold drapery, besides being Sanders' Bank! A descendant of this versatile trading family thinks that the linen sails used for Cook's great voyages into the unknown were made here, in a back-yard workshop. With the name Sanders still engraved on its fanlight, the shop stands nearly opposite the Town Hall—a quaint seventeenth-century building illustrated on the firm's banknotes.

One is still walking in Cook's footsteps on passing through the remainder of Church Street and up the 199 steps to St. Mary's Church and the Abbey Plain beyond.

Rooted in Norman times, this astonishing church corresponds to an old tale—say one of the traditional Mumming Plays—which has been carved about and added to until the original is all but lost to view. In the seventeenth and eighteenth centuries this gull-haunted sanctuary on the East Cliff acquired curious galleries reached by exterior staircases, enormous box-pews, large wall-boards painted with Biblical texts, cabin-like windows and pillars resembling ships' masts. The town's fishermen had taken the church in hand; they and the local shipwrights were determined to make the place big enough and congenial for themselves and their families. In all England there is surely no other church quite so redo-

33   St. Mary's, Whitby—the Georgianised interior

lent of those who go down to the sea in ships, whether these be fishermen's cobles or vessels of high renown, like Cook's *Endeavour*, *Resolution* and *Discovery*—all three built here, beside the upper harbour.

In crossing the short space between St. Mary's Church and the Abbey one exchanges a distinctly plebeian atmosphere for the remnants of thirteenth-century austerity. The Abbey is grandly situated, facing the sea, and sufficiently recalls the earlier days of Abbess Hilda and of her swineherd, Caedmon, who miraculously turned poet overnight. Thirteen hundred years have passed since Caedmon sang to Hilda his beautiful Song of Creation, but any day of an English summer people still enjoy the imagery of his thought by stepping over to the Caedmon Cross—at the head of the Church Stairs—and gazing upon the birds and other creatures that inspired him. This so richly carved cross was unveiled by the Poet Laureate in 1898.

The Abbot's Book, covering much of the Abbey history from very early times, is treasured in the town's museum in Pannett Park. Finely preserved and still readable, it takes its place in Whitby's long pageant of Time, as represented in this wonderful museum. First, some magnificent fossil saurians discovered hereabouts by men prospecting for alum and jet; then some type ammonites from the coast between Staithes and Ravenscar. Beehive querns of about 200 B.C. found beneath Whitby houses; the dedication stone of the Roman fort at Ravenscar; samples of Whitby jet-ware, ranging from rosary beads and witch-charms to a lovely nineteenth-century chess-table—there is no dearth of interest. Quite likely the shipping section will require another afternoon's visit!

It is in this shipping section, of course, that Captain Cook sails the seas again, so to speak—also those two great whaling captains, William Scoresby, who invented the 'crow's-nest', and his scientist son, another William. While in the Arctic, Scoresby junior would make crayon drawings of Greenland whales and of the ice-bound fleet of whalers; some of the drawings are here in the museum, a striking foil for his pen-and-ink drawings of snow crystals—surely the first of their kind? His microscope went with him everywhere. Even in the ship's log-books, this flair for illustration found expression. Each whale is represented by a fish-tail. If the whale was captured, the tail goes into mourning with an overall wash of black ink. If the tail remains a sketchy outline, it signifies one that eluded the harpooners and 'got away'.

Whitby's latest tribute to its bygone whalers is a pair of whale jaw-bones set up like an arch on the West Cliff, near Cook's bronze statue.

34 *Flamborough Head—an essay in chalk*

Very aptly they frame most of the old town, across the harbour, and spell forgotten adventure to a new generation.

Today, there is no more stirring experience at Whitby than watching from the same vantage point as the herring fleet leaves harbour after nightfall. The harbour bridge swings slowly open, and the boats, thirty or forty of them, sail past silently in single file, later to form a fan-shaped pattern—picked out with mast-head lights—in the off-shore fishing ground.

Some of the Books Consulted

Many are acknowledged in the text. Others include the following:

Letters of Charles Waterton, edited by R. A. Irwin (who also supplied me with useful notes); Rockcliff, 1955.

Marshalls of Leeds, Flax Spinners, W. G. Rimmer; Cambridge University Press, 1960.

Ralph Thoresby, *Diary*; edited by J. Hunter, 1930.

Oliver Heywood, *Diary*; edited by J. H. Turner, 1881–5.

Letters of Thomas Gray; edited by Duncan C. Tovey, 1900–12.

The Silent Traveller in the Yorkshire Dales, Chiang Yee; Methuen, 1941.

The Striding Dales, Halliwell Sutcliffe; Warne, 1929.

With Dickens in Yorkshire, T. P. Cooper; Ben Johnson, York, 1923.

The Story of Fountains Abbey, Canon C. C. Bell; Raphael Tuck, 1932.

Guide to Aldborough and Boroughbridge, Lady Lawson-Tancred (local handbook only).

Testament of Friendship, Vera Brittain; Macmillan, 1940.

History of the Parish and Manor House of Bishopthorpe, J. R. Keble, 1905.

A York Miscellany, I. P. Pressly; A. Brown & Sons, Hull, 1942.

Index

The numerals in **heavy type** refer to the **figure numbers** of the illustrations

206 South Riding